# THE THIRD VOICE

## MODERN
## BRITISH AND AMERICAN
## VERSE DRAMA

### BY DENIS DONOGHUE

"I shall explain at once what I mean by the 'three voices.' The first is the voice of the poet talking to himself—or to nobody. The second is the voice of the poet addressing an audience, whether large or small. The third is the voice of the poet when he attempts to create a dramatic character speaking in verse; when he is saying, not what he would say in his own person, but only what he can say within the limits of one imaginary character addressing another imaginary character."—T. S. ELIOT, *The Three Voices of Poetry* (1953)

PRINCETON, NEW JERSEY

PRINCETON UNIVERSITY PRESS

1959

Donoghue, Denis. The third voice: modern British
and American verse drama. Princeton, N.J.,
Princeton University Press, 1959. 286 p. 20 cm.
1. English drama—20th cent.—Hist. & crit. 2.
American drama—20th cent.—Hist. & crit.
PR736.D6 (822.9109) 59—5595 ‡ Library of
Congress.

Publication of this book has been aided by
the Ford Foundation program
to support publication, through university presses,
of works in the humanities
and social sciences.

Printed in the United States of America

Second Printing 1966

# CONTENTS

# CONTENTS

# THE THIRD VOICE

MODERN BRITISH AND AMERICAN

VERSE DRAMA

Poetic drama, verse drama, prose drama, dramatic verse, dramatic poetry—we have a generous supply of terms, yet we confuse our speech by blurring their outlines.

"Poetic drama," for instance, is a term of praise used so loosely in critical writings that it no longer bears a reasonably stable meaning. Mr. Eliot, an agile rhetorician, relates it so closely to "verse drama" that he implies a firm equation of these terms.[1] This equation is rejected, however, by Mr. Granville-Barker: "What *is* Poetic Drama? Not simply drama written in verse, . . ."[2] Agreed. "Verse drama" is a purely technical phrase: it makes no implications whatever as to the quality of the script or of the play as a whole. Unlike "poetic drama," it is entirely neutral in its application.

It is customary (and appropriate) to describe as poetic dramas certain plays such as Shaw's *The Apple Cart*, Synge's *Riders to the Sea*, and Ibsen's *An Enemy of the People*, the texts of which are in prose. The phrase would also be used to describe, in terms of form, a great silent film such as Dreyer's *The Passion of Joan of Arc*. It would appear, therefore, that the phrase is characteristically applied in recognition of the validity of certain dramatic structures which are not necessarily verbal at all. We shall return to this point, but first (for clarification) a word about "prose drama."

The adoption of prose as the sole verbal medium of "realistic drama" may be seen in the French *tragédie domestique et bourgeoise* in the middle of the eighteenth century. Diderot's early writings on the drama—in association with *Le Fils Naturel* and *Le Père de Famille*—are mainly pleas for a realistic drama

---

[1] T. S. Eliot, "The Aims of Poetic Drama," *Adam International Review*, November 1949, p. 14.

[2] Harley Granville-Barker, *On Poetry in Drama*, Sidgwick and Jackson, 1937, p. 3.

in opposition to the conventions of the French tragic theatre.[3] They are manifestoes of a genre which was new in France but which had immediate models in Lillo's *The London Merchant* (1731) and Edward Moore's *The Gamester* (1753). Characteristically, the *drame bourgeois* differs from conventional "high" tragedy in its selection of subject matter, in its chosen "decorum" of style, and in its avoidance of the grand or heroic tone.

In the English theatre such playwrights as Lillo, Moore, and Charles Johnson repudiated a convention in the theory and practice of "high" tragedy which goes back as far as Diomedes and the mimes of Herodas. In the third Book of the *Ars Grammatica* Diomedes wrote: ". . . Tragoedia est heroicae fortunae in adversis conprehensio. . . . Comoedia est privatae civilisque fortunae sine periculo vitae conprehensio. . . . Comoedia a tragoedia differt, quod in tragoedia introducuntur heroes duces reges, in comoedia humiles atque privatae personae; . . ."[4] Dryden wrote in similar terms in the Preface to the second edition of *The Indian Emperor* (1668): "Were there neither judge, taste, nor opinion in the world, yet they (i.e. Tragedy and Comedy) would differ in their natures; for the action, character, and language of tragedy, would still be great and high; that of comedy, lower and more familiar. Admiration would be the delight of one, and satire of the other."[5]

But there are certain early tragedies in the English theatre, such as *Arden of Feversham, A Warning for Fair Women, The Yorkshire Tragedy, The English Traveller*, and *A Woman Killed with Kindness*, in which the convention that the chief characters should be of princely or at least of noble rank is violated. The author of *Arden of Feversham*, dramatising a famous murder-story, claims that "simple trueth" is on his side. At the end of

[3] Denis Diderot, *Writings on the Theatre* (in French), edited by F. C. Green, Cambridge University Press, 1936.

[4] *Grammatici Latini*, edited by Heinrich Keil, Leipzig, Tevbner, 1857 I, 487-88. See J. V. Cunningham, *Woe or Wonder*, University of Denver Press, 1951, p. 45 *et passim*.

[5] John Dryden, Preface to the second (1668) edition of *The Indian Emperor, Works*, edited by Walter Scott, Edinburgh, Ballantyne, 1808, II, 275.

the play, when Alice has been sent to Canterbury to be burned, Franklin speaks an Epilogue:

> Gentlemen, we hope youle pardon this naked Tragedy,
> Wherin no filed points are foisted in
> To make it gratious to the eare or eye;
> For simple trueth is gratious enough,
> And needes no other points of glosing stuffe.[6]

Clearly, if the spirit of decorum is to be observed, such plays should yield up the "high" style of traditional tragedy, but this limitation is not always maintained. Even in *Arden of Feversham* there are several passages which reveal the inability of "domestic tragedy" to achieve a genuine "high" style within its own terms: when Mosbie soliloquises he speaks in a style whose artifice is similar in kind to that of *The Spanish Tragedy*:

> Disturbed thoughts dryves me from company
> And dryes my marrow with their watchfulnes;
> Continuall trouble of my moody braine
> Feebles my body by excesse of drinke,
> And nippes me as the bitter Northeast wind
> Doeth check the tender blosoms in the spring.
> Well fares the man, how ere his cates do taste,
> That tables not with foule suspition;
> And he but pines amongst his delicats,
> Whose troubled minde is stuft with discontent.
> My goulden time was when I had no gould.[7]

Such plays as *Arden of Feversham* and *The Yorkshire Tragedy* are domestic tragedies because the chief character in each is a private person of middle class, far below the rank of the traditional tragic hero. It follows that Lillo, Moore, and Johnson, in rejecting the convention of "high" characters in tragedy, were preserving a minority tradition in the English theatre which goes back to the end of the sixteenth century; they were not

---

[6] *The Shakespeare Apocrypha*, edited by C. F. Tucker Brooke, Oxford, Clarendon Press, 1908, p. 35.

[7] *Ibid.*, p. 18.

merely answering a demand from the rising middle-class. Furthermore, since Lillo selected his tragic hero, like Arden, from the merchant class, and since he intended to eschew the "high" style, it seemed a small additional gesture to abandon verse altogether. This is the only essential difference between the constructive processes of *Arden of Feversham* and those of *The London Merchant*.[8]

"Prose drama" as a special genre, then, claims to be "like life" in its style and organisation; to deal with characters in social rank far below royalty or nobility; and to reject artifice in its language. These are the claims which William Archer, for example, advanced in *The Old Drama and the New* and, by implication, in his translation of the "prose dramas" of Ibsen. In the theory of verse drama which Mr. Eliot has developed in recent years each of these claims is made explicitly or by implication. Indeed, Mr. Eliot has implied—however benignly— that verse drama in the contemporary theatre can improve on Lillo and on Henry Arthur Jones as skilfully as it can avoid the pitfalls of "poetical" drama from Coleridge to Gordon Bottomley.

The "poetry" of poetic drama is not necessarily or solely a *verbal* construct; it inheres in the structure of the play as a whole. That is, the "poetry" is not in any one part of the play, or any one of its elements, separately exhibited, but in the manner in which, and the degree to which, all the elements act in cooperation. This conception of poetic drama is exemplified in Cocteau's theoretical writings. In the "Préface de 1922" to *Les Mariés de la Tour Eiffel* he wrote: "L'action de ma pièce est imagée tandis que le texte ne l'est pas. J'essaie donc de substituer une 'poésie de théâtre' à la 'poésie au théâtre.' La

---

[8] Domestic tragedy as a special genre, including some plays by Dekker, Ford, and Heywood, has been studied by Henry H. Adams in *English Domestic or Homiletic Tragedy 1575 to 1642*, Columbia University Press, 1943. See also *Woe or Wonder, supra*, footnote 4. The eighteenth-century developments of the genre are treated in Ernest Bernbaum's *The Drama of Sensibility*, Boston, Ginn, 1915.

poésie au théâtre est une dentelle délicate impossible à voir de loin. La poésie de théâtre serait une grosse dentelle; une dentelle en cordages un navire sur la mer. . . . Les scènes s'emboîtent comme les mots d'un poème."[9]

Applying such insights to the plays of Ibsen and of Chekhov, Francis Fergusson describes the "poetry" of poetic drama: ". . . not a poetry of words, but a poetry of the rhythmic relationship and contrast of 'scenes' established by the performers' make-believe, and appealing to the histrionic sensibility of the audience."[10] Of *The Cherry Orchard* he writes: "Chekhov's poetry, like Ibsen's, is behind the naturalistic surfaces; but the form of the play as a whole is 'nothing but' poetry in the widest sense: the coherence of the concrete elements of the composition."[11] We would here endorse this "slant," reserving until much later any local modifications it appears to need.

A poem consists of words. Whatever we choose to regard as the unit of poetic composition—the single word, the syntactical unit, the verse-line—is necessarily verbal. But the unit of a play is not encompassed within the verbal realm. If one isolates a moment from the thousands of contiguous moments in a play, one should regard as the unit of theatrical composition everything that is happening in that moment, simultaneously apprehended. Words are being spoken, gestures are being made, the plot is pressing forward, a visual image is being conveyed on the stage itself. The term which encompasses all these elements is "situation": the play is a succession of enacted situations so chosen and arranged as to constitute the objective equivalent of the motive which is the "action" of the play.

Arguing back again. A word, phrase, image, or stanza in a poem acquires its highest value not when it is apprehended

[9] Jean Cocteau, *Théâtre I*, Paris, Gallimard, quinzième édition, p. 45. See also his *D'un Ordre Considéré comme une Anarchie*, 1923, *Le Rappel à l'Ordre*, Paris, Stock, 1926, p. 257.

[10] Francis Fergusson, *The Idea of a Theater*, Princeton University Press, 1949, p. 207.

[11] *Ibid.*, p. 165.

in itself as an independent verbal particle but when its function in the complete poem is estimated. This is generally conceded. What one asks of a word in a poem is that by virtue of grammar, syntax, association, contrast, or some other internal principle, it make an essential contribution to the "perfection" of the poem. Similarly one asks that each situation in a play shall make an essential contribution to the "perfection" of the composition. The ideal implied in such requirements is that of "organic unity," or of what Coleridge in *Table Talk* called "fusion."[12] It could also be derived from Aristotle's conception of *entelechy*.

Such unity pleases because it appeals to one's taste for whatever is "finished," complete in itself, suffering neither fracture nor excess, enjoying its own completeness. It pleases also because it exhibits the operation of perfect relationships; it is an instance of full cooperation between several forces, each of which *might* have been recalcitrant, a rogue calf.

Ibsen's *The Pillars of Society* offers distinguished examples of such cooperation. We shall treat one briefly. The fourth act of the play takes place in the garden-room in Consul Bernick's house. It is a stormy evening, already half dark and growing darker. Rummel, who is arranging a demonstration in support of the Consul, says to a servant: "Only every second candle, Jacob. The place mustn't look too brilliant; it is supposed to be a surprise, you know. And all these flowers—? Oh yes, let them stand; it will seem as if they were there always."[13]

The theme of "seeming" and deception, thus inaugurated in word and act, is elaborated in a conversation between Consul Bernick and Lona Hessel, Mrs. Bernick's step-sister, later in the same act. The Consul sees no escape from the deception which he has committed. When the demonstration is about to begin, the blinds in the garden-room are drawn up. The entire street is found to be illuminated, with signs reading "Long

---

[12] S. T. Coleridge, *Specimens of the Table Talk*, Murray, 1851, pp. 264-65.

[13] Henrik Ibsen, *Samfundets Stötter, The Pillars of Society*, translation by William Archer, The Scott Library, edited by Havelock Ellis, Scott, n.d., p. 87.

Live Karsten Bernick, the Pillar of our Society." Confronted with this spectacular setting for new deception, the Consul rushes from the windows, crying: "Away with the mocking words, I say! Do you not see all these lights are gibing at us? . . . All these are the lights in a dead room." A little later Mrs. Bernick, having recovered her son, is reconciled to her husband. Addressing the crowd he confesses his crime. The crowd disperses, the street-illuminations are extinguished; Mr. and Mrs. Bernick, Lona Hessel, and Martha Bernick are together in the room:

MRS. BERNICK: Now they are all gone.
BERNICK: And we are alone. My name no longer shines in the transparencies; all the lights are put out in the windows.
LONA: Would you have them lighted again?
BERNICK: Not for all the world . . .

Bernick's new moral life is presented in terms of vision. The play ends when the false, external illuminations have been extinguished, and a real, inner light of Truth is established in Bernick's character. Instead of lights in a dead room there is now, outside, the honest darkness of night; inside, the new and growing light in Bernick's soul. At this point the dark and stormy night is seen to brighten—empathetically—as the light of Truth in Bernick spreads out into the entire new society which he represents:

MARTHA: How the sky is clearing; how it grows light over the sea . . .
LONA: . . . the spirits of Truth and of Freedom—these are the Pillars of Society.

This is one of the internal relationships which, acting together, constitute the "poetry" of Ibsen's play: the relationship between the *scene* and the moral *act* which the central agent, Bernick, undertakes. At every point the scene exhibits—in its own terms—the *quality* of the hero's moral condition. Poetic

*9*

drama characteristically reveals such relationships since they are the immediate, local manifestations of the unity which is the "poetry" of the play. A play is "poetic," then, when its concrete elements (plot, agency, scene, speech, gesture) continuously exhibit in their internal relationships those qualities of mutual coherence and illumination required of the words of a poem.

We have invoked Aristotle, reminding ourselves of his entelechial *myth*. If there is any "lesson" to be drawn from the following studies, it is that in the modern English and American theatres those men who are most gifted as writers have only a faltering grasp of the *myth* behind such phrases as "organic unity," "entelechy," "coherence," and "perfection," or of the exhibition of this *myth* in terms of theatre. Most good poets write plays, bad plays. One thinks of Wallace Stevens, of Auden, of William Carlos Williams. Yeats is the greatest exception, thus providing a shadowy continuity with Ibsen, whose own theatre-poetry Yeats was very slow to acknowledge.

# CHAPTER ONE. ON VERSE IN DRAMA:
## A "NEUTRAL" SURVEY

THERE is no "pure" theory on the matter. Arguments for or against the use of verse in drama have depended on such considerations as the state of contemporary non-dramatic verse, particular methods of acting and stage-production, the use of rhyme, and the extent of the authority of the Ancients. "Theory" is therefore dialectical, medicinal. Stendhal's advocacy of prose, for instance, was directly related to his distaste for the shallowness of contemporary French verse: "Ces tragédies—là doivent être en prose. De nos jours, le vers alexandrin n'est le plus souvent qu'un cachesottise."[1] In drama, Stendhal argued, prose is preferable also because its freedom from "rules" facilitates "ce mot propre, unique, nécessaire, indispensable."[1]

Stendhal was not the first to argue along these lines: a similar case for prose against verse (without special regard to drama) had been put forward in the first years of the eighteenth century by the "rationalists," Trublet, Fontenelle, and La Motte. In the revived quarrel between the Ancients and the Moderns, La Motte, for example, adopted a sternly "modernist" attitude. In his *Discours sur Homère* (1714), while conceding that a good verse translation of the *Iliad* was *possible*, he maintained that a prose translation was greatly to be preferred: "Jamais la tyrannie de la rime ne permettra de suivre les tours & les expressions d'un Auteur, aussi exactement que la prose le peut faire."[2] Furthermore, prose was more flexible than verse, more natural, free from "rules." Again: "L'ordre, la précision, les convenances ne seroient plus à la merci de regles tyranniques que ne maitrisent pas toûjours les plus grands génies."[3] La

[1] Henri Beyle, *Racine et Shakespeare* edited by L. Delbos, Oxford, Clarendon Press, 1907, p. 1. See also pp. 70-71.
[2] *Oeuvres de Monsieur Houdar de la Motte*, Paris, 1754, II, 117-18.
[3] *Quatrième Discours a l'occasion de la Tragédie d'Oedipe, Oeuvres, supra*, IV, 394, 392.

Motte's "realism" is especially evident in the prefatory "Discours" to his prose version of *Oedipe*. There, enumerating the advantages of prose in tragedy, he asserts: "Premièrement: l'avantage de la vraisemblance qui est absolument violée par la versification: car pourquoi, en faisant agir des hommes, ne les pas faire parler comme des hommes? n'est—il pas, j'ose le dire, contre nature, qu'un Héros, qu'une Princesse asservissent tous leurs discours à un certain nombre de sillabes?"[3]

An attitude similar to those of La Motte and Stendhal was expressed by Ibsen in 1883. A friend, the actress Lucie Wolf, had requested him to write a prologue for a festival performance at the Christiania Theatre. Ibsen declined, pointing out that his convictions and his "art-principles" forbade him: "Prologues, epilogues, and everything of the kind ought to be banished from the stage. The stage is for dramatic art alone; and declamation is not dramatic art."[4] Ibsen assumed that the prologue "would have to be in verse; for such is the established custom," and he declined to support the convention: "Verse has been most injurious to dramatic art. A scenic artist whose department is the drama of the present day should be unwilling to take a verse into his mouth."[4]

Ibsen considered it highly improbable that verse would be employed "to any extent worth mentioning" in the drama of the immediate future: "the aims of the dramatists of the future are almost certain to be incompatible with it." It was therefore doomed to extinction, "just as the preposterous animal forms of prehistoric times became extinct when their day was over."[4] Here the author of *The Wild Duck* is castigating the author of the verse plays up to *Peer Gynt*. Ibsen concludes by declaring that "for the last seven or eight years" he has "exclusively cultivated the very much more difficult art of writing the genuine, plain language spoken in real life."[4]

Ibsen's attitude, and almost his exact words, determined the

---

[4] *The Correspondence of Henrik Ibsen*, the translation edited by Mary Morison, Hodder and Stoughton, 1905, p. 367. Letter dated 25th May 1883.

*12*

characteristic bias of his English apologist, William Archer. In *The Old Drama and the New* (1923) Archer declared that in Elizabethan drama "the established custom of writing in verse, good, bad, or indifferent, enabled and encouraged the dramatists to substitute rhetoric for human speech."[5]

An important aspect of the question of verse drama was contemplated when Edmund Wilson asked, "Is Verse a Dying Technique?" Mr. Wilson pointed out that verse was once made to serve many purposes for which prose would now be used. Solon had expounded his political ideas in verse; Hesiod had used verse in writing his shepherd's calendar. *La Tentation de Saint Antoine* would probably have been written in verse if Flaubert had lived in an earlier age. After Ibsen "the dramatic 'poets'—the Chekhovs, the Synges and the Shaws . . . wrote almost invariably in prose." Mr. Wilson continued: "It was by such that the soul of the time was given its dramatic expression: there was nothing left for Rostand's alexandrines but fireworks and declamation."[6] Finally: "Is it possible to believe, for example, that Eliot's hope of having verse reinstated on the stage —even verse of the new kind which he proposes—is likely ever to be realised?"[7]

The most recent adverse comment on verse drama has been offered by Yvor Winters. He argues, like Poe, that the short lyric is the only essentially poetic form, the only form in which "the most powerful and the most sensitive mode of writing can be used efficiently throughout." Every other form, including that of Shakespearean tragedy, necessitates a certain amount of inferior writing. The epic and the verse drama have long been dead, due to defects "in the nature of the forms." One of the snags in the use of verse in a long work is that the verse *as such* imposes on the slack or transitional parts of the work an excessive degree of emphasis and weight: Professor Winters refers to "the tyrannic overemphasis of materials proper only to

[5] *The Old Drama and the New*, Heinemann, 1923, p. 47.
[6] *The Triple Thinkers*, New York, Oxford University Press, 1948, pp. 15, 24.
[7] *Axel's Castle*, Scribner, 1931, p. 120.

prose."[8] On this latter point: the problems involved in the transitional parts of a verse play have been considered by Mr. Eliot over a period of several years. The solution he offers in *The Cocktail Party* and *The Confidential Clerk* involves making the verse-norm rather slack and tightening it whenever an unusual degree of emotion is to be expressed. Provided that an impression of an unified language persists throughout the play, the strategy would seem feasible. The procedure will be examined later.

One of the problems involved in verse drama is the relation between the verse (in particular, its syntax, diction, and rhythm) and the characteristic speech of the audience to which it is addressed. This problem, which assumes priority in Eliot's later theories, was the subject of discussion in sixteenth-century Italian criticism. Giraldi Cinthio, for example, citing Aristotle, Horace, Ariosto, and Trissino in support of his contention that prose was not at all adapted to tragedy, argued that the verse should be in harmony with everyday speech. The verses used in comedy should be like the speech of the common people, and those of tragedy like the language of the great and noble.[9]

Castelvetro also accepted the use of verse in drama on the authority of the Ancients. In addition, in his commentary on Aristotle's *Poetics,* he advanced a mechanical consideration: ". . . il verso, che è parlare maraviglioso, & dilettevole, per molte cagioni, alcuna delle quali è gia stata detta, cio è per potere senza sconvenevolezza alzare la voce in palco si, che il popolo tutto agiatamente oda. . . ."[10] It should be recalled, in this connexion, that Castelvetro's prime concern was: by what means can the play or poem be made to please an unlettered audience,

[8] "Problems for the Modern Critic of Literature," *Hudson Review,* Vol. IX, 3, Autumn 1956, p. 359 *et passim.*

[9] *Discorsi intorno al comporre de i romanzi, delle commedie, e delle tragedie,* Venice, 1554, p. 228. A. H. Gilbert, editor and translator, *Literary Criticism: Plato to Dryden,* American Book Company, 1940, pp. 247, 259, 260.

[10] *Poetica d'Aristotele vulgarizzata et sposta,* Basle, second edition, 1576, p. 30.

"rozza moltitudine"?[11] That the sound-patterns of verse facilitated the audience's hearing and, thence, understanding the speeches was a consideration of great importance.

Corneille, like Cinthio, was concerned with the relation between verse and common speech. In the "Examen" to *Andromède* (1650) he wrote: "J'avoue que les vers qu'on récite sur le théâtre sont présumés etre prose: nous ne parlons pas d'ordinaire en vers, et san cette fiction leur mesure et leur rime sortiroient du vraisemblable. Mais par quelle raison peut-on dire que les vers alexandrins tiennent nature de prose, et que ceux des stances n'en peuvent faire autant?" Appealing to Aristotle: "Si nous en croyons Aristote, il faut se servir au théâtre des vers qui sont les moins vers, et qui se mêlent au langage commun, sans y penser, plus souvent que les autres. C'est par cette raison que les poetes tragiques ont choisi l'ïambique plutôt que l'hexamètre, qu'ils ont laissé aux épopées, parce qu'en parlant sans dessein d'en faire, il se mêle dans notre discours plus d'ïambiques que d'hexamètres."[12]

The appropriate *degree* of correspondence between the verse in a play and the current norms of speech has always proved difficult to settle. In the Preface to the second edition of *The Indian Emperor* Dryden opposed the use of prose in drama on grounds which, if permanently valid, would operate against the verse of *The Cocktail Party* and *The Confidential Clerk*: ". . . one great reason why prose is not to be used in serious plays, is, because it is too near the nature of converse: there may be too great a likeness; as the most skilful painters affirm, that there may be too near a resemblance in a picture. . . . Thus prose . . . is by common consent deposed, as too weak for the government of serious plays."[13]

[11] Bernard Weinberg, (1) *Castelvetro's Theory of Poetics; Critics and Criticism: Ancient and Modern*, edited by R. S. Crane, University of Chicago Press, 1952. (2) "From Aristotle to pseudo-Aristotle," *Comparative Literature*, Vol. v, 2, Spring, 1953.

[12] "Examen" to *Andromède* (1650), *Oeuvres Complètes*, edited by Ch. Marty-Laveaux, Paris, Hachette, 1862, v, 309-10. See also *Discours sur la poésie dramatique, ibid*, I.

[13] *The Works of John Dryden*, edited by Walter Scott, Edinburgh, Ballantyne, 1808, II, 269-70.

That verse commands a wider range of expression than prose, and more subtle nuances of meaning, is the central argument proposed by its advocates. In the Preface to *Cromwell* Victor Hugo declared: "Le vers est la form optique de la pensée." As to the qualities which this verse should possess: "Que si nous avions le droit de dire quel pourrait être, à notre gré, le style du drame, nous voudrions un vers libre, franc, loyal, osant tout dire sans pruderie, tout exprimer sans recherche."[14] One is reminded of Eliot's search for a form of verse and an idiom in which everything that needed to be said could be said naturally, without recourse to prose, verse which would be "capable of unbroken transition between the most intense speech and the most relaxed dialogue."[15]

Eliot's ideas on verse drama have developed over many years, from the essay on *Rhetoric and Poetic Drama* (1919) to *The Three Voices of Poetry* (1953).[16] The central idea in his argument is that the human soul in intense emotion strives to express itself in verse. It is interesting to find that here Eliot repeats an argument offered many years ago by Bernard Shaw. Unlike Eliot, Shaw found Shakespearean blank verse "as natural a form of literary expression as the Augustan English" of Dublin or "the latest London fashion in dialogue."[17] But Shaw and Eliot, unlike William Archer, emphasise the "naturalness" of verse speech. Shaw advised young actors to "leave blank verse patiently alone until you have experienced emotion deep enough to crave for poetic expression, at which point verse will seem

[14] *Cromwell*, edited by Edmond Wahl, Oxford at the Clarendon Press, 1909, p. 44.

[15] *Poetry and Drama* (1950); *Selected Prose*, Penguin Books, 1953, pp. 82-83.

[16] For convenience, the following may be listed here: *"Rhetoric" and Poetic Drama* (1919); *A Dialogue on Dramatic Poetry* (1928); *The Music of Poetry* (1942); *Introduction to S. L. Bethell's "Shakespeare and the Popular Dramatic Tradition"* (1944); *The Aims of Poetic Drama* (1949); *Poetry and Drama* (1950); *The Three Voices of Poetry* (1953).

[17] "Cymbeline Refinished: A Variation," *The London Mercury*, Vol. xxxvii, 1938, p. 376.

*16*

an absolutely natural and real form of speech to you."[18] Eliot
has declared that Ibsen, Strindberg, and Chekhov were ham-
pered by the limitations of prose. Verse, he maintains, has several
advantages over prose: for example, the exciting effect of verse
rhythms operating on the mind of the listener without his being
conscious of it; and the possibility of reinforcing and deepening
the dramatic effect by the musical effect of a varied pattern of
style. Everything that prose can do in the theatre, verse can do
also, he argues, and it is the privilege of dramatic verse to show
us several planes of reality at once. Verse both imposes a form
to which the author must submit himself, and releases more
unconscious force than prose can: "The poetry of a great verse
drama is not merely a *decoration* of a dialogue which could, as
drama, be as well put in prose; it makes the drama itself different—and more dramatic."[19]

Words, words, words: each one offered as "pure" argument,
each one by definition "impure." We would seek here to frustrate
the theorists (conceding them a bare hearing), hoping that the
"idea" of verse drama will emerge more "realistically"—however
vaguely, or unmanageably—from the "image" of certain modern
verse plays. Proceeding with a banal thought: if these verse plays
turn out to be seriously inadequate, it will little matter whether
the theories on which they are based are sound or not.

[18] *Dramatic Opinions and Essays*, Constable, 1907, I, 27.
[19] "The Aims of Poetic Drama," *Adam International Review*, November 1949, pp. 14-15.

## CHAPTER TWO. FIVE ANECDOTES
## TO STAND FOR MANY

THERE is no evading the nineteenth century. Whether one uses it, as Gordon Bottomley used it, in a pious endeavour to go through it to Shakespeare or to mythology, or as Mr. Eliot uses it, as something to react against—the thing is still *there*. Its theatre is still *there*, confused, naïve, often absurd, chaotic—but chaotic in ways that reveal our own chaos. Our preoccupations are inherited from the ones the nineteenth century acknowledged or failed to acknowledge; our theatre is just as unsatisfactory as the one which distressed Henry James.

### I.

In 1821 Shelley was working on *Charles the First*, seeing the assignment, piously, as an occasion to imitate Shakespeare's central tragedies. To Trelawny he declared that in style and manner he would "approach as near our great dramatist as my feeble powers will permit." His model was *King Lear*, "for that is nearly perfect." Shelley's piety was his own, but it was also the piety of an age, issuing in earnest plays by Wordsworth, Beddoes, Keats, Southey, Miss Baillie, and practically every English poet from Coleridge to Swinburne. To us the venture seems peculiarly misguided, and we admire Byron and Hopkins for holding out against it, forgetting (as we do) that one has to imitate *something* and that even deliberately to write *against* something is to take one's bearings from it. Behind Shelley there is the curious force that interpreted experience through the formulation of a Shakespearean tragic soliloquy, a force that expressed itself also in the critical writings of Jeffrey, the Schlegels, Goethe, and Hugo. And surely a great part of the *spirit* of the nineteenth century could be invoked through the third Book of *Wilhelm Meisters Lehrjahre*, in which we read of Wilhelm's first experiences with the tragedies of Shakespeare.

There are *degrees* of imitation, of course, *kinds* of imitation, and perhaps what we dislike in *The Cenci* is not so much the inferiority of the play itself as the mean, timorous procedures which it exhibits. It is well known that in *The Cenci* and again in *Ginevra* Shelley borrowed extensively from *Romeo and Juliet* and from Shakespeare's central tragedies.[1] But such borrowings mean very little in themselves: the *complexity* of a writer cannot be dissolved into the simplification of his sources. It is more revealing to observe that Shelley's procedure, like Wordsworth's in *The Borderers* (the worst of Shakespearean imitations, surely) was to use the *diction* of one Shakespearean play in treating of a *situation* borrowed from another. For instance: in Act II, Scene iv of *King Lear*, the King, challenged by Goneril and Regan as to the necessity of retaining even a single follower, answers:

> O, reason not the need: our basest beggars
> Are in the poorest thing superfluous:
> Allow not nature more than nature needs,
> Man's life's as cheap as beasts': . . .

Othello, accepting the Duke's direction to undertake an expedition against the Turks, says:

> The tyrant custom, most grave senators,
> Hath made the flinty and steel couch of war
> My thrice-driven bed of down . . . (I, iii, 230-32)

In the second act of *The Cenci* Shelley, with Lear's situation in mind, uses Othello's language:

>                                                    . . . If you,
> Cardinal Camillo, were reduced at once
> From thrice-driven beds of down, and delicate food,
> An hundred servants, and six palaces,
> To that which nature doth indeed require?

[1] Cp. Beach Langston, "Shelley's Use of Shakespeare," *Huntingdon Library Quarterly*, Vol. XII, 1949, pp. 163-90.

What *The Cenci* lacks is *character*: it has so little momentum of its own that it cannot use the energy borrowed from Shakespeare. There are a few fine passages of blank verse—notably Beatrice's speech in prison—but the play as a whole is a wraith: it stays in the mind (if at all) for its "atmosphere," its Jacobean-and-Gothic pastiche, its succession of high-pitched dialogues.

For Shelley, as for so many nineteenth-century poets, the limits of drama were set by his apprehension of Shakespeare. Like Coleridge, Schiller, and A. W. Schlegel, he practically equated drama with tragedy and, in turn, tragedy with its Shakespearean manifestations. For these writers there could be no question, for instance, of taking bourgeois tragedy seriously. Hazlitt spoke for his time and for Shelley when he said that "tragic poetry" was "the most impassioned species of it" and that impassioned poetry was "an emanation of the moral and intellectual part of our nature, as well as of the sensitive." By contrast, bourgeois tragedy appealed "almost exclusively" to one's sensibility.[2] There was no way out: one had to return to the source. From the first performance of *Remorse*, therefore, in 1813 to that of *A Blot in the 'Scutcheon* in 1843, verse dramatists in the English theatre (Byron excepted) had in mind a single neo-Shakespearean idea of "high" tragedy.

## II.

Browning attended Macready's performances of Shakespeare in 1835 and 1836; by 1836 Macready hoped that he had stimulated in Browning "a spirit of poetry whose influence would elevate, ennoble, and adorn our degraded drama."[3] In May 1837 Macready produced *Strafford*.

It is clear from Macready's Diary and from Browning's Letters that the actor and the poet were much more radically opposed in their conceptions of drama than they at any time

[2] *On Poetry in General; Lectures on the English Poets, Works,* edited by A. R. Waller and Arnold Glover, Dent, 1903, v, 5.
[3] *The Diaries of W. C. Macready 1833-1851,* edited by William Toynbee, Chapman and Hall, 1912, I, 277.

realised. Browning was an experimental dramatist, trying to clarify and exploit ideas of drama which Macready would have found bewildering. Macready's influence on the poet was, on the whole, unfortunate. Of *Strafford* he wrote in his *Diary*: "I had been too much carried away by the truth of character to observe the meanness of plot, and occasional obscurity." His conception of plot, however, was merely a taste for multiplicity of incident. As a result, Browning wasted a lot of time rewriting parts of *Strafford* at least five times, adding "incident" and improving the play to no extent whatever.

Browning invariably yielded to Macready. When he found that Macready wanted a "Shakespearean" tragedy, he laid aside his experiments and composed *A Blot in the 'Scutcheon*, a romanticised version of *Romeo and Juliet*.[4] Writing to Macready about the new play he assured him that there was "*action* in it, drabbing, stabbing, *et autres gentillesses*." The fact is that there is little but pastiche in it. It is clear that Browning's deliberate attempt to placate Macready with a "Shakespearean" tragedy caused him in this instance to compose blank verse of far poorer quality than much of the verse he had already written. Mildred's death-speech is a case in point:

> As I dare approach that Heaven
> Which has not bade a living thing despair,
> Which needs no code to keep its grace from stain,
> But bids the vilest worm that turns on it
> Desist and be forgiven,—I—forgive not,
> But bless you, Thorold, from my soul of souls!
> There! Do not think too much upon the past!
> The cloud that's broke was all the same a cloud
> While it stood up between my friend and you;
> You hurt him 'neath its shadow: but is that
> So past retrieve? I have his heart, you know,

[4] Cp. James Patton McCormick, "Robert Browning and Experimental Drama," *Publications of the Modern Language Association*, Vol. LXVIII, 5, December, 1951, pp. 982-91.

I may dispose of it: I give it you!
It loves you as mine loves! Confirm me, Henry!

(*Dies*).

There is very little energy in the movement of the iambics: the
sprightliness of the diction ("I have his heart, you know") is
belied by the rhythm. Much of the verse in *A Blot in the
'Scutcheon* reads like a parody of early Shakespeare, mere ap-
prentice-work. Yet Browning had already written the remarkable
couplets of *Sordello*:

> And every eve, Sordello's visit begs
> Pardon for them; constant at eve he came
> To sit beside each in her turn, the same
> As one of them, a certain space; and awe
> Made a great indistinctness till he saw
> Sunset slant cheerful through the buttress-chinks,
> Gold seven times globed; surely our maiden shrinks
> And a smile stirs her as if . . .[5]

The distinction in this writing may be seen in the discreet
handling of the rhymes. In the second and third lines, for instance, the syntax at "same" directs the reader's mind forward,
offsetting the tendency of the rhyme to make it sink to rest at
that point. In the fifth line the substitution of an ionic foot for
the first two expected iambics throws coordinate stresses on
"great" and the first syllable of "indistinctness," and after this
flurry of syllables the caesura comes in the middle of the
penultimate foot. The narrative movement takes up again at
"till": the feeling of expectancy hovers at "saw" and glides
beautifully into the trochaic "sunset" of the next line. There is
nothing to compare with this *ease* in *A Blot in the 'Scutcheon*.

[5] Ezra Pound in *ABC of Reading*, London, Faber and Faber, 1951
edition, pp. 181-91, cites a long passage which includes these lines; then
comments: "There is here a certain lucidity of sound that I think you
will find with difficulty elsewhere in English, and you very well may
have to retire as far as the Divina Commedia for continued narrative
having such clarity of outline without clog and *verbal* impediment."

Browning came closer than any other poet-dramatist to the *invention* of a theatre-form answerable to the dominant motives of his time. He was the only writer who realised, for instance, that a neo-Shakespearean drama based primarily on the idea of "painting the passions" would be perverse. "Painting the passions" virtually dominated English verse drama in the years following *A Blot in the 'Scutcheon*: the poets insisted on the assumption that Shakespeare's own procedures favoured this emphasis.

This was not, of course, a new development: the difference was one of degree, not of kind. We find a similar tendency in late seventeenth-century tragedies, notably in *Venice Preserved,* where Otway's main impulse is to press as much emotion as possible into the local situation, with little regard for the larger coherence of the play. As a result, the play tends to break down into isolated, grandiloquent *scenes*,[6] such as that between Belvidera and Jaffeir at the beginning of the fourth act:

Oh inconstant man!
How will you promise? How will you deceive?
Do, return back, re-place me in my Bondage,
Tell all thy Friends how dangerously thou lov'st me,
And let thy Dagger doe its bloudy office.
Oh that kind Dagger, Jaffeir, how 'twill look,
Struck through my Heart; drench'd in my bloud to th' hilts.

The partial interpretation of Shakespeare represented by *Venice Preserved* continued in the nineteenth century to dominate such a play as *A Legend of Florence*. It also revealed itself clearly in Coleridge's Shakespearean criticism. Coleridge, deviating from Aristotle, enumerated the parts of the drama as three: language, passion, character. There is in his theoretical, if to a less extent in his practical, criticism a conscious denigration of plot.[7] Similarly, Wordsworth declared that in writing *The Borderers* his care (in this like Shelley, Hazlitt, Beddoes,

[6] Cp. Moody E. Prior, *The Language of Tragedy*, Columbia University Press, 1947, p. 189.
[7] *Coleridge's Shakespearean Criticism*, edited by T. M. Raysor, London, Constable, 1930, I, 205-06.

and Stevenson) "was almost exclusively given to the passions and the characters."

The impulse to "paint the passions" found its appropriate form in Browning's dramatic monologues. Browning erred frequently and seriously as a dramatist, but it is part of his lasting achievement that he eventually realised the only proper form for the dominant motive in the drama of his time. Northrop Frye has pointed out[8] that in the nineteenth century the tragic vision was practically identical with the ironic vision; hence, nineteenth-century tragedies tend to be either *Schicksal* dramas dealing with the arbitrary ironies of fate, or (clearly the more rewarding form) studies of the frustration of human activity by the combined pressures of a reactionary society without and a disorganised soul within. This irony, tending toward a stasis of action, culminates in lyric. The tendency—symbolically enacted in a Shakespearean soliloquy—is seen most clearly in Browning's monodramas (such as *Porphyria's Lover*) which are gestures of isolation, successions of romantic-ironic moments. These monodramas may be regarded as the point of contact between nineteenth-century tragedy and one of the characteristic *situations* of "high" Romantic poetry. It is as if one element in *Hamlet*, the tension between the hero and his environment, were abstracted to become a source of nineteenth-century romantic irony. Ultimately, the ideal hero would be a Chatterton or a Christopher Smart.

There is no evidence that later nineteenth-century poets realised the significance of Browning's monodramas. Tennyson, Swinburne, and Bridges continued the weary struggle to imitate Shakespeare. Hopkins was quick to note the archaism in the diction of Bridges's *Ulysses*, and he might well have commented similarly on the neo-Elizabethan verse of Tennyson's *Becket* (1884) while remarking, as he did, the dramatic poverty of *The Promise of May* (1882). Tennyson, according to his son, "was aware that he wanted intimate knowledge of the mechanical

[8] "A Conspectus of Dramatic Genres," *Kenyon Review*, Vol. XIII, 4, Autumn, 1951, p. 550.

details necessary for the modern stage." His plays were written, therefore, "with the intention that actors should edit them for the stage, keeping them at the high poetic level." This was the basis on which Irving "arranged" the script of *Becket* in 1893. Browning, however, recognising that the impulse to "paint the passions" led to soliloquy, exploited the impulse artistically by means of the monodrama. Tennyson and Swinburne dissipated the Shakespearean tragic form by retaining its mechanical semblance and turning it into a series of interrupted monologues. The defect has been described by Henry James in another context: in the Preface to *The Tragic Muse* he notes: "No character in a play (any play not a mere monologue) has, for the right of the thing, a *usurping* consciousness; the consciousness of others is exhibited exactly in the same way as that of the 'hero.' " The example he offers is that of Hamlet, whose "prodigious consciousness, the most capacious and most crowded, the moral presence the most asserted, in the whole range of fiction, only takes its turn with that of the other agents of the story, no matter how occasional these may be."[9] The dominant tendencies in the later nineteenth-century theatre conspired to render this ideal impossible.

## III.

James himself, of course, is the greatest rejected lover in the nineteenth-century theatre. Like Keats, like Hopkins, he was fascinated by the dramatic forms; he considered the drama "the ripest of all the arts, the one to which one must bring most of the acquired as well as most of the natural." For reasons which are more easily explained by his biography than by his "nature" he sought to be a dramatist by studying Sardou and the contemporary French theatre. He could hardly have chosen a less fruitful model, except perhaps Shakespeare—one is free to speculate at large on this point. At all events he learned how to compose a "well-made" play; in addition he made it "well-written." But the results, fascinating to lovers of James

[9] *The Art of the Novel*, New York, Scribner, 1935, p. 90.

and interesting to connoisseurs of failure, are wooden, graceless plays. Of the several reasons for which *Guy Domville* might have pleased the audience at the St. James's Theatre in January 1895, few are of any relevance today: distracted by Sardouism, James contrived to compose a play which, however well-written or well-made, is rhetorically gross. One tinkers with the idea that James as dramatist had no conception of the art of rhetoric, of ingratiation; instead of fulfilling the desires inaugurated in the first act James grossly thwarted them and then blamed the "yelling barbarians" for rejecting him and relishing Wilde.

The failure of *Guy Domville* was not the end of James's work for the theatre, but we may see it as making explicit what the theatre may well have "sensed" (since it has its own "feel" and is rarely "wrong"); that James, while willing to "learn the trade," was unable radically to translate his skills into the unique language of theatre. James's procedures were quantitative, cumulative; his "translation" was never qualitative. It was as if he reasoned thus: "take a fastidious master of words, add to him the tricks of the theatrical trade, and the result must be a superb dramatist." In our own day Eliot has suffered from a similar misconception, though he has more manfully tried to overcome it, being inhibited now, it would seem, by factors which are so deeply involved in his temperament as to be beyond his own diagnosis. Of the art of "translation" Cocteau is surely our most agile master, and he has been fortunate in acquiring at an early stage in his life an insight into the radically different *languages* in which artists in theatre, ballet, cinema, or literature must think. This insight was not available to James; instead he acknowledged what was always fundamental in himself, a rift between Drama and Theatre. After *Guy Domville* he wrote: "I may have been meant for the drama—God knows!—but I certainly wasn't meant for the theatre."[10] The acknowledged rift (or, in our terms, the inability to "translate") was not as serious for James as it proved for Beddoes, Taylor, Kingsley,

[10] *The Letters of Henry James*, edited by Percy Lubbock, Macmillan, 1920, I, 232.

and Hardy. For one thing, he could still utilise, in the later novels, his own "feel" for the dramatic *myth* as an ordering insight into motives and relationships: the gross business of "theatre" could not deny that vision in all its suggestiveness and scope, nor could it prevent the development of James's novels in modes arising directly from his sense of "the dramatic way," his recognition of the "scenic" principle. In others, like Hardy, the rift between Drama and Theatre could issue only in glum rejections, frustrations, dark forebodings. It is a painfully common experience in the nineteenth-century theatre.

## IV.

If we would believe Harley Granville-Barker, we owe the modern revival of "poetic drama" to Maeterlinck. Certainly, it is proper to associate Maeterlinck's early plays with Yeats's *The Shadowy Waters*, and the association, if extended, provides a minor "tradition" to which such a play as Gordon Bottomley's *Gruach* may be referred. It is necessary to bear in mind, however, that such a "tradition" would be based merely on a single element in Maeterlinck, the transcendentalism which appears again in his essay on Emerson and which is in large measure derived from that source. There are indeed other respects in which a putative relation between Maeterlinck and the early Yeats is justified, Maeterlinck's devaluation of plot, for instance, and his refusal to interest himself in the motivation of Shakespeare's tragic heroes: "Aussi, n'est-ce pas dans les actes, mais dans les paroles que se trouvent la beauté et la grandeur des belles et grandes tragédies."[11] This beauty and greatness, Maeterlinck declared, are not to be found solely in the words that render the action; there must be, as it were, a dialogue of the "second degree": "On peut même affirmer que le poème se rapproche de la beauté et d'une vérité supérieure, dans la mesure où il élimine les paroles qui expliquent les actes pour les rem-

---

[11] *Le Tragique Quotidien, Le Trésor des Humbles,* Paris, Société du Mercure de France, ninth edition, 1896, pp. 193, 194.

placer par des paroles qui expliquent non pas ce qu'on appelle un 'état d'âme' mais je ne sais quels efforts insaisissables et incessants des âmes vers leur beauté et vers leur vérité."[11]

In Maeterlinck, as in Yeats's early plays, there is an impulse to eliminate denotation, to make the words answerable only to connotation, in particular to "état d'âme." A similar urge in both writers prompted such stratagems as that of hanging a gauze veil between the audience and the stage in order to emphasise the "distance from life."

The mooted "tradition," however, while preempting Maeterlinck's "atmosphere," would have no place for the prime motive of his early plays, Fear. There is in these plays a pervading sense of disintegration: an impression of the human soul, in a nightmare other-world, torn by dragons. The urge to remove his characters from the quotidian world is, in Maeterlinck, dialectical; in the early Yeats, pastoral and to some extent nostalgic. Perhaps we must argue, with this perspective in mind, that Maeterlinck's "influence" on the modern theatre has been retrograde: misread, attenuated, he has surely been to some extent responsible for pushing verse plays away from the "urgencies of actuality" (Robert Penn Warren's phrase, in a different context) into realms of filigree, fantasy, whimsy, "delicacy," the esoteric, the "cultivated," the decorative. Wherefore until recently a poetic play was expected to exhibit a pampered, elegant "mood," but no contact at all with the human, the ordinary, the natural, the solid stuff of actuality. A tentative explanation would go somewhat as follows: Maeterlinck's plays operate within the realm of *pathos* rather than *praxis*: the Aristotelian *act*, issuing from the *moto spiral*, is here reduced to a *scene*, or even to an "atmosphere," which in turn, as compensation, takes unto itself (to sustain its new burden) the rarefied tone, the esoteric "colour"; in short, the Georgian. From Maeterlinck to Barrie and Flecker. We push the argument to extremes, to make a point which we hope to qualify in a later chapter on the Mood Play.

## V.

We invoke Masefield for our last anecdote to remind ourselves that while Yeats's recourse to the French symbolists is an
important factor in modern literature and drama, the main formal influences on the early developments of modern English
verse drama were English. French literature made no particular
impact on Stephen Phillips, Flecker, or on Masefield himself.
Only in Eliot's plays (and, embarrassingly, in Tennessee Williams) has a French tradition—ultimately that of the novel of
Stendhal and Flaubert—penetrated modern English drama. The
blank verse of *Paolo and Francesca* (1902) looks back through
Tennyson's *Queen Mary* (1875) to Shakespeare. Similarly the
soliloquising tendency of nineteenth-century verse drama culminates in the arias which Flecker distributes in *Don Juan*:

> In vain, O day with rose of battle shining
> You drive upon the dome your ancient car:
> In vain you hope your golden head reclining
> To breathe the fire and hear the shout of war:
> In vain, O day, with rose of battle shining.

Masefield seldom wrote album-verse as bad as this, but his
work suffers at least as much from the absence of any viable
decorum for his plays. Hence the pervading unevenness of his
dramatic writing: he moves from one arbitrary mode to another,
hoping that something will turn up. In *The Tragedy of Nan*
(1908) he sought to compose a poetic play by exploiting the
"poetry" of English rustics; the result is one of the most em-
barrassing plays in the modern theatre:

"They was eight maids in white when they carried 'er. Then
they was women. Beautiful they were. Then they grew old. One
by one. And then their 'ouses were to let, with the windows
broke. And grass and grass. They be all gone. When I be gone
there'll be none to tell the beauty of my vlower. There'll be
none as knows where 'er body lies. I 'ave 'er little grave all done
up with shells. And the vlowers that do come up, they be little

words from 'er. Little zhining words. Fifty-nine year them little words come."

Besides the desire to emulate Hardy's novels or Tennyson's dialect-play *The Promise of May, The Tragedy of Nan* shows that Masefield's conception of *poésie de théâtre*, like Flecker's, consisted only of the identification of the poetic and the picturesque. Formal considerations did not weigh heavily.

*Good Friday* (1916) is a better play and the best of Masefield's Biblical dramas. It is clear, however, that the adoption of the rhyming couplet for the dialogue was an error. There was nothing in Masefield's play which demanded or could use up the characteristic "qualities" of the couplet, its ability to hold two ideas or situations in poise, its grasp of sharp distinctions or qualifications. Professor Fergusson has pointed out in his essay on Racine that the couplet, characteristically, "feels" conclusive, as the perfect, aphoristic summary. Blank verse, on the other hand, less "perfect" and more flexible, can reflect much more of the psyche's subtle posturings. And *terza rima,* with its endlessly interlocking rhymes, reflects at any moment only a provisional unity: as the angle of vision shifts, it follows the process of change. The fine balance, the intricate symmetry, of the Alexandrine couplet give an impression of final order, though it often has the illusion of variety and change:

"The 'order' would appear to be that of the logical contradiction: stress equal and opposite to counterstress, thesis to antithesis. The contradiction is never substantially transcended—the third term, the synthesis on another level, is never provided—there is only another couplet. . . . But the oppositions *seem* to be transcended by the very clarity with which they are put, much as the manner of salon or stage offers a surface so perfect as to 'transcend' the tragic split which makes it possible."[12]

The material of *Good Friday*, and the play's characteristic modes, are not those which the couplet is peculiarly fitted to render. As a result, there is a superflux in the couplet which

[12] "Action as Rational," *Hudson Review*, Vol. I, 2, Summer, 1948, p. 201. *The Idea of a Theater*, Princeton University Press, 1949.

overhangs the material of the play and weighs it down: the form imposes on the rhymed words a degree of emphasis and "point" which their meaning cannot support. The form is too "perfect" for the matter:

> I have no part nor parcel in his end.
> Rather than have it thought I buy my ease,
> My body's safety, honour, dignities,
> Life and the rest at such a price of pain
> There
> > *(She stabs her arm with her dagger)*
> > is my blood, to wash away the stain.
> There. Thère once more. It fetched too dear a price.
> O God, redeem that soul in paradise.

We have been discussing fragmentary insights, half-truths, truths touched without recognition. Hence our fragmentary mode of exposition. Hence also our devoted emphasis on Browning, since he was the only poet in the English theatre of his time who was sensitive to formal incongruities, the only *inventor* among the dramatic poets. His inventions are precious to us today not because they provide a viable theatre-form for our time and for our own preoccupations (they do *not*) but because we may yet be inspired by the myth of formal coherence and unity which impelled Browning. And with this myth in mind we are struck once again by the most serious disaster in the modern English theatre: that the English reception of Ibsen's plays stopped with the mere recognition of *theme* and *argument*. Modern theatre-poetry struggles to be born (it is Professor Fergusson's phrase) in the shadow of this failure.

# CHAPTER THREE. YEATS AND THE
# CLEAN OUTLINE

■■■■■■■■■■■■■■■■■

"... to me drama ... has been the search for more
of manful energy, more of cheerful acceptance of
whatever arises out of the logic of events, and for clean
outline, instead of those outlines of lyric poetry that
are blurred with desire and vague regret."—
W. B. YEATS, Preface to *Poems, 1899-1905*

■■■■■■■■■■■■■■■■■

WE would examine Yeats's development as a verse dramatist,
concentrating on *The Shadowy Waters, The Hour Glass, At the
Hawk's Well,* and *A Full Moon in March.*

The first edition of *The Shadowy Waters* appeared in 1900,[1]
but Yeats is known to have begun work on the play many years
before.[2] This version of the play is characteristic of the earliest
phase in Yeats's writing for the theatre. *A Full Moon in March*
first appeared in 1935;[3] it embodies a conception of drama
which Yeats had clarified by trial and error over a period of
many years. Thus the beginning and the end. In the 1913 version of *The Hour Glass*[4] we would see an important stage in
this development, leading to the *Plays for Dancers. At the
Hawk's Well* (1916), the earliest of these, reveals most clearly
their characteristic structure.[5]

[1] *The Shadowy Waters,* London, Hodder and Stoughton, 1900, pp. 7-57.
This text first appeared in *The North American Review,* May 1900.

[2] *The Letters of W. B. Yeats,* edited by Allan Wade, London, Rupert
Hart-Davis, 1954, p. 237 and p. 237n.

[3] *Poetry,* Chicago, March 1935. *A Full Moon in March,* London, Macmillan, 1935, pp. 3-22.

[4] *The Mask,* Florence, April 1913. *The Hour Glass,* Dundrum, Cuala
Press, 1914, pp. 1-35.

[5] *At the Hawk's Well* was first published, under the title "At Hawk's
Well or Waters of Immortality" in *Harper's Bazaar,* March 1917. In
the same year it was included in *The Wild Swans at Coole,* Cuala Press.
The first English publication of the play was in *Four Plays for Dancers,*
Macmillan, 1921.

We also wish to examine in the four plays a preoccupation
(which is also profoundly active in Yeats's poems) with the
diverse claims of Soul and Body, the Ideal and the Actual.
Yeats's development, both as poet and as dramatist, was a
painful and by no means unswerving movement toward a conception of life which would do justice to its seemingly rival
elements:

> Labour is blossoming or dancing where
> The body is not bruised to pleasure soul . . .[6]

But he never achieved a definitive image of such harmony in
*words*: he came closer to it in *gesture*.

Yeats worked on *The Shadowy Waters* at intervals from
about 1885 to 1899; in 1905 he rewrote the play completely.[7]
For many, however, it remains "the least successful of Yeats's
verse plays":[8] a widely held view has been expressed by Mr.
Eliot: "*The Shadowy Waters* seems to me one of the most
perfect expressions of the vague enchanted beauty of the (pre-
Raphaelite) school: yet it strikes me . . . as the western seas
descried through the back window of a house in Kensington,
an Irish myth for the Kelmscott Press; and when I try to visualise
the speakers in the play, they have the great dim, dreamy eyes
of the knights and ladies of Burne-Jones."[9] Guilt by association.
True, Yeats's Forgael and Dectora do not lend themselves to
"visualisation," but *The Shadowy Waters* is not *The Voysey
Inheritance*. The characters in *The Shadowy Waters* are im-
palpable: Yeats meant them to be so. His aim was: "to create
for a few people who love symbol a play that will be more a
ritual than a play, and leave upon the mind an impression like

---

[6] "*Among School Children*" (1927), stanza VII, 1.1-2; *October Blast*,
Cuala Press, 1927. *Collected Poems*, Macmillan, 1950, p. 244.

[7] Thomas Parkinson in his *W. B. Yeats: Self-Critic*, University of
California Press, 1951, Ch. 2, presents the revisions as illustrating Yeats's
progress toward formal clarity.

[8] Lennox Robinson, *Ireland's Abbey Theatre*, Sidgwick and Jackson,
1951, p. 40.

[9] T. S. Eliot, *Selected Prose*, Penguin Books, 1953, p. 202.

that of tapestry where the forms only half-reveal themselves amid the shadowy folds."[10]

Forgael is unreal inasmuch as he does not endorse the reality of human life; his function is to testify to the existence of a reality free from the limitations of nature and circumstance. *The Shadowy Waters* is characteristic of Yeats's earliest plays (his Maeterlinckian plays) in that its action arises from an imputed tension between two realities: that of the circumstantial world as we know it, and a reality of Essence or Idea toward which Forgael's will strains. The play presents a conflict between these two worlds. The sailors are the static representatives of the natural world; Forgael bears witness to a special kind of transcendence. The movable parts of the play are Aibric and Dectora. Aibric, associated with Forgael at the beginning, eventually yields to the rational Order. Dectora, the queenly enemy, is at last won over to vindicate the higher Order of Forgael's aspiration.

There is no mistaking Yeats's dialectic. Indeed, a comparison of the 1900 version of the play with the standard acting version as first performed in 1906 shows that the revisions were designed not only to strengthen the structure of the play but also to emphasise still further the conflict of Forgael's aspirations with those of the other characters.

The theme is love. When Forgael speaks of the promises of the human-headed birds, Aibric rebukes him:

> I know their promises. You have told me all.
> They are to bring you to unheard-of passion,
> To some strange love the world knows nothing of,
> Some Ever-living woman as you think,
> One that can cast no shadow, being unearthly.
> But that's all folly. Turn the ship about,
> Sail home again, be some fair woman's friend;
> Be satisfied to live like other men,

[10] Programme-note on the play, printed in *Inis Fail*, August 1905. See also Yeats's letter to Frank Fay (?20 January, 1904), *Letters*, edited Wade, *supra*, p. 425.

And drive impossible dreams away. The world
Has beautiful women to please every man.

Forgael rejects this kind of love with its "brief longing and deceiving hope"; but he is answered again by Aibric:

All that ever loved
Have loved that way—there is no other way.

Forgael protests:

Yet never have two lovers kissed but they
Believed there was some other near at hand,
And almost wept because they could not find it.

At this point Aibric's attitude hardens:

When they have twenty years; in middle life
They take a kiss for what a kiss is worth,
And let the dream go by.

Forgael, seizing on the "dream," answers with the largest idealistic gesture in the whole play:

It's not a dream,
But the reality that makes our passion
As a lamp shadow—no—no lamp, the sun.
What the world's million lips are thirsting for
Must be substantial somewhere.[11]

Professor Ellis-Fermor has quoted these passages from the standard acting version, arguing that in *The Shadowy Waters* "the central theme is realisation of ideal love in terms of, not by the superseding of, natural love. . . ."[12] It is hard to agree. When Aibric insists that there is only one kind of love, Forgael

---

[11] *Collected Plays*, Macmillan, 1952, pp. 150-51. This is the "acting version" of *The Shadowy Water* which was first performed on 8 December 1906 and published in London by A. H. Bullen in the following year. Allan Wade in his *A Bibliography of the Writings of W. B. Yeats*, Rupert Hart-Davis, 1951, p. 77, writes: "Written partly in verse, partly in prose: the prose seems to be largely the work of Lady Gregory."

[12] Una Ellis-Fermor, *The Irish Dramatic Movement*, Methuen, second edition, 1954, p. 102.

protests, crying out not for a deeper penetration of human love, but for a new "way" of love altogether:

> Yet never have two lovers kissed but they
> Believed there was some other near at hand,
> And almost wept because they could not find it.

It is necessary to argue, therefore, that Forgael's love, like that of the Ghost of Cuchulain in *The Only Jealousy of Emer*, is transcendental love: not natural love ennobled, refined, or exalted, but a new kind of love altogether. This appears also in the 1900 version of the play, in which Forgael says:

> When I hold
> A woman in my arms, she sinks away
> As though the waters had flowed up between;
> And yet, there is a love that the gods give,
> When Aengus and his Edaine wake from sleep
> And gaze on one another through our eyes,
> And turn brief longing and deceiving hope
> And bodily tenderness to the soft fire
> That shall burn time when times have ebbed away.
> The fool foretold me I would find this love
> Among those streams, or on their cloudy edge.[13]

Later, in the same version, Dectora asks:

> Where are these boughs? Where are the holy woods
> That can change love to imperishable fire?[13]

In terms of Time, the tension between Yeats's two worlds is that between the transience of the natural world and the idea of permanence; in terms of Space, between Aibric's "habitable world" and Forgael's country at the end of the world "where no child's born but to outlive the moon"; in natural terms, between the body and that "mysterious transformation of the flesh"

[13] As at footnote 1, above, p. 19 and pp. 49-50.

which Yeats rather gnomically invoked.[14] Each of these aspirations is part of a larger movement toward an ideal existence envisaged symbolically as the fusion of lily and rose, of Forgael and Dectora.

At this point Yeats is dangerously close to what Allen Tate has called "the angelic fallacy." When Forgael presses toward transcendental love, he not only evades the limitations of human love but sidesteps the entire human condition. The state which Tate finds in Poe's major stories, particularly in *Ligeaia* and *The Fall of the House of Usher*, is present also in *The Shadowy Waters*: "The hero professes an impossibly high love of the heroine that circumvents the body and moves in upon her spiritual essence. All this sounds high and noble, until we begin to look at it more narrowly, when we perceive that the ordinary carnal relationship between man and woman, however sinful, would be preferable to the mutual destruction of soul to which Poe's characters are committed."[15]

Yeats's Forgael, Poe's Roderick, and Marlowe's Faustus are "overreachers": the disease in each case is hypertrophy of the will. *The Shadowy Waters* is weak, however, not because its hero or its author is philosophically "wrong," but because the dialectical abstraction named Forgael is subjected to nothing but fondling. There is no serious testing of its aspirations, no irony. Yeats treats it as a pet child.

Indeed, the delicate blur which the play leaves in the mind reveals its real deficiency. Certainly it would be absurd to describe *The Shadowy Waters* as a "solid" play in the sense which Professor Empson had in mind in one of his homely generalisations. A solid play, he argued, which can give the individual a rich satisfaction at one time, and therefore different satisfactions at different times from different "points of view," is likely to be a play that can satisfy different individuals and can face an

---

[14] *The Arrow*, 24 November 1906. See Richard Ellman, *The Identity of Yeats*, Macmillan, 1954, p. 81, and *The Irish Dramatic Movement, supra*, Chapter v.

[15] "The Angelic Imagination," *Kenyon Review*, Vol. XIV, 3, Summer 1952, pp. 457-58.

audience: ". . . the trouble with plays like Maeterlinck's is that they are only good from one 'point of view.' "[16] In the case of *The Shadowy Waters*, if through a rational or instinctive distrust of transcendentalism one sides with Aibric more than with Forgael (and this is a reasonable attitude), if one resists the Yeats-Forgael rhetoric, the play crumbles. Its texture is so precariously thin that it cannot bear the slightest ironical pressure. This distinguishes *The Shadowy Waters* from, say, *Man and Superman*. It is possible to find the "argument" of these plays equally unacceptable, but *Man and Superman* is so solid in texture that it holds fast as a play even under the most ironical scrutiny.

The "thinness" of *The Shadowy Waters*—as of *Poems* (1895), *The Wind among the Reeds* (1899), and *In the Seven Woods* (1903)—arises from the tendency of the poems and the play alike to offer images of a disembodied state which represents the spirit or the soul. Even in *The Tower* (1928) Yeats failed to present a relation between Soul and Body in which both elements would simultaneously thrive. In the early poems the putative harmony of Body and Soul is disrupted, the Body and the entire human order being willed out of existence, just as Forgael, supported by the rhetorical bias of his play, finds in human love not a path to ideal love but a trap. This impulse to slough the human mode of action is expressed in several early poems:

> I am haunted by numberless islands, and many a
> Danaan shore,
> Where Time would surely forget us, and Sorrow
> come near us no more;
> Soon far from the rose and the lily and fret of the
> flames would we be,
> Were we only white birds, my beloved, buoyed out
> on the foam of the sea![17]

[16] William Empson, *Some Versions of Pastoral*, Chatto and Windus, second edition, 1950, p. 66.

[17] *The White Birds*, 1892, *The Countess Cathleen and Various Legends and Lyrics*, 1892; *Collected Poems*, Macmillan, 1933, pp. 46-47.

In the Crazy Jane sequence, on the other hand, there is an almost frenetic adhesion to simple Matter, to Body; these poems fail to penetrate the natural or the finite by means of a deep analogical act.

One of the most distinctive features of *A Full Moon in March* —to be dealt with later—is that it comes very close to the enactment of a movement of the sensibility in which the discordant elements are held in energetic tension. One does not simply cancel its rival, as in *The Shadowy Waters*. Instead we pass through the knot of the "intrigue" (*through* the discordant elements) to an image of vital harmony which is the dance itself. The "free" gesture of the dance is the resolution, the fulfilment, the "way out."

The 1900 version of *The Shadowy Waters* was written entirely in verse. In revising the play Yeats saw that it would be possible to increase its tension by juxtaposing prose and verse passages. The sailors, for instance, who in the early version had spoken lines like

> How many moons have died from the full moon
> When something that was bearded like a goat
> Walked on the waters and bid Forgael seek
> His heart's desire where the world dwindles out?[18]

now speak in prose, thereby "reducing" their own status: "What is the use of knocking about and fighting as we do unless we get the chance to drink more wine and kiss more women than lasting peaceable men through their long lifetime . . ."[19]

Throughout the standard acting version prose is used for those parts of the dialogue which mirror the "merely" human world. Correspondingly, the Higher Reality expresses itself only in verse. In at least one passage the dichotomy between the two worlds is strongly underlined by this means: when Aibric and the sailors move away from Forgael and his birds, prose-

---

[18] As at footnote 1, above, p. 14.
[19] *Collected Plays, supra*, pp. 149-50.

reality and poetry-reality simultaneously claim the audience's attention, though Forgael alone holds the stage:

SECOND SAILOR: There is nobody is natural but a robber. That is the reason the whole world goes tottering about upon its bandy legs.

AIBRIC: Run upon them now, and overpower the crew while yet asleep.

Aibric and the sailors go out. Confused voices and the clashing of swords are heard from the other ship, which cannot be seen because of the sail. Forgael, who has remained at the tiller, cries out:

> There! there! They come! Gull, gannet, or diver,
> But with a man's head, or a fair woman's.
> They hover over the masthead awhile
> To wait their friends, but when their friends have come
> They'll fly upon that secret way of theirs,
> One—and one—a couple—five together . . .[20]

Yeats's dramatic instinct served him well in the decision to offset prose and verse in the acting version of *The Shadowy Waters*, because the jolt in moving from one to the other reinforces the implication of the play. When he passes from prose to verse in this play (and he makes these changes abruptly, "raising" the tone of the language) he gives a strong impression of the inadequacy of the human or circumstantial world. The strategy of prose-and-verse serves his rhetorical purpose.

The procedure needs to be used very carefully, however. We would argue that the use of prose and verse in a play is likely to be fruitful in four main ways; some of these are obvious and may be noted without special illustration.

First, prose may be used to apply an ironical corrective to any rhetorical excess which the verse-plot may include. Frequently a corrective of this kind is necessary to exorcise an

[20] *Ibid.*, p. 153.

ironical, unregenerate spirit in the audience: one may cite the impulse of the spectator to resist, by laughter, what he feels to be a particularly tender love-scene or an excessively heroic gesture. The use of prose in such cases also helps to strengthen the texture of the play, to give it a certain "roughage."

Second, as an extension of this procedure, prose may be useful in a verse play which employs a double plot, especially if the secondary plot is in any sense a burlesque version of the main plot. "Comic relief" often takes a similar form.

Third, the dramatist may offset prose and verse if he wishes unobtrusively to confront the actual with the ideal, the "partial" view of life with the "full" truth. *The Shadowy Waters* is a case in point. Also, as we shall see, *September Lemonade*.

Finally, there are plays such as Delmore Schwartz' *Shenandoah* in which verse is used for the ritual, quasi-choric commentary of the title-role (that of a privileged spectator), and prose for the naturalistic parts (such as the disagreement between Walter Fish and Nathan Harris over the naming of the newborn child).[21] The following is a typical instance. Dr. Adamson says: "Ah, this is the house blessed by the birth of a child; what a wonderful thing it is to bring a human being into the world . . ."

Shenandoah, whose words are heard only by the audience, comments:

> Here is the man of God: what will he say?
> How relevant are his imperatives?
> Can he express himself in modern terms?
> And bring this conflict to a peaceful end?
> His insights, old as Pharaoh, sometimes work,
> But there is always something wholly new,

[21] "I would classify as naturalistic that type of realism in which the individual is portrayed not merely as subordinate to his background but as wholly determined by it." Philip Rahv: "Notes on the Decline of Naturalism," *Perspectives*, Vol. 2, Winter 1953, p. 153. In *Shenandoah* the Fish family and their relatives are in this sense determined by their Jewish background.

Unique, unheard-of, unaccounted for,
Under the sun, despite Ecclesiastes . . .

After this choric interlude the plot continues: Dr. Adamson is still speaking: "But why did I hear such shouting and angry voices? What must God think, seeing anger in the house of a newborn child? Men were not born to fight with one another . . ."[22]

The juxtaposition of prose and verse is clearly a fertile procedure, but it often involves the dramatist in an oversimplification of the issues arising in the play. For instance, no mature attitudes could be as *simpliste* as those Yeats uses in *The Shadowy Waters*, and this simplification is intensified by the juxtaposition of prose and verse. One may readily see, therefore, why Eliot has in recent years eschewed entirely the mixture of verse and prose in a single play. We should not, of course, discount the possibilities of the procedure.

*The Shadowy Waters* does not answer any important questions for the verse dramatist. In particular, it fails to point toward a viable dramatic language. At the end of the play we find Forgael and Dectora tossing mere wool-balls of pre-Raphaelite lyricism. Dectora, on the edge of an "other" world of love, says:

> The mist has covered the heavens, and you and I
> Shall be alone for ever. We two—this crown—
> I half remember. It has been in my dreams,
> Bend lower, O king, that I may crown you with it,
> O flower of the branch, O bird among the leaves,
> O silver fish that my two hands have taken
> Out of the running stream, O morning star,
> Trembling in the blue heavens like a white fawn
> Upon the misty border of the wood,
> Bend lower, that I may cover you with my hair,
> For we will gaze upon this world no longer.

[22] *Shenandoah*, New Directions, 1941, p. 23.

The harp begins to burn as with fire. Forgael, gathering Dectora's hair about him, answers:

> Beloved, having dragged the net about us,
> And knitted mesh to mesh, we grow immortal;
> And that old harp awakens of itself
> To cry aloud to the grey birds, and dreams
> That have had dreams for father, live in us.[23]

This, as dramatic language, is in no respect an advance on any characteristic passage from Beddoes; it represents no real improvement on the following lines, for instance, from Tennyson's *The Foresters*, in which Marian protests her fidelity to Robin Hood:

> Forget *him*—never—by this Holy Cross
> Which good King Richard gave me when a child—
> Never!
> Not while the swallow skims along the ground,
> And while the lark flies up and touches heaven!
> Not while the smoke floats from the cottage roof,
> And the white cloud is roll'd along the sky!
> Not while the rivulet babbles by the door,
> And the great breaker beats upon the beach!
> Never—[24]

One does not account for the weakness of Yeats's lines by simply asserting that blank verse has lost its validity as theatre-speech. This idea has gained currency mainly because of Mr. Eliot's authority, but we should be slow to accept it. The fact that one rejects the neo-Shakespearean pastiche in such plays as *Otho the Great*

> I do believe you. No, 'twas not to make
> A father his son's debtor, or to heal
> His deep heart-sickness for a rebel child.

[23] *Collected Plays, supra*, pp. 166-67.
[24] *The Foresters*, I, ii, *The Works of Alfred Lord Tennyson*, Macmillan, 1907, p. 811.

'Twas done in memory of my boyish days,
Poor cancel for his kindness to my youth,
For all his calming of my childish griefs,
And all his smiles upon my merriment.
No, not a thousand foughten fields could sponge
Those days paternal from my memory,
Though now upon my back he heaps disgrace.[25]

is not enough to prove that blank verse as such is disabled in
the modern theatre. It is difficult, for instance, to accept the
view that blank verse or even iambic pentametre with rhyme
has no means of contact with the colloquial speech of the
present century. One may cite, as a test case, a short passage
from Karl Shapiro's *The Intellectual*:

> . . . I'd rather be
> A milkman walking in his sleep at dawn
> Bearing fat quarts of cream, and so be free
> Crossing alone and cold from lawn to lawn.
>
> I'd rather be a barber and cut hair
> Than walk with you in gilt museum halls,
> You and the puma-lady, she so rare
> Exhaling her silk soul upon the walls.
>
> Go take yourself apart, but let me be
> The fault you find with everyman. I spit,
> I laugh, I fight; and you, *l'homme qui rit,*
> Swallow your stale saliva, and still sit.[26]

Finally, two lines from Robert Frost; in *The Witch of Coös*
the son says to the narrator:

> Mother can make a common table rear
> And kick with two legs like an army mule.[27]

[25] *Otho the Great*, I, iii, *The Poetical Works of John Keats*, edited
by H. W. Garrod, Oxford, Clarendon Press, 1939, p. 327.
[26] *V-Letter and other Poems*, Random House, 1944, p. 52.
[27] Robert Frost, *Collected Poems*, Henry Holt and Co., 1949, p. 247.

Here the stress on "like" (exacted by the metre alone, not by the grammar) stiffens the rhythm, strengthening the impression of the "kicking" table-legs. This is the kind of effect which a regular metrical scheme facilitates; the relation between the metre and the rhythm enables the writer partially to promote or to suppress a word, when necessary, in the interests of greater precision of statement. These examples from Shapiro and from Frost suggest that, provided diction and syntax are strongly "contemporary," the writer for the theatre may avail himself of the full resources of blank verse without fear of archaism or of Elizabethan echoes. Although traditional metres have indeed suffered a severe loss of authority during the past thirty years, it is much too early to decide that the dramatist must yield up blank verse. On the technical level (which is also the level of meaning and expressiveness) the loss of blank verse would constitute one of the most serious limitations in modern verse drama.

But the verse itself must not remain neutral, external. The weakness of the lines from *The Shadowy Waters* arises not from blank verse as such but from the fact that the metre is merely passive. It does not impinge on the other elements in the passage, and therefore plays no part in defining the feeling. Instead of engaging with the diction and the syntax to form a complex whole, it falls away from those elements, remaining detached, inert. We may illustrate this more clearly by reading the first stanza of Donne's *Love's Usury*:

> For every hour that thou wilt spare me now,
>    I will allow,
> Usurious God of Love, twenty to thee,
> When with my brown, my gray hairs equal be;
> Till then, Love, let my body reign, and let
> Me travel, sojourn, snatch, plot, have, forget,
> Resume my last year's relict: think that yet
>    We'd never met.[28]

[28] *The Songs and Sonets of John Donne*, edited by Theodore Redpath, Methuen, 1956, p. 14.

In the sixth line the metre directs the reader's mind swiftly through the stages of an erotic *geste*: the sensual licence is apprehended all the more strikingly because its far-ranging effects are encompassed within the span of a single line. This impression, conveyed by the metre as such, is inseparable from the "meaning" of the line.

Summing up: *The Shadowy Waters* is structurally defective. When the conflict between the values represented by Forgael and by Aibric has been presented, there is no further tension. The contrived disagreement in the Forgael-Dectora passages merely repeats the issues which Forgael and Aibric had already canvassed; the climax had passed. Inevitably thereafter the characters, each bearing a heavy symbolic burden, have no issue on which conflict is possible. Even when we work out the meanings of the symbols[29] we are still left with the foregone, undramatic conclusion of Forgael's golden net. We think of Villiers d l'Isle Adam;[30] in short, Yeats's conceptions in *The Shadowy Waters* were lyrical rather than dramatic.

There are moments in the 1913 version of *The Hour Glass* in which prose and verse are juxtaposed for purposes similar to those we have seen in *The Shadowy Waters*. In one of these the Wise Man questions his wife in verse:

> But sometimes, when the children are asleep
> And I am in the school, do you not think
> About the martyrs and the saints and the angels,
> And all the things that you believed in once?

His wife answers: "I think about nothing. Sometimes I wonder if the linen is bleaching white, or I go out to see if the crows are picking up the chickens' food."[31]

Here the change of diction (more than a change of rhythm, the use of a radically different selection of words) emphasises

[29] *The Identity of Yeats, supra*, pp. 80-84.

[30] Harry Goldgar, " 'Axel' de Villiers d l'Isle Adam et 'The Shadowy Waters' de W. B. Yeats," *Revue de Litterature Comparée*, Vol. XXIV, 1950, pp. 563-74.

[31] *Collected Plays, supra*, p. 317.

the rift between the Wise Man's new values and his wife's. "All" rebukes "nothing"; "martyrs," "saints," and "angels" are grotesquely answered by "crows" and "chickens." The rhetoric of the passage is similar to that employed in the prose sections of *Murder in the Cathedral*.

The 1902 version of *The Hour Glass* was in prose. In 1903 Yeats told Lady Gregory that he proposed to put in verse the soliloquies and the part which featured the Angels. With these changes he aimed "to lift the 'Wise Man's' part out of a slight element of platitude."[32] Ten years later he described the revised version as "practically a different work of art."[33]

The scheme of conflict between two worlds used in *The Shadowy Waters* is employed again in *The Hour Glass*, but the area of conflict has been altered. This time it is no longer a question of transcendental as opposed to natural love, but of Reason against Faith. Within the Morality form (and with echoes from *Doctor Faustus* and from *King Lear*) Yeats draws a dramatic pattern of conversion. The point of departure is the Wise Man's assertion:

> There's nothing but what men can see when they are awake.
> Nothing, nothing . . .

The pattern is completed when the Wise Man says:

> The last hope is gone,
> And now that it's too late I see it all:
> We perish into God and sink away
> Into reality—the rest's a dream.

The conception is familiar in a number of Yeats's poems, such as *The Coming of Wisdom with Time*:

> Though leaves are many, the root is one;
> Through all the lying days of my youth

[32] *Letters*, edited Wade, *supra*, p. 391.
[33] *Ibid.*, p. 576. The prose-and-verse play was completed only in 1913. Both texts were given in *Plays in Prose and Verse*, 1927, but only the prose-and-verse play was included in the 1934 and subsequent editions of *Collected Plays*.

I swayed my leaves and flowers in the sun;
Now I may wither into the truth . . .[34]

The burden of significance in "wither" is carried by this
word again in *The Hour Glass*, when the Wise Man says: "The
beggar who wrote that on Babylon wall meant that there is a
spiritual kingdom that cannot be seen or known till the facul-
ties, whereby we master the kingdom of this world, wither away
like green things in winter."

The opposition of "reality" and "dream" in the lines

We perish into God and sink away
Into reality—the rest's a dream . . .

points to the central motive of *The Hour Glass*, and to a preoccupation which Yeats emphasises in several ways. First, he
draws the audience's attention away from questions of personality or character-development: the "characters" are anonymous and, from the beginning, fully developed. In addition,
he exploits the pastoral and metaphysical implications in the
opposition of Wise Man and Fool (Reason and Faith; Intellect
and Folk-Intuition). Finally, the metaphysical theme is located
with ironic significance in the word "dream."

This word is developed very suggestively in the play. Near
the beginning the Wise Man ponders the feared existence of a
spiritual world. He has dreamed of it twice; if it were true,
everything he has done would be undone, his speculation would
be reduced to nothing:

Twice have I dreamed it in a morning dream,
Now nothing serves my pupils but to come
With a like thought. Reason is growing dim;
A moment more and Frenzy will beat his drum
And laugh aloud and scream;
And I must dance in the dream . . .

[34] *The Green Helmet and Other Poems*, 1910; *Collected Poems*, 1950,
p. 105.

When the Wise Man sees the Angel he cries out:

> . . . What are you? Who are you?
> I think I saw some like you in my dreams,
> When but a child. That thing about your head,—
> That brightness in your hair—that flowery branch;
> But I have done with dreams, I have done with dreams.

This is the moment of conversion. The Wise Man's violent rejection of the world of dreams is the last occasion on which he will use that word as an Act of Unbelief in the existence of a spiritual world. When he next speaks the word, it becomes a gesture of Faith:

> We perish into God and sink away
> Into reality—the rest's a dream.

One feels how much the word has gone through to bear this final affirmation. From this moment the Wise Man's Knowledge and Will move in the same direction.

In *The Hour Glass* Yeats found an easy solution to the problem of a theatre-form by borrowing one from *Everyman*. The comparison immediately reveals, however, the naïvete and slackness of Yeats's play: its brightest light is reflected from the earlier masterpiece. *The Hour Glass* is nobly conceived, but it does not render any vision of a "deep of the mind" such as Yeats hoped to achieve in his Noh plays.[35] He has whittled away until very little is left. At the same time *The Hour Glass* is a considerable advance on *The Shadowy Waters*: its plot is coherent and quite free from the repetition which marred the earlier play. Furthermore, at least a few passages show that Yeats during these years was beginning to realise in practice, as he had already concluded in theory,[36] that the application of lyrical verse to a plot would not cause the mixture to spring

---

[35] Introduction to *Certain Noble Plays of Japan*, Cuala Press, 1916, p. 5.

[36] See Preface to *Poems 1899-1905*, London, A. H. Bullen; Dublin, Maunsel, 1906, p. xii.

into dramatic form and life. The following passage is characteristic:

ANGEL: You have to die because no soul has passed
    The heavenly threshold since you have opened school,
    But grass grows there, and rust upon the hinge;
    And they are lonely that must keep the watch.
WISE MAN: And whither shall I go when I am dead?
ANGEL: You have denied there is a Purgatory,
    Therefore that gate is closed; you have denied
    There is a Heaven, and so that gate is closed.
WISE MAN: Where then? For I have said there is no Hell.
ANGEL: Hell is the place of those who have denied . . .

Predictable, yes; and one should not claim too much for the writing; it is largely the result of deleting the merely decorative metaphors of *The Shadowy Waters* and relying on the validity of the Morality form. But it remains a substantial improvement. Even allowing for the borrowings, the passage has something of the tension which arises from an intellectual issue keenly argued. It has at least the possibility of drama.

We would invoke, at this point, in examining one of the *Plays for Dancers*, the provisional description of poetic drama offered in an earlier chapter. We propose, therefore, to consider the inter-relation of the concrete elements of *At the Hawk's Well* and to enquire into the degree of mutual illumination which they exhibit.

The action or motive of *At the Hawk's Well* is to wrest immortality from its Guardians. It is the impulse to transcend one of the great limitations of the natural world. Pointing to this motive, the plot utilises one of the traditional "commonplaces" of literature, the romantic Quest. Young Cuchulain journeys over the seas to the Hawk's Well of Immortality, where he finds the Well, dry; the Guardian of the Well; and an old man who for fifty years has been cheated into sleep by the fairy-dancers whenever the well has been filled with the miraculous water. When again the water is about to come, the Guardian of the Well dances, the old man is put to sleep, and Cuchulain, possessed, is beguiled into leaving the fountain.

The prime agent in the play is Cuchulain, "young in body and in mind," with "proud step" and "confident voice." He boasts of his good fortune:

> I will stand here and wait.
> Why should the luck
> Of Sualtam's son desert him now? For never
> Have I had long to wait for anything.[37]

The Guardian sits on an old grey stone beside the well:

> Worn out from raking its dry bed,
> Worn out from gathering up the leaves,
> Her heavy eyes
> Know nothing, or but look upon stone.

Similarly, the old man, "withered," shares the quality of the desolate scene:

> He is all doubled up with age;
> The old thorn trees are doubled so
> Among the rocks where he is climbing.

Indeed, he is scarcely to be distinguished from the barren scene in which he is found. Cuchulain addresses him:

> You should be native here, for that rough tongue
> Matches the barbarous spot . . .

and again,

> You seem as dried up as the leaves and sticks,
> As though you had no part in life.

Details of the scene itself are embodied so strikingly in the text that in symbolising the limitations of the natural world they present that world not as an inert *context* but as a positive *cause* of the enacted events:

---

[37] *Collected Plays, supra,* p. 213. All the quotations from *At the Hawk's Well* are taken from this edition.

> I call to the eye of the mind
> A well long choked up and dry
> And boughs long stripped by the wind, . . .

Similarly, the scene and the agents illumine one another: the desolation of the scene envelops the old man and the Guardian. The scene is therefore a fit "container" for the old man and for the Guardian because it shares their essential quality.[38] One effect of this relationship is to present the young Cuchulain in stark contrast as the heroic warrior, the Challenger. At the beginning of the play he scorns the natural limitations represented by the scene, by the old man, and by the Guardian of the Well; in the end, they ensnare him.

Another instance of the congruence of scene and agency in *At the Hawk's Well* may be mentioned. Yeats, regarding Cuchulain as "a half-supernatural legendary person,"[39] and setting the play in the Irish heroic age, uses masks to emphasise the strangeness of the play-world, its "distance from life."[39] It is because of a feeling for such congruence that Yeats, at least up to the publication of *The Winding Stair* (1929) was one of the most scrupulous modern masters of decorum.

Speech and gesture may be considered together. All the movements in the play are non-mimetic. The dances, the drum-taps, the music of zither and gong, the movements of the musicians, even the cries of the Hawk, are ritual and symbolic gestures, designed to excite and liberate the audience. In *The Symbolism of Poetry* (1900) Yeats had expressed the idea that the purpose of rhythm is "to keep us in that state of perhaps real trance, in which the mind liberated from the pressure of the will is unfolded in symbols."[40] When this liberation has been achieved, the action and the words of the play can make their effect. Dance, music, masks, and costume, in addition to their

[38] See in another connexion Kenneth Burke, *A Grammar of Motives,* Prentice-Hall, 1945.

[39] *Plays and Controversies*, Macmillan, 1923, p. 417.

[40] *Ideas of Good and Evil*, A. H. Bullen, 1903, p. 247. "The Symbolism of Poetry" first appeared in *The Dome*, April 1900.

parts "within the play," prepare the audience to receive the full impact of the drama. In this respect they illumine the theatre-form by preparing the audience to experience it in the most sensitive, will-less spirit.

The elements cohere; their coherence is the poetry of the play. Indeed, the defects in *At the Hawk's Well* are in the text itself: they are not in the organisation of the play as a whole, or in the inter-relation of its elements, but in the fact that on occasion the speech is inadequate to the feeling it serves. For example, when the Hawk has gone out, the Old Man, now awake, creeps up to the Well and finds it empty:

> The accursed shadows have deluded me,
> The stones are dark and yet the well is empty;
> The water flowed and emptied while I slept;
> You have deluded me my whole life through.
> Accursed dancers, you have stolen my life.
> That there should be such evil in a shadow!

It is far less than the full expression of pain which is needed. The drama has hidden itself in the softness of the words; there is little here of that remarkable fidelity of word to emotion which one finds in *The Only Jealousy of Emer*, when Cuchulain, waking, turns not to his wife but to his mistress, and cries out:

> Your arms, your arms. O Eithne Inguba,
> I have been in some strange place and am afraid.[41]

Gesture alone, histrionically so rich, would almost have sufficed here to indicate the nature and the depth of the emotion, but the lines of speech serve beautifully to define the emotion more accurately by pointing to the fear in it. With this distinguished example of Yeats's histrionic sense before us we may say that the defect of the passage quoted from *At the Hawk's Well* is not that it does not say enough, or that its speech is feeble, but that it does not sufficiently trust gesture to do its own work. The words merely repeat what the natural gesture

[41] *Collected Plays, supra,* p. 294.

at this point would have "said" (the pain, the deceit), neither intensifying the emotion nor defining it more accurately.

The *Plays for Dancers* strike us as beautiful and, to a large extent, successful plays because so much of Yeats's heroic material has been used up in the form. We would not argue that Yeats, given this material and his own theatrical interests, required the Noh form rather than any other. Indeed, any ancient heroic type of play, such as the Indian Nataka,[42] might have served his purpose. The Noh plays provided Yeats with three things, (a) a theatre-form of proved validity, a means of organising and therefore of realising his material, a means of perceiving the forms and shapes latent in it; (b) a way of undercutting the mere representation of the surface of life (though in this there is loss as well as gain); and (c) an elaborate store of non-verbal expression which could liberate the mind from the will by the ritual nature of its eloquence.

In *The Shadowy Waters* Yeats presents Forgael's urge toward some state—impossible to render except by symbol—which is felt to contain the fullness and totality lacking in the natural world. The play is the enactment of a *moto spiral* to move beyond nature to a world of transcendence (hardly, in Yeats's case, to be described in terms of Grace or even in terms of quasi-Divine Charity). Even today it is feasible to posit an order of Grace or of Charity and to work piously within its terms, but the difficulty is to do this without repudiating the finite, concrete order which one must strive to penetrate. The ideal contemporary play would present the order of Grace not as replacing but as adhering dynamically to the order of Nature, finding its values, however exalted, through the human condition. Allen Tate has reminded us that "the reach of our imaginative enlargement is perhaps no longer than the ladder of analogy, at the top of which we may see all that we have brought up with us from the bottom, where lies the sensible world."[43]

[42] V. Raghavan, "The Aesthetics of the Ancient Indian Drama," *World Theatre*, Vol. v, 2, Spring 1956, p. 105.
[43] *The Angelic Imagination, supra*, p. 475.

This dichotomy between the natural and the transcendental pervades Yeats's plays. Forgael the absolutist longs to replace human love by a new kind of love on an immeasurably higher plane with different conditions and richer satisfactions. *A Full Moon in March* presents ideal love again in terms of totality, but, this time, a kind of totality that owes nothing to an "other world" or to a vision of essence or transcendence. It is perhaps not too crude to say that *A Full Moon in March* implies that love is real and full only when it is the completed act not just of the heart but of the whole body. Yeats had written in *The Thinking of the Body* (1906): "Art bids us touch and taste and hear and see the world, and shrinks from what Blake calls mathematic form, from every abstract thing, from all that is of the brain only, from all that is not a fountain jetting from the entire hopes, memories, and sensations of the body."[44] It is important to bear in mind, however, that no definitive adhesion to this view can be shown in Yeats's work. Several years after *The Thinking of the Body*, in *All Souls' Night* (1921) and in *Sailing to Byzantium* (1927) Yeats was to be found violently repudiating the commitment to the body and clinging with poignant intensity to an order of disembodied thought:

> Such thought, that in it bound
> I need no other thing,
> Wound in mind's wandering
> As mummies in the mummy-cloth are wound.[45]

This is nothing like the existence in which "Body is not bruised to pleasure Soul"; rather, it adheres to a self-enclosed order of meditation.

We do not offer these comments as an exhaustive account of this dichotomy in Yeats. They are designed merely to indicate that Yeats was forced into interim and contradictory positions by the problem. One observes, however—reminded by Hugh

[44] *The Thinking of the Body*, 1906; *Discoveries*, Dundrum, Dun Emer Press, 1907; *The Cutting of an Agate*, New York, Macmillan, 1912; London, Macmillan, 1919, p. 104.
[45] *Collected Poems*, 1950, *supra*, p. 259.

Kenner—that in his later years Yeats found the commitment to disembodied thought too radical, too narrow. *A Full Moon in March* represents a very late stage in the movement toward this view. In the volume of poems of the same name one reads *A Prayer for Old Age* (1934):

> God guard me from those thoughts men think
> In the mind alone;
> He that sings a lasting song
> Thinks in a marrow-bone.[46]

Here and in practically every page of his work Yeats is concerned with one of the most radical problems of the present century, the disintegration of personality. It is significant that in the play *A Full Moon in March* ideal love is presented as the fusion of Queen and Swineherd, of "crown of gold" and "dung of swine." When the Second Attendant asks, "What can she lack whose emblem is the moon?" the First Attendant answers, "But desecration and the lover's night."[47] The emphasis is not, however, mere reversion to "Crazy Jane Talks with the Bishop":

> For love has pitched his mansion in
> The place of excrement.[48]

The "desecration" in *A Full Moon in March* is enacted in the climax of the play when the Queen dances before the severed head of the Swineherd: her "virgin cruelty" is repudiated in the kiss. In the dance of adoration the Queen dances with the severed head while the drum-taps grow ever faster and more intense. The stage directions at this point read: "As the drum-taps approach their climax, she presses her lips to the lips of the head. Her body shivers to very rapid drum-taps. The drum-taps cease. She sinks slowly down, holding the head to her breast." This is a fitting climax to Yeats's best play. The feeling at this point is so intense that speech is too crude, too circum-

---

[46] *Collected Poems, supra,* p. 326.

[47] *Collected Plays, supra,* p. 630.

[48] *The Winding Stair and Other Poems,* Macmillan, 1933; *Collected Poems, supra,* p. 295.

scribed, to express it. Instead, the Queen's commitment is enacted by means of silent, symbolic gesture. One is reminded that in several Noh plays the final scene "depends more upon the dance than on the words."[49] It is difficult, then, to agree with Eric Bentley that in *A Full Moon in March* Yeats "employs the non-verbal arts while subordinating them to the word."[50] This applies to *The Dreaming of the Bones* but not to *A Full Moon in March*; in the latter play the dance, with its climactic kiss, is the most eloquent event. Speech alone, for once, is insufficient. It is the dance which vibrates as symbolic enactment of the complete, the "perfect" life.

The verse in *A Full Moon in March* exhibits something of the strength which Yeats envisaged when he wrote that "the element of strength in poetic language is common idiom."[51] Indeed, while the play is "distinguished, indirect and symbolic"[52] it goes a considerable distance toward wider reference by the use of "common idiom" and of a verse-manner which imitates the rhythms of traditional ballads:

> He swore to sing my beauty
> Though death itself forbade.
> They lie that say, in mockery
> Of all that lovers said,
> Or in mere woman's cruelty
> I bade them fetch his head.

> O what innkeeper's daughter
> Shared the Byzantine crown?
> Girls that have governed cities

[49] Ernest Fenollosa and Ezra Pound, *"Noh" or Accomplishment*, Macmillan, 1916, p. 9.

[50] Eric Bentley, "Yeats as a Playwright," *Kenyon Review*, Vol. x, 2, Spring 1948, pp. 196-208.

[51] Letter to John Quinn, 16 September 1905, *Letters, supra*, p. 461.

[52] Yeats wrote in his Introduction to *Certain Noble Plays of Japan, supra*, p. 2: "In fact with the help of these plays translated by Ernest Fenollosa and finished by Ezra Pound I have invented a form of drama, distinguished, indirect and symbolic, and having no need of mob or press to pay its way—an aristocratic form."

Or burned great cities down,
Have bedded with their fancy-man
Whether a king or clown.[53]

The imitation is probably deliberate. Yeats's interest in ballad-material and in ballad-style—which one finds in *The Wanderings of Oisin and other Poems* (1889)—continued even up to *Last Poems* (1936-1939). It is probable that the feature of ballad-verse which appealed most to him was its syntactical strength. Writing to Professor Grierson in 1926 Yeats emphasised the importance of "natural momentum in the syntax."[54] We need not suggest that Yeats owed to ballad-verse the remarkably supple use of syntax which one finds in such poems as *Leda and the Swan* (1923):

> A shudder in the loins engenders there
> The broken wall, the burning roof and tower
> And Agamemnon dead . . .[55]

but it is at least possible that in *A Full Moon in March* he invoked the ballad-style so as to compose language with a strong syntactical spine.

*A Full Moon in March* is Yeats's best play, finer than *Purgatory* (1938) or *On Baile's Strand* (1905), but it is imperfect. By the time Yeats's conception of dramatic form had moved from theory into mature practice, he had ceased to be a great poet. In *A Full Moon in March* some element has gone out of the words which had rendered them dynamic in *The Tower* seven years before. In common with the *Last Poems* the verse of *A Full Moon in March* exhibits the "slackening of tension" which Dr. Leavis has noted.[56] A short passage will illustrate the defect:

[53] *Collected Plays, supra*, p. 627.
[54] *Letters, supra*, p. 710.
[55] *The Cat and the Moon and Certain Poems*, Cuala Press, 1924; *Collected Poems*, 1950, *supra*, p. 241.
[56] F. R. Leavis, "The Great Yeats, and the Latest"; *Scrutiny*, Vol. VIII, 4, March 1940, pp. 437-40.

I owe my thanks to God that this foul wretch,
Foul in his rags, his origin, his speech,
In spite of all his daring has not dared
Ask me to drop my veil. Insulted ears
Have heard and shuddered, but my face is pure.
Had it but known the insult of his eyes
I had torn it with these nails.

Here the Queen's anger is almost contradicted by the flat,
mechanical movement of the verse: the lines give little impression
of a vehemence straining against a formal verse structure.

None of Yeats's verse plays is a complete success: *A Full
Moon in March* narrowly misses the mark. As in *At the Hawk's
Well*, the script is the weakest part of the play. Mr. Eliot has
noted with satisfaction that in *Purgatory* Yeats moved toward
the repudiation of the blank verse in which he had trusted for
so many years. The point is well made. Finding such difficulty
in composing a new-minted, echo-free blank verse, Yeats had
no choice but to move as far away from that form as possible.
As partial compensation for the loss, he attained a degree of
flexibility which had previously eluded him:

It's like—no matter what it's like.
I saw it a year ago stripped bare as now,
So I chose a better trade.
I saw it fifty years ago
Before the thunderbolt had riven it,
Green leaves, ripe leaves, leaves thick as butter,
Fat, greasy life. Stand there and look,
Because there is somebody in that house . . .[57]

As a dramatist Yeats was a good short-story writer: Aristotelian "magnitude"—if it interested him—was beyond his
range. Instead of a large dramatic action which might be the
focus of a civilisation in all its complexity he offers something

[57] *Collected Plays, supra*, p. 686.

more enclosed: he has described it in a beautiful and moving poem:

> Character isolated by a deed
> To engross the present and dominate memory.[58]

A further limitation is the fact that Yeats's theatre has proved, up to the present, to be coterie-drama, intelligible only to the "sensitive minority"[59] which enjoys the esoteric. These are serious limitations, they do not to the same extent apply to the theatres of Brecht, Eliot, or Giraudoux.

Yeats's importance as a dramatist consists in the fact that in a theatre-form of great distinction he dramatised one of the crucial preoccupations of the twentieth century. The heroic material which he used in such plays as *A Full Moon in March* should not deceive us into thinking that his theatre is beautiful but irrelevant. Essentially, Yeats's later plays, like the poems in *The Tower*, are as relevant to contemporary problems as, say, the *Pisan Cantos, Ash Wednesday, Ulysses, Sunday Morning, The Cocktail Party*, or *Joseph and his Brothers*. This is not generally conceded: the formalism of Yeats's plays, and their Japanese origin, have given many people the impression that the plays are akin to rites in an exotic and unfamiliar religion. André Gide expressed something of this feeling in connexion with Jacques Copeau's pursuit of an ideal form of theatre. Copeau's immense effort, Gide asserted, remained without any direct relation to the epoch; while claiming not to, he was working "pour une elite": "Il voulait mener à la perfection, au style, à la pureté, un art essentiellement impur et qui se passe de tout cela."[60]

Copeau told Gide that he was never closer to achieving his aim than in the Japanese Noh drama he was presenting: "Une pièce sans aucune relation avec nos traditions, nos contumes,

---

[58] "The Circus Animals' Desertion," *Collected Poems*, 1950, p. 392.

[59] Walter Kerr, "Killing Off the Theater," *Harper's Magazine*, April 1955, p. 62: "The theater was not created by a sensitive minority for a sensitive minority."

[60] André Gide, *Journal 1889-1939*, Paris, Gallimard, 1948, pp. 1020-21. I should like to acknowledge that my attention was drawn to this entry (of 15 January 1931) by Eric Bentley.

nos croyances; où, facticement, il obtenait sans trop de peine
une 'stylisation' arbitraire d'une exactitude incontrôlable,
totalement artificielle, faite de lenteurs, d'arrêts, de je ne sais
quoi de guindé vers le surnaturel dans le ton des voix, dans les
gestes et dans l'expression des acteurs."[60] Gide's conception of
relevance is unduly restricted. The dramatic knot of *At the
Hawk's Well*—to take a corresponding example—exists for its
own sake and for the sake of its untying, but if the question of
further relevance is raised, we must assert that the play is, in
fact, didactic. It engages itself strenuously with the deceit of
"the Gods" and with the pathetic longing to circumvent the
limitations of the natural world:

> O lamentable shadows,
> Obscurity of strife,
> I choose a pleasant life,
> Among indolent meadows;
> Wisdom must live a bitter life.

One need not overload the argument. If in *At the Hawk's
Well* one accepts Cuchulain and the Old Man as "emblems"
(Yeats's word), they are emblems of "those profound emotions
that exist only in solitude and silence."[61] The point at which
their stark beauty becomes, in Gide's terms, *contrôlable* is the
point at which one finds that in himself they have reached down
into a "deep of the mind." This moment is surely reached in
*The Dreaming of the Bones* when, after Dermot and Dervorgilla
have gone out, the young Irishman says:

> I had almost yielded and forgiven it all—
> This is indeed a place of terrible temptation.[62]

*A Full Moon in March* is a more "enclosed" play than *The
Cocktail Party*, but both exorcise the deepest tensions in life
by naming and enacting them. One part of the difference is
that Yeats was engrossed by these tensions—as dramatist—only
in their most climactic manifestations.

[61] *Plays and Controversies, supra,* p. 417.
[62] *Collected Plays, supra,* p. 444.

# CHAPTER FOUR. *DRAME À THÈSE*:
## AUDEN AND CUMMINGS

*A Full Moon in March* and *The Ascent of F6* were composed almost simultaneously. They have scarcely anything in common. Yeats's drama appears to exhibit a self-subsistent Order, and while we may indicate the relevance of the play to the largest human concerns we recognise also that there was no social event or situation in the 1930's to which the play could be directly referred. Its resonance is not "local." An attempt has recently been made to show that Yeats's last plays spring directly from his conception of the political situation in modern Ireland, but this idea imposes a severe strain on the texts.[1] In *The Ascent of F6*, on the other hand, one finds contemporaneity brandished in theme, diction, and tone. Whereas Yeats looked to an ancient aristocratic theatre-form to enable him to penetrate far below the surface of human life, Auden sought, with the aid of Eliot's *Sweeney Agonistes*, a means of remaining on that surface and cutting through its superficiality. Yeats's impulse was formalist; the force behind Auden was social consciousness.

In an earlier chapter we tried to show that one of the ways in which Yeats used language in his prose-and-verse plays, notably in *The Hour Glass*, involved calling attention, moment by moment, to the verbal medium then being used, not for its intrinsic interest or satisfaction, but in order to evoke in the audience, for the time being, a special kind of response. He assumed, for example, that the audience would respond to the differentia of verse with a special kind of attention. A similar aim may be seen in *Ulysses* and in *Finnegans Wake*: the language, including its visual representation on the page, is designed (as Dr. Williams has noted) to force the reader into a

[1] Donald R. Pearce, "Yeats's Last Plays," *English Literary History*, Vol. XVIII, I, March 1951.

special frame of mind favourable to the apprehension of the work. The special frame of mind is one in which most of the reader's attention is directed to Joyce's words as such, that is, as things with a life in themselves beyond the life they mirror. In Joyce and in Yeats the visible and audible signs of the medium determine to some extent the response exacted from the audience: the words are at once the means and the end of this special attention. We shall see that Eliot has tended to eschew this potentiality of verse so as to keep the audience's response as "natural" as possible.

In *The Ascent of F6* Auden and Isherwood again use verse as a rhetorical aid, to jerk the audience into new kinds of attention at certain moments in the play. The chosen moments are those in which the audience is confronted, not with a new direction in the plot, but with a recognition of its deeper implications; not with a new act in the sequence, but with a new revelation of is meaning. For example, when Ransom, after the discussion with the Abbot, withdraws into himself, pondering meaning and responsibility:

Is it too late? Pretence? It is too late for that;
I recognise my purpose.
There was a moment in the Lakeland Inn;
There was a choice then and I made it wrong;
And if I choose now, I must choose alone—
Not for my friends: I cannot turn them back.
O you, who are the history and the creator
Of all those forms in which we are condemned to suffer;
To whom the intelligent and necessary is also the just;
Show me my path, show all of us, that each upon
This mortal star may feel himself the danger
That under his hand is softly palpitating.[2]

The plot proceeds in prose: committee-meetings, censored news conveyed to the British public by radio announcers, con-

[2] W. H. Auden and Christopher Isherwood, *The Ascent of F6*, Faber and Faber, 1936, pp. 72-73.

versations between Ransom and his friends. For instance, the words which follow the passage just quoted are spoken by Gunn: "Has the old boy gone? Good. I was afraid I might be butting in; but Ian and the others threw me out. And I didn't much like the idea of sitting by myself in the dark, with all those monks around . . ." This is clearly one of the ways in which prose and verse may be employed in a play. It is appropriate, for instance, that in *The Ascent of F6* the crucial conversation between Ransom and his mother (after he has rejected his brother's proposal in regard to F6) is in verse, so as to differentiate as sharply as possible the relationship between mother and son from all other relationships in the play. Similarly in *On the Frontier* (1938) the verses of love spoken by Eric and Anna in ii.i are protected, by the formality of their diction, from the grotesque political world which has just spoken in slogan-prose. Again, in *The Ascent of F6*, when Auden wishes to show how the expedition to F6 impinges on the British public, he emphasises the *representative* function of Mr. and Mrs. A by having them speak with the formal fixation of rhyme:

> Nothing to tell to impress your friends—
> The old old story that never ends:
> The eight o'clock train, the customary place,
> Holding the paper in front of your face,
> The public stairs, the glass swing-door,
> The peg for your hat, the linoleum floor,
> The office stool and the office jokes
> And the fear in your ribs that slyly pokes.

The tone of these verses arises, obviously, from a joyless attempt to imitate certain parts of Mr. Eliot's early verse. Indeed, we have been reminded by Dr. Leavis that *The Ascent of F6* is "heavily parasitic upon both the Eliot of *Sweeney Agonistes* and the Eliot of the Choruses."[3] It is necessary, however, to enquire more closely into the relationship.

[3] F. R. Leavis, "Mr. Auden's Talent," *Scrutiny*, Vol. v, 3, December 1936, p. 325.

In *Sweeney Agonistes* Sweeney talks to Doris:

> You'd be bored.
> Birth and copulation, and death.
> That's all the facts when you come to brass tacks:
> Birth, and copulation, and death.
> I've been born, and once is enough.
> You don't remember, but I remember,
> Once is enough.[4]

If we compare these lines with the passage just quoted from *The Ascent of F6*, bearing in mind the context in each case, we realise that Auden has taken Sweeney's words and flattened them out. The malaise in the characters of *Sweeney Agonistes* is hysterical and neurotic: the words are like sore places on the body which, touched, send out waves of pain, suffusing the entire area with that rawness which is caught in the rhythm of Eliot's lines. Auden dissipates the pain with more words; the rawness is dulled to mere lassitude.

One understands, then, why Hugh Kenner in his study of Ezra Pound includes Auden in the category of "diluters," those who, as Pound said, "follow either the inventors or the 'great writers,' and who produce something of lower intensity."[5] Indeed, one of the more disquieting conclusions which issue from a study of *The Dance of Death* and *The Dog beneath the Skin* is that these plays, like *The Ascent of F6,* exhibit the dilution of Eliot's "style" into a "manner." The manner is acquired by retarding the pace of the style and spreading its characteristic qualities over a larger area.

Insofar as the text alone is under consideration there is very little to add to Dr. Leavis's damaging account of *The Ascent of F6*, published more than twenty years ago. One may cavil, however, at his description of Mrs. Ransom's early verse-speech as "the Tennysonian pathetic":

[4] T. S. Eliot, *Sweeney Agonistes,* Faber and Faber, 1932, pp. 24-25.
[5] Ezra Pound, *Polite Essays,* Faber and Faber, 1937, p. 167. Hugh Kenner, *The Poetry of Ezra Pound,* Faber and Faber, 1951, p. 28.

I have no purpose but to see you happy,
And do you find that so remarkable
What mother could deny it and be honest?
I know my son the greatest climber in the world;
I know F6 the greatest mountain in the world.
May not a mother come at once to bring
Her only gift, her love? When the news came,
I was in bed, for lately
I've not been very well. But what's a headache
When I can stand beside my son and see him
In the hour of his triumph?

The whine in the verse encourages us to reject Mrs. Ransom, to turn away from her as her son rejects her embrace later in the same scene. The spuriousness in her is revealed in the syntax, culminating in the rhetorical question at the end of the speech. Auden is in fact parodying the Tennysonian pathetic.

The uncertainty of tone and poise which Dr. Leavis finds in the verse of *The Ascent of F6* is evidence of a crucial weakness in the play, and the passage which he cites from II.iv is a particularly clear example of a defect which exhibits itself even in more impressive passages:

O senseless hurricanes,
That waste yourselves upon the unvexed rock,
Find some employment proper to your powers,
Press on the neck of Man your murdering thumbs
And earn real gratitude! Astrologers,
Can you not scold the fated loitering star
To run to its collision and our end?
The Church and Chapel can agree in this,
The vagrant and the widow mumble for it
And those with millions belch their heavy prayers
To take away this luggage . . .

Solemn Shakespearean parody, as Dr. Leavis describes it. But this is not the entire truth. Recall the context: Lamp has been killed, Shawcross has thrown himself over the precipice, and now Gunn has expired in a hurricane almost at the summit of F6. "Scenario" undoubtedly calls for a burst of eloquence from Ransom at this point. Thinking about this, one realises the basic flaw in the verse: it is not so much the Shakespearean pastiche as the fact that the verse norm of *The Ascent of F6* is unable to find for itself a genuine "high" style when it needs one. Similarly with early bourgeois tragedy, as we have seen. Where Shakespeare "raises" his style and where Eliot "tightens" his, Auden can merely parody the former, just as in the speeches of Mr. and Mrs. A he mimics the latter. The verse has none of the flexibility or the range necessary to serve a wide variety of dramatic situations. This is particularly revealing because in the composition of Ransom's first soliloquy Auden shows the firm possession of a "high" style *in prose*. Ransom has been reading a translation of the *Inferno*, Canto Twenty-Six, and he ponders—with little insight, indeed—the line "Ma per seguir virtude e conoscenza":

"Who was Dante—to whom the Universe was peopled only by his aristocratic Italian acquaintances and a few classical literary characters, the fruit of an exile's reading—who was Dante, to speak of Virtue and Knowledge? It was not Virtue those lips, which involuntary privation had made so bitter, could pray for; it was not Knowledge; it was Power. Power to exact for every snub, every headache, every unfallen beauty, an absolute revenge; with a stroke of the pen to make a neighbour's vineyard a lake of fire and to create in his private desert the austere music of the angels or the happy extravagance of a fair."

Perhaps it is a little too high. One thinks of a greater "high" speech, Father Mapple's sermon in *Moby Dick*, where the grandeur of Melville's prose, like the great description of the storm in *The Nigger of the Narcissus*, is sanctioned by the sheer scale of the story. Ransom's meditations have no corresponding support. The least that may be claimed for the passage, however, is that even at its "highest" it maintains a relation to Ransom's other prose-speeches: they all exhibit the same kind of language, raised here, lowered there, but essentially a unified mode of speech. The defect of the "senseless hurricanes" lines is that they are quite unrelated to Ransom's verse-norm; they therefore lack its sanction.

*The Ascent of F6* is crudely organised. Dr. Leavis has noted that in this play Auden lacks "the organisation corresponding to his local vitality." Bearing in mind the qualitative parts of a play as Aristotle outlined them, one observes that the diction of *The Ascent of F6* is occasionally impressive, the plot never so; the characters, with the exception of Ransom himself, are ciphers; the play is poor in thought and melody, it offers a certain interest in the "spectacle." The weakness of the plot is particularly serious: instead of inventing a sequence of dramatic situations which would have its own intergrity first and thereafter, if he so wished, a moral, Auden merely uses the characters and the plot as allegory. It is symptomatic that in recent discussions of *The Ascent of F6* he has interested himself only in the "meaning" of the play, or the lessons to be drawn from it. He does not reveal any deep concern for the elements of the play as "things," or for their organic coherence, or for the theatre-form which they serve. Here, for instance, is part of a discussion between Auden and Howard Griffin:

G: In connexion with *The Ascent of F6*, I would like to ask you a question about the protagonist. Was that figure based on Colonel Lawrence?

A: Yes: The ascent of the mountain is a symbol of the *geste*, it can also be a symbol of the act of aggression.

G: Then you look on Lawrence definitely as a jingoist?

A: Oh no, he was surely in sympathy with the Arabs.

G: Yes, but only up to a point. He concurred with England's imperialist policies. Also, he regarded war as a game, a sport—

A: There is a difference between regarding war as sport and being jingoistic. With the business of unconditional surrender modern warfare cannot be regarded as a game . . .

When Mr. Griffin mentioned that he was a little perplexed by the mother-image which reveals itself on the mountain in *The Ascent of F6* Auden explained: "It seems to me that in man's search for God he erects before him a number of images. I believe that the mother-image is one of the last to be outgrown. . . . In this play the protagonist dies after the appearance of the mother on the mountaintop."[6]

If *The Ascent of F6* is *drame à thèse* Mr. Auden is more interested in the *thèse* than in the *drame*: witness the movement away from the play as a thing in itself toward the psychological lessons that may be abstracted from it. One of the snags in this habit is that themes which sound interesting and resonant in discussion (such as the mother-image) are found to be, in the play—where formal considerations insist on priority—merely mechanical "business" designed to fabricate a climax. One honours Auden as poet and moralist; one attends to the allegory in *The Ascent of F6* of man's spiritual journey; but one is compelled to recognise that Auden has failed to construct a coherent play. He has failed to realise his conceptions in dramatic terms or to grasp a theatre-form which, enjoying its own vitality, could carry those conceptions without strain.

This may account for the fact that the interest of Auden's plays is "historical" and "sociological" rather than intrinsic. One is tempted to study them as symptoms rather than as plays. One is interested in their representative qualities inasmuch as they reflect a preoccupation with music-hall, with German expressionistic drama, and, above all, with a partisan social message. Their interest as drama is marginal.

Kenneth Burke has pointed out[7] that a drama considered as *agon* is analytically subdivided into competing principles, of protagonist and antagonist. Their competition adds up to one overall cooperative act, as the roles of Iago and Othello "dove-

[6] Howard Griffin, "A Dialogue with W. H. Auden," *Hudson Review,* Vol. III, Winter 1951, pp. 583, 591.

[7] Kenneth Burke, *The Philosophy of Literary Form,* revised edition, Vintage Books, 1957, p. 64.

tail" to compose the total progression of the tragedy. In addition, each of the "principles" possesses satellites, or adjuncts; some of these are strongly identified with one or other of the principles, as Antony was unequivocally the adjunct of Caesar. There are other characters, indeterminate, who shade off into a general overlapping background, as with the shifting role of the mob which Brutus and Antony alternately swayed. Such a set of "mediating" characters is necessary as a common ground of persons through which the cooperation of the competing principles can take place. Hence, no matter which of the three the dramatist begins with (agon, protagonist, or antagonist) he cannot compose a coherent drama unless he imaginatively encompasses the other two. The simpler forms of "proletarian" literature suffer from the fact that the poet, beginning with a strong attitude toward protagonist or antagonist, features this attitude throughout and, as a result, fails to bring the two other terms to full development.

In *The Ascent of F6* Auden clearly entered into his envisaged drama through the character of Michael Ransom. None of the other characters evokes any real interest or gives the impression of having interested their creator. Despite moments of insecurity Auden has succeeded, by and large, in establishing Ransom; as protagonist he stands, palpable, in the centre of the play. But the antagonist principle is hardly presented at all: the scheming politicians are absurd; the treatment of Mrs. Ransom, issuing in her appearance on the mountain, is evasive. Finally, there is a mere mechanical presentation of the agon itself; far from being imaginatively encompassed it has remained, inert, at the schematic stage.

By contrast, E. E. Cummings's *Santa Claus* (1946) encompasses, with imaginative vigour, the three terms, agon, protagonist, and antagonist. *Santa Claus*, like *The Ascent of F6*, is *drame à thèse*; indeed both plays are equally *lebensnah*, but Mr. Cummings had the histrionic instinct to recognise that the terms of his *thèse*, stark and "committed," suited the conventions of a Morality play. Auden, on the other hand, tried to insinuate into his play incidents and material foreign to its decorum.

Mr. Cummings proceeded into his drama—we would guess—through an imaginative realisation of its agon. The terms in which the theme appeared to him may be gauged from his description of its "scene." In a lecture delivered in 1953 Mr. Cummings spoke of "a spiritually impotent pseudocommunity enslaved by perpetual obscenities of mental concupiscence; an omnivorous social hypocrisy, vomiting vitalities of idealism while grovelling before the materialisation of its own deathwish: a soi-disant free society, dedicated to immeasurable generosities of love; but dominated by a mere and colossal lust for knowing, which threatens not simply to erase all past and present and future human existence but to annihilate (in the name of liberty) Life Herself."[8] From this context of feeling an agon might have issued in any of several forms corresponding to the fourth Book of *Gulliver's Travels*, or to a satire by Rochester, or to Mr. Cummings's own *Eimi*, or to *Bartholomew Fair*. But Mr. Cummings, feeling, above all, the conflicting principles involved, penetrated his material by means of a Morality play in five scenes.

Mr. Cummings's attitudes are, as we have seen, partisan. He seems to write in the hope that what he hates will be obliterated by the sheer profusion of his words. But his dramatic instinct saves him from falsifying the issue: in *Santa Claus* protagonist and antagonist are genuinely and coordinately realised. Hence the validity of the conflict.

The protagonist is Santa Claus. When the play begins he is dispirited. No one wants the only commodity he has to give, Understanding. The antagonist, Death, advises Santa Claus to give the Mob what it wants, mere Knowledge. Thus Understanding, in its distress and bewilderment, reduces itself to Knowledge, wears the face of Death, decries the human in humanity, loses the power of love, and can no longer understand why people turn into monsters. But the Child recognises the truth of Understanding even when its face is masked by Death; and the Mob, without vision, mistakes Death for Santa Claus and

---

[8] E. E. Cummings, *i: six nonlectures*, Harvard University Press, 1954, p. 103.

kills him. Santa Claus, restored to his own nature and his full humanity, finds the Child, who is his daughter. At the end of the play they both find, in the Woman, their Love.

*Santa Claus* is an intensely moving play. From the moment in which Death addresses Santa Claus as "brother" to the moment in which Santa Claus, the Woman, and the Child find one another, we are engaged by their acts. Cummings's "ciphers" are much more firmly established in human terms than the "characters" of *The Ascent of F6*, perhaps because they move gracefully in a form of drama which accommodates them.

Again we may have recourse to an Aristotelian view. The *plot* is organised with the economy and formality of a Noh play: the knot is tied and at last untied with a quality of skill which Yeats would have admired. Formally, the play is spare and chaste. The *characters* are rendered palpable because their speeches are sensitive mirrors of their acts. Santa Claus, for example, while he is possessed by Understanding, speaks in bruised tones, without rancour: "I have so much to give; and nobody will take." But when his understanding is degraded to Knowledge his voice utters only slogans:

> —Just a moment. Friends,
> it never shall be said that Science favoured
> or slighted anyone. Remember: Science
> is no mere individual. Individuals
> are, after all, nothing but human beings;
> and human beings are corruptible:
> for (as you doubtless know) to err is human.
> Think—only think! for untold centuries
> this earth was overrun by human beings!
> Think: it was not so many years ago
> that individuals could be found among us! . . .

Much of the *thought* of *Santa Claus* is Wordsworthian in its concern for Understanding in preference to Knowledge, for Love in preference to Big Business. Death, for instance, while having no notion of Love, appreciates at least the extent to which the world cooperates with him, doing part of his work:

> You're speaking of a true or actual world.
> Imagine, if you can, a world so blurred
> that its inhabitants are one another
> —an idiotic monster of negation:
> so timid, it would rather starve itself
> eternally than run the risk of choking;
> so greedy, nothing satisfies its hunger
> but always huger quantities of nothing—
> a world so lazy that it cannot dream;
> so blind, it worships its own ugliness:
> a world so false, so trivial, so unso,
> phantoms are solid by comparison.[9]

This is simple, and representative. The material with which Cummings deals in *Santa Claus* is much "easier" than in the earlier play *Him* (1927) because the protagonist and antagonist compete as starkly as any "principles" in a Morality play. As a result there are in *Santa Claus* none of the wide-ranging speculations which one finds in *Him*, no speeches comparable to this one, for example:

"All my life I've wondered if I am any good. If my head and my heart are made out of something firmer or more living than what I see everywhere covering itself with hats and with linen.—If all the capable and little and disgusting minds which, somehow, are responsible for the cities and the countries in which I exist, have not perhaps also manufactured this thing— this bundle of wishes—which I like to call 'myself.' If my arms dreams hands exist with an intensity differing from or beyond the intensity of any other arms dreams hands. . . . You cannot imagine how disagreeable it is to wonder—to look about you, at the eyes and the gestures which promenade themselves in streets and in houses, and to be afraid. To think: 'Am I also one

---

[9] E. E. Cummings, *Santa Claus: A Morality*, New York, Henry Holt and Co. 1946, pp. 3, 9, 4.

of these, a doll, living in a doll world, doomed to be undressed, dressed, spanked, kissed, put to bed?' "[10]

*Diction*: the text of *Santa Claus* modulates between fragments of conversation and slogan-speeches. Most of the thought of the play is in the slogans and the ideas which are invoked, in all reverence, to destroy the slogans. The "humanity" of the play issues in single-line conversations, notably between Santa Claus and the Child. In such passages the style is transparent:

SANTA CLAUS:                    Why are you going?
CHILD:                                        Don't be afraid:
          we'll find her.
SANTA CLAUS:                        I should never be afraid
          of anything in the sky and on the earth
          and anywhere and everywhere and nowhere,
          if I were only sure of one thing.
CHILD:                                        What?
SANTA CLAUS: Who was that somebody else?
CHILD:                                  That somebody
          we lost?
SANTA CLAUS:                    Yes.
CHILD:                          Can't you guess who?
SANTA CLAUS:                      Can I?
CHILD:                                You.

*(She dances away)*

*Melody*: the metre is what Robert Frost calls "loose iambic pentametre." In the case of *Santa Claus* this means that each line, characteristically, has five feet, basically iambic, except that anapaests are frequently substituted for iambics even in positions in which such substitution is not found in traditional blank verse:

> Now I'll abide by the verdict of that little girl
> over there, with the yellow hair and the blue eyes.
> I'll simply ask her who I am; and whoever
> She says I am, I am: is that fair enough?

[10] E. E. Cummings, *Him*, New York, Liveright Publishing Corporation, 1927, p. 95.

*Spectacle*: no indications are given in the printed text as to the "scene," apart from the traditional costumes worn by Death and by Santa Claus. In production the "quality" of each scene would probably be most accurately conveyed by various coloured lights. Apart from this, the production would strive for the degree of simplicity and starkness featured in the plot.

Cummings is a *poète de théâtre*. *Him* and *Santa Claus* exhibit in their author a remarkable flair for the theatre as a medium of expression, for the theatre as such, not for the theatre as a receptacle into which lyric verse may be insinuated. This is probably what Professor Fergusson had in mind when he attributed "style" to the author of *Him*: style in the first instance theatrical rather than merely verbal.[11] Mr. Cummings has not discussed the theatre as a medium of expression in its own right and with its own potentialities, but his practice has been in this respect admirable.

[11] Francis Fergusson, "Eugene O'Neill," *Hound and Horn*, iii, 145-60, reprinted in Morton Dauwen Zabel, *Literary Opinion in America*, Harper, revised edition, 1951.

# CHAPTER FIVE.

## T. S. ELIOT AND THE COMPLETE CONSORT:

### *MURDER IN THE CATHEDRAL*

What we call the beginning is often the end
And to make an end is to make a beginning,
The end is where we start from. And every phrase
And sentence that is right (where every word
    is at home,
Taking its place to support the others,
The word neither diffident nor ostentatious,
An easy commerce of the old and the new,
The common word exact without vulgarity,
The formal word precise but not pedantic,
The complete consort dancing together)
Every phrase and every sentence is an end
    and a beginning,
Every poem an epitaph.

*Little Gidding* (v)[1]

AT this point we would show that *Murder in the Cathedral*, to which a crucial influence on the development of modern verse drama has frequently been attributed, is an unsuccessful play; that its text evades, rather than solves, the problems of dramatic verse; and that its structural flaws are similar to those of certain late nineteenth-century verse plays.

In doing so we would have recourse to Kenneth Burke's distinction between the "psychology of form" and the "psychology of information." Form, as he presents it, is the creation of an appetite in the mind of the auditor, and the adequate satisfaction of that appetite. This satisfaction—so complicated is the human mind—at times involves temporary frustration, but in the end this frustration proves to be simply a more involved kind of

---

[1] *Four Quartets*, London, Faber and Faber, 1944, pp. 42-43.

satisfaction and serves to make the satisfaction of fulfilment more intense. In information, the interest of the matter is intrinsic; it follows that the methods of maintaining interest which are most natural to the psychology of information are surprise and suspense. In form, the interest of the matter is extrinsic; the method of maintaining interest which is most natural to the psychology of form is eloquence, or formal excellence. In this sense eloquence involves the minimising of interest in fact *per se*; instead, the elements of surprise and suspense are refined, carried down into the writing of a line or a sentence, until in all its smallest details the work bristles with disclosures, contrasts, restatements with a difference, ellipses, images, aphorisms, sound-values—in short, all that wealth of minutiae which in their line-for-line aspect we call style and in their broader outlines we call form.[2]

One of the examples cited by Mr. Burke is the transition in *Macbeth* from the murder scene to the porter scene. Here the presence of one quality calls forth the demand for another, rather than one tangible incident of plot awaking an interest in some other possible tangible incident of plot. The relation between the scenes is not logical but is emotionally natural: the audience's feeling of horror demands and receives relief, temporarily, in the comic grotesquerie of the porter. Similarly in *The Waste Land* the oppressively trivial conversation in the public house calls forth in the poet a memory of a line from *Hamlet*:

> Goonight Bill. Goonight Lou. Goonight May.
> Goonight. Ta Ta. Goonight. Goonight.
> Good night, ladies, good night, sweet ladies, good night,
> good night.[3]

Here the poet, feeling his release, drops into another good night, a good night out of what was, within the conditions of the poem at least, a graceful and irrevocable past. The Shakespearean

[2] "Psychology and Form," *The Dial*, July 1925; reprinted in *Counter-statement*, 1931.
[3] *Collected Poems*, London, Faber and Faber, 1936, p. 67.

world and its language answer the reader's desire for relief from the pain of vulgar triviality. The transition, by verbal correspondence, is all the more affecting if the line recalls Ophelia's situation: one kind of insanity, beautiful and pathetic, imposes moral judgment on another, monstrous kind, of which the poem itself provides definitive critique.

A final instance of formal perfection may perhaps establish the rhetorical principle which we would use in our consideration of *Murder in the Cathedral*. In the fourth act of *Cymbeline* the royal brothers intone a lament over the grave of Fidele. Arviragus says:

> With fairest flowers
> Whilst summer lasts, and I live here, Fidele,
> I'll sweeten thy sad grave: thou shalt not lack
> The flower that's like thy face, pale primrose, nor
> The azur'd harebell, like thy veins: no, nor
> The leaf of eglantine, whom not to slander,
> Outsweet'ned not thy breath: the ruddock would
> With charitable bill . . .

Up to this point we, the audience, are with him: the words deputise graciously for our sorrow. But discomfort is at hand: Arviragus continues:

> With charitable bill (O bill, sore shaming
> Those rich-left heirs, that let their fathers lie
> Without a monument!) bring thee all this; . . .

The parenthesis is a distraction, what Matthew Arnold might have called a provincialism, a movement away from the "tone of the centre" which our notion of elegiac decorum exacts. The floral catalogue continues, displeasing now by excess; our idea of propriety intervenes and at this moment finds in the younger brother, delightfully, a spokesman. Guiderius interrupts:

> Prithee, have done,
> And do not play in wench-like words with that
> Which is so serious.[4]

---

[4] New Arden Shakespeare edition by J. M. Nosworthy, London, Methuen, 1955, pp. 137-38.

Formal excellence is here exhibited in the sympathetic relation between Guiderius's act and the audience's desires; the temporary frustration caused by Arviragus's excess makes fulfilment more joyous.

In *Murder in the Cathedral* the "psychology of information" and its characteristic methods (suspense and surprise) are not involved. The broad outlines of the plot, as in Aeschylus, are known to the audience before the play begins. The first audience at Canterbury in 1935 knew at least that Thomas Becket became a Christian martyr some hundreds of years before. When one considers the "psychology of form," however, one finds in *Murder in the Cathedral* little of the eloquence or formal excellence cultivated by Aeschylus and Shakespeare. By comparison with the rhetorical finesse exhibited in the passages quoted from *Cymbeline* and *The Waste Land*, the organisation of *Murder in the Cathedral* is pedestrian.

The play, in fact, consists of a number of expressive segments which are related only on the conceptual level: there is no unity of drama and metaphor as there is in, say, *The Tempest*. We would cite, for instance, a passage from the long chorus directly before the priests bring the Archbishop to vespers:

> I have smelt them, the death-bringers, senses
>         are quickened
> By subtle forebodings; I have heard
> Fluting in the nighttime, fluting and owls,
>         have seen at noon
> Scaly wings slanting over, huge and ridiculous.
>         I have tasted
> The savour of putrid flesh in the spoon.
>         I have felt
> The heaving of earth at nightfall, restless,
>         absurd. I have heard
> Laughter in the noises of beasts that make strange
>         noises: jackal, jackass, jackdaw; the
>         scurrying noise of mouse and jerboa; the

laugh of the loon, the lunatic bird. I have
 seen
Grey necks twisting, rat tails twining, in the
 thick light of dawn. I have eaten
Smooth creatures still living, with the strong
 salt taste of living things under sea; I
 have tasted
The living lobster, the crab, the oyster, the
 whelk and the prawn; and they live and
 spawn in my bowels, and my bowels dissolve
 in the light of dawn. I have smelt
Death in the rose, death in the holyhock,
 sweet pea, hyacinth, primrose and
 cowslip . . .[5]

In the chorus from which these lines are quoted the inva-
sion by animal-death of the senses of sight, hearing, touch,
taste, and smell makes up a quasi-lyrical segment. It is effective
and "in character" but it remains a segment, linked to the other
parts of the play by concept—mechanically—but not by image,
metaphor, symbol, or rhythm. That is, the *qualitative* relation
of parts is lacking. Mr. Eliot has in this passage written an almost self-contained block of choric verse whose "form" is defective in that it makes the final chorus of faith sound lifeless.
The evocation of death in the lines quoted arouses in the audience a correspondingly keen appetite for "life": when this life
is eventually rendered in the final chorus it emerges, disappoint-
ingly, as a new departure, with no verbal relation to the death
from which it arose:

Forgive us, O Lord, we acknowledge ourselves
 as type of the common man,
Of the men and women who shut the door and sit
 by the fire;
Who fear the blessing of God, the loneliness
 of the night of God, the surrender required,
 the deprivation inflicted;

[5] *Murder in the Cathedral*, London, Faber and Faber, 1935, pp. 63-64.

Who fear the injustice of men less than the
    justice of God;
Who fear the hand at the window, the fire in the
    thatch, the fist in the tavern, the push into
    the canal,
Less than we fear the love of God.
We acknowledge our trespass, our weakness,
    our fault; we acknowledge
That the sin of the world is upon our heads;
    that the blood of the martyrs and the
    agony of the saints
Is upon our heads.
Lord, have mercy on us.
Christ, have mercy on us.
Lord, have mercy on us.
Blessed Thomas, pray for us.

These lines are weak, not because their tone is that of a mechanical or conventionally religious gesture, but because that tone is not presented as issuing from all that went before. We miss the feeling that the new vision of faith has been won from the chorus of despair. The verbal life, and hence the spiritual experience, of the Chorus is not continuous throughout the play.

This may seem to be merely a quarrel about the texture of the verse, but the defect involves the entire organisation of the play.

The determining flaw in *Murder in the Cathedral* is that the imitation of its action is complete at the end of Part One, when the Archbishop says:

I shall no longer act or suffer, to the sword's end.
Now my good Angel, whom God appoints
To be my guardian, hover over the swords' points.

When this moment is reached, approximately halfway through the play, the dramatic pattern has been traced. One realises this more vividly by noting, with Kenneth Burke, that in

Christian martyrdom an important variation is imposed on the characteristic tragic rhythm. Regarding the tragic rhythm (or an archetypal version of it) as a movement, on the part of the hero, from Purpose through Passion to Perception, we note that in Christian martyrdom the first two of these stages become simultaneous equivalents, inasmuch as the *act* of self-sacrifice is identical with the *passion* or sufferance. Further: that in *Murder in the Cathedral* Thomas has first suffered temptation (*pathema*); he has detected and resisted this temptation (*poiema*); and the perception (*mathema*) gained from the trial equips him for martyrdom.[6] This rearrangement of the phases is important, but it is even more important to observe that each of the three phases is completed at the end of Part One. In fact, everything after Part One is structurally superfluous. Even the distinguished prose sermon and the speech of the assassins, intrinsically so interesting, are *tours de force* and, structurally, redundant.

Even if one were to reject the description of the tragic pattern as proposed, one would still be compelled to recognise that in *Murder in the Cathedral* the coherence and integrity of plot, Henry James's "divine principle of the Scenario,"[7] are violated.

This is not to imply that *Murder in the Cathedral* is an insignificant play—on the contrary. But its significance lies in its "meaning," not in the integrity of its action. Like *The Ascent of F6* it offers itself more readily as a locus of sociological discourse than as an imitation of a coherent action. There is strong temptation, then, in considering *Murder in the Cathedral*, to pursue its social and documentary implications rather than to enquire into its validity as a play. Richard Blackmur, for example, presents the play as a drama of "the Church struggling against society towards God," the way of the Church against the way of the World. From this point of observation—true—

---

[6] *A Grammar of Motives*, New York, Prentice-Hall, 1945, p. 265.
[7] *The Notebooks of Henry James*, edited by F. O. Matthiessen and Kenneth B. Murdock, New York, Oxford University Press, 1947, p. 188.

the play reveals the awful harm as well as the good done men and women in the course of the struggle. It is this harm and this good, he argues, this sense of irreparable damage and intransigent glory, as it is in contact with the struggle, that makes the drama actual. It is not spiritual drama, like Dante's drama of damnation, penance, and beatitude; it is the drama of human emotions actualised in the light of spiritual drama. Spirit, intellect, and theology are there, he argues, but they are there through actualised emotions of the experience of good and evil, of fraud and ambition, self-deceit and nobility, and the communal humility of the poor.[8]

There is no difficulty, then, in allowing the play a high degree of meaning, but the meaning is broad and begins to operate only when the individual agents of the play have been equated with their corresponding institutions. Thus, despite the lauded "actuality," Thomas is "the Church," the assassins are "society," and the play is then available as an illuminating document. The value of a play, however, is not to be equated with the degree to which it offers scope for socio-historical discourse. *Murder in the Cathedral* has too much of this kind of meaning; its validity in terms of dramatic action is in no way strengthened by its profound relevance as a social text.

This defect is probably related to the essentially expository nature of the play. Sensing this, Professor Fergusson described the play as a "demonstration and expression" of the "right reason" for martyrdom, and, on a wider basis, of the right doctrine of human life in general—orthodoxy.[9] The play is therefore "theology as drama," but the determining bias is that of the theologian. This is not, of course, to deny either the value of Mr. Eliot's world-view, or the propriety of having one. In *King Lear* there is, ultimately, a world-view, as orthodox as that of *Murder in the Cathedral*, but it does not frustrate the drama: the determining act is that of the dramatist.

[8] *Language as Gesture*, London, Allen and Unwin, 1954, p. 183.
[9] *The Idea of a Theater*, Princeton University Press, 1949, p. 210.

We have met a reference to *Murder in the Cathedral* as "a drama of human emotions actualised in the light of spiritual drama." This claim is not generally conceded. More often the characters in the play are regarded as being, at least in their initial conception, "roles in the life of the schematic community."[10] Similarly, Eliot is often rebuked for sacrificing some of Thomas's humanity "in order to lay emphasis upon the martyrdom of the saint."[11] Miss Helen Gardner, for instance, has argued that Thomas's main function in the play is to give an Addisonian demonstration of "how a Christian can die." Thomas, she maintains, is less a man than an embodied attitude, "for there is in this play an almost Gnostic contempt for personality and its expression in acts."[12] This seems harsh, however: there is more in Thomas than an embodied attitude. Perhaps Miss Gardner has not taken sufficient account of those factors in the play which are designed for the prime purpose of indicating Thomas's character. There are, for instance, such passages as the First Priest's early speech:

> I saw him as Chancellor, flattered by the King,
> Liked or feared by courtiers, in their overbearing fashion,
> Despised and despising, always isolated,
> Never one among them, always insecure;
> His pride always feeding upon his own virtues,
> Pride drawing sustenance from impartiality,
> Pride drawing sustenance from generosity,
> Loathing power given by temporal devotion,
> Wishing subjection to God alone.

Or, again, Thomas's own confession, in words whose rhythm enacts the superficiality described:

> Thirty years ago, I searched all the ways
> That lead to pleasure, advancement and praise.

[10] *Ibid.*, p. 213.
[11] Patricia M. Adair, "Mr. Eliot's *Murder in the Cathedral*," *Cambridge Journal*, November 1950, p. 86.
[12] *The Art of T. S. Eliot*, London, Cresset Press, 1949, p. 135.

Delight in sense, in learning and in thought,
Music and philosophy, curiosity,
The purple bullfinch in the lilac tree,
The tiltyard skill, the strategy of chess,
Love in the garden, singing to the instrument,
Were all things equally desirable . . .

Finally,

While I ate out of the King's dish
To become servant of God was never my wish.

The most effective indications of Thomas's character are, of course, his own acts; and, ultimately, it is sufficient to acknowledge that a clear and consistent relation is maintained between Thomas's character and his deeds. That character is not as rich in contingent traits as a St. Teresa or a St. Elizabeth of Hungary, because Thomas's role in the play does not require such contingency. We may be content to reflect that, at the very least, the presentation of Thomas would have satisfied Aristotle's requirements for *ethos*. We are audacious if we demand more.

If from this account Eliot's idea of "character" appears puny, one should recall the function of the four Tempters. It is important to note that the main function of the first three Tempters is not so much to influence the Archbishop's future behaviour as to provide a summary of his past; the mechanical nature of their roles is similar to that of the Tempters in *Samson Agonistes* or the *confidante* in French classical drama. There is no question of Thomas's yielding to any of the three; their real function is to show to what extent he has been susceptible to the attractions they represent. These are:

(a) "the good time"

Old Tom, gay Tom, Becket of London . . .

(b) "Power"

Shall he who held the solid substance
Wander waking with deceitful shadows?

(c) "Treachery"

THOMAS

To what does this lead?

TEMPTER

To a happy coalition
Of intelligent interests.

The nature of the Archbishop's character and of his past life is filled out by such means; his present spiritual condition is clarified, both to himself and to his audience, by the fourth Tempter. These, then, are the functions of agents whose presence in the plays seems at first sight a rather trite association of Thomas with the tempted Christ.

Thomas's "character" is adequately presented, but several of his speeches exhibit a defect which we find in certain late nineteenth-century verse plays, particularly those of Swinburne. The terms in which Henry James indicated the structural weakness of *Chastelard* apply also to *Murder in the Cathedral*: "Chastelard descants in twenty different passages of very florid and eloquent verse upon the intoxicating beauties of his mistress; but meanwhile the play stands still."[13]

Thomas's speeches are, in themselves, more interesting than Chastelard's: we enter more readily into his experience of the spirit than into Chastelard's of the flesh; but the structural flaw persists and accounts for the feeling that the play, in performance, moves by fits and starts. When Thomas descants, the play stands still. (When Antony addressed the Roman mob, the play rushed forward.)

This impression is strengthened by a certain "anonymity" in Thomas's voice. It is worthwhile remarking the resemblance between the Archbishop's voice and that anonymous voice which is heard so pervadingly in Eliot's early non-dramatic poetry, particularly in *Ash Wednesday*. One thinks, for example, of Thomas's first speech:

They know and do not know, what it is to act or suffer.
They know and do not know, that acting is suffering

[13] *The Nation*, 18 January 1866; *Complete Plays*, edited by Leon Edel, Philadelphia and New York, J. B. Lippincott Company, 1949, p. 33.

And suffering is action. Neither does the actor suffer
Nor the patient act. But both are fixed
In an eternal action, an eternal patience
To which all must consent that it may be willed
And which all must suffer that they may will it,
That the pattern may subsist, for the pattern is the action
And the suffering, that the wheel may turn and still
Be forever still.

And this from *Ash Wednesday*:

Because I know that time is always time
And place is always and only place
And what is actual is actual only for one time
And only for one place
I rejoice that things are as they are and
I renounce the blessed face
And renounce the voice
Because I cannot hope to turn again
Consequently I rejoice, having to construct something
Upon which to rejoice . . .[14]

Thomas and the anonymous speaker are not saying the
same things, but they are speaking in the same voice. It would
be impertinent to suggest that it is Mr. Eliot's own voice, but
it is necessary to observe that between this dramatic and that
non-dramatic voice there is no essential difference. In both
passages we have the feeling that the words are heuristic, that
of themselves they are engendering poetic life, and that they are
doing this almost without functional restraints. In the case of
*Murder in the Cathedral* the words seem to operate almost apart
from the character and situation they are designed to serve.
They are intrinsically fine, moving easily out of their context
into an autonomous poetic existence; and this is a measure of
their weakness as dramatic verse. In *The Music of Poetry* Eliot
referred to "the profound difference between dramatic and all

[14] *Collected Poems, supra*, p. 93.

other kinds of verse."[15] A sense of this difference (which the early Yeats lacked) has taken a central position in Eliot's recent theory of verse drama, but it played little part in the composition of *Murder in the Cathedral*.

It is worthwhile considering this point in the light of Eliot's own comments on the language of *Murder in the Cathedral*. It seemed to him that the vocabulary and style should not be precisely those of modern conversation, since he wanted to take his audience back to an historical event. Yet he felt that the language should not be archaic, since he wished to emphasise the contemporary "point" of the situation. The style, therefore, had to be neutral, committed neither to the past nor to the present. As regards versification, he believed that the essential aim was to avoid any echo of Shakespeare: blank verse, after extensive use in non-dramatic poetry, seemed to him to have lost its flexibility and its easy relation to conversation: "Therefore what I kept in mind was the versification of 'Everyman,' hoping that anything unusual in the sound of it would be, on the whole, advantageous."[16] Eliot declared, finally, that the verse of *Murder in the Cathedral* had only a negative merit, inasmuch as it avoided what had to be avoided. To the extent that it solved a problem it did so only for that one play, and it offered no indication of the kind of verse he should use in another play.

Faced with these difficulties, Eliot seems unconsciously to have slipped into a verse-manner which he had already used in his early poems. We would argue, in fact, that the relation between the verse of *Murder in the Cathedral* and that of *Ash Wednesday* is much too close; similarly in the case of Yeats there is not enough difference between the verse of *The Shadowy Waters* and that of *He tells of a Valley full of Lovers*. And note too how little is required of the verse in *Murder in the Cathedral*. Given the prose of the sermon and the prose speeches of the assassins, the remaining verse, whether it is the voice of despair

---

[15] *Selected Prose*, London, Penguin Books, 1953, p. 63.
[16] *Ibid.*, pp. 76-77.

or, later, the cry of faith, is largely in one tone: its density is unvaried. It grapples with the profound, the philosophical, the "large" statement, but it is not asked to extend its range to include the transitional or the commonplace. Those who find a lot of "poetry" in *Murder in the Cathedral* are right, but the deeper insight is Eliot's, who has seen that at all costs he must achieve a verse-style in which, as he puts it, everything that any dramatic character might have to say, whether high or low, "poetical" or "prosaic," may be said quite naturally.[17]

He has *Antony and Cleopatra* in mind as an exemplary play in this respect; we may glance at two characteristic passages, the first "mean," the second "high." In the first (I.iv) Octavius, when he has received a letter informing him of Antony's behaviour in Alexandria, says to Lepidus:

> You may see, Lepidus, and henceforth know,
> It is not Caesar's natural vice to hate
> Our great competitor. From Alexandria
> This is the news: he fishes, drinks and wastes
> The lamps of night in revel: is not more manlike
> Than Cleopatra, nor the queen of Ptolemy
> More womanly than he: hardly gave audience, or
> Vouchsafed to think he had partners: you shall find there
> A man who is the abstract of all faults
> That all men follow.[18]

An eighteenth-century critic, considering this passage, would praise the style for being pure, chaste, and "easy," emphasising its power and flexibility, power so confident of itself that it does not need to gesticulate. We may illustrate these qualities in the verse by pointing to the unobtrusive yet determining nature of the rhythm. The opening lines, answering to Octavius's vaunted moderation, move quietly and easily, as if with reserves of energy. But as soon as Octavius begins to give details of Antony's

[17] *Ibid.*, p. 63.
[18] New Shakespeare edition by J. Dover Wilson, London, Cambridge University Press, 1950, p. 16.

behaviour, the increased severity of his tone is defined in the
rhythm, which now strains against the metre. Inevitably, the
details are offered so as to permit the gesture of moral distaste
in

> hardly gave audience, or
> Vouchsafed to think he had partners . . .

where the rhetorical pause after "or" mimics Antony's lofty
superciliousness. At this point the tension between metre and
rhythm is resolved. In the next line rhythm and metre move
together to endorse a rebuke very different from the almost
casual tone of Octavius's opening remarks:

> you shall find there
> A man who is the abstract of all faults
> That all men follow.

The close relation between this verse and Octavius's speaking voice exemplifies the quality which Eliot would seem to
admire in *Antony and Cleopatra* generally, and which he failed
to secure in *Murder in the Cathedral*. This relation operates in
terms of diction, syntax, and rhythm. As far as diction is concerned, the single phrase which seems to parade its literary
affiliation, "the lamps of night," is so common in Elizabethan
literature that, while slightly "enlarging" the range of Octavius's
remarks, it does not destroy the tonal unity of his speech. For
the rest, the passage is manipulated conversation; however
formal, it takes its bearings from the habits of refined discourse.

The kind of achievement represented by this passage, the
certainty of touch in handling common speech, may be seen
even in the most exalted moments in the play. When Antony
dies in Cleopatra's arms, a "high" speech is called for by convention, scenario, and rhetorical considerations. Shakespeare's
remarkable achievement consisted in providing such a speech
without the clangour which Tamburlane made at the death of
Zenocrate. Furthermore, a "high" speech was required which
would yet end, without bathos, as fit preparation for the next

scene in Octavius's camp. Shakespeare solved these problems by concentrating the "high" quality of Cleopatra's speech on her sense of loss, her feeling that with Antony dead all greatness is cut to the common level:

> Noblest of men, woo't die?
> Hast thou no care of me? shall I abide
> In this dull world, which in thy absence is
> No better than a sty? O, see, my women,

(*At this moment Antony dies*)

> The crown o' th' earth doth melt. My lord!
> O, withered is the garland of the war,
> The soldier's pole is fall'n: young boys and girls
> Are level now with men: the odds is gone,
> And there is nothing left remarkable
> Beneath the visiting moon.

At this point Iras moans, "Royal Egypt, Empress," but Cleopatra rejects the fancy that greatness of any kind yet persists:

> No more but e'en a woman, and commanded
> By such poor passion as the maid that milks
> And does the meanest chares. It were for me
> To throw my sceptre at the injurious gods,
> To tell them that this world did equal theirs
> Till they had stol'n our jewel. All's but naught;
> Patience is sottish, and impatience does
> Become a dog that's mad: then is it sin,
> To rush into the secret house of death,
> Ere death dare come to us? . . .[19]

This is surely one of the most economical speeches in all "high" drama. One exults at the fitness of the procedure by which Cleopatra rejects the whole world of hyperbole which she has made, traditionally, her own. In terms of "form" the surprise of this rejection is carried down into the detail of the

[19] *Ibid.*, pp. 105-06.

writing, exhibiting itself in such phrases as "poor passion" and in the association of Cleopatra with "the maid that milks/ And does the meanest chares."

We have here, then, two passages of Shakespearean blank verse, differing widely in tone and diction, and yet recognisably a single language. The metre as such, of course, contributes to this impression of unity, but is not, in itself, sufficient to guarantee it. Ultimately, one must search for the determining principle in the relation between metre, diction, rhythm, syntax, trope, the nature of the speaker, and the nature of the dramatic situation in which the words are spoken. It is this unified language, however, which Eliot has come to regard as the ideal of speech toward which modern verse dramatists must strive. He himself may well have been urged toward the extension of his range in *The Cocktail Party* by recognising in Cleopatra's speech the dramatic potentialities of common language.

The demands made on the verse of *Murder in the Cathedral* are slight; we have now to consider whether a corresponding limitation applies to the burden and scope of the entire play.

*Murder in the Cathedral* is an act of piety before it is a work of art. By contrast *Four Quartets* is a work of art which, having satisfied artistic criteria, is thereafter seen to be also an act of piety. The distinction is worth considering briefly.

One of Eliot's great achievements as a poet has been to preserve the inclusiveness of his operative vision. Richard Blackmur has reminded us that as a poet Eliot is compelled to know and deal with, what as a Christian he perhaps has only to know and transcend, all that knowledge and experience which is not Christian and which is so much greater in quantity than the Christian.[20] One would have expected that the dramatic form would lend itself most readily to the treatment of knowledge and experience in these terms; and yet it has tended otherwise in *Murder in the Cathedral*. There can be little doubt that the order of Grace and Orthodoxy within which the play operates

[20] *Language as Gesture, supra,* p. 209.

imposes severe limitations on the elements of experience hostile to that order. *Four Quartets*, on the other hand, grapples at large not merely with the order of Grace, separately, or with the order of Nature, separately, but with the complex involvement of both. *Murder in the Cathedral* transcends the quantity of experience which is not Christian. *Four Quartets* deals with that experience, conceding to it its full and dangerous rights: hence its characteristic mode of "exploration."

# CHAPTER SIX. THE FAMILY REUNION

SOME of the most penetrating strictures on *The Family Reunion* were expressed by Eliot himself, looking back after eleven years. We shall consider some of these in detail, but to begin with, perhaps we should test the single positive claim which Eliot has made for his play. In retrospect he thought that in *The Family Reunion* he had made a good deal of progress in finding a form of versification and an idiom which would serve all his purposes and which would be capable of unbroken transition between the most intense speech and the most relaxed dialogue.[1] We have already discussed this aim, offering instances from *Antony and Cleopatra*. We have also argued that the problem was evaded rather than solved in *Murder in the Cathedral*. In his more recent plays Eliot has been forced to tackle the parallel problem of relating modern dramatic verse to contemporary speech: first, because his themes are derived from contemporary situations; second, because a close relation to contemporary speech is suggested by the decorum of those plays. In making these experiments Eliot has faced, for his generation, a problem which in former ages had engaged the attention, as we have seen, of such theorists as Cinthio, Castelvetro, and Corneille. It is one of our aims to show that Eliot achieved the versification and idiom he describes not in *The Family Reunion* or even in *The Cocktail Party* but in *The Confidential Clerk*.

The problem concerns words and the feelings and thoughts which the words serve. The main difficulty arises from the nature of words themselves. For words, unlike feelings, are, if not exact, at least sharp, definite in outline, positive and committed. Words have form; feelings sprawl to such an extent that their verbal formulation involves "clarification," hence distortion. In many cases the thought or the feeling is not nearly as "formed" as the words which must be used to represent it if

[1] *Poetry and Drama* (1950); *Selected Prose*, Penguin Books, 1953, pp. 82-83.

*94*

it is to be represented at all. We cite a well-known passage from *Ulysses*:

MRS. THORNTON

(*In nursetender's gown*) Embrace me tight, dear. You'll be soon over it. Tight, dear. (*Bloom embraces her tightly and bears eight male yellow and white children. They appear on a redcarpeted staircase adorned with expensive plants. All are handsome, with valuable metallic faces, wellmade, respectably dressed and well-conducted, speaking five modern languages fluently and interested in various arts and sciences. Each has his name printed in legible letters on his shirtfront: Nasodoro, Goldfinger, Chrysostomos, Maindoree, Silversmile, Silberselber, Vifargent, Panargyros . . .*)[2]

Edmund Wilson has argued that Joyce here goes beyond the probable in the vocabulary which he allows Leopold Bloom to command. Yet he does not suppose that Joyce means us to think of Bloom as actually formulating these *words* and *names* in his mind. Rather, it is Joyce's way of conveying a vision which on Bloom's part must have been much less distinct or at least much less "literary" than these words.[3] To grasp, with ideal accuracy, Bloom's drunken fancy, the reader must subtract something from the words Joyce uses to represent it, and this "something" is the sharp clarity which the words *as words* impose on the fancy. The passage would seem to fail, therefore, because the reader, while reading, has no way of knowing whether or to what extent Bloom's vision is less distinct or less literary than the words used to convey it, especially as in earlier episodes involving Bloom the reader feels no difficulty and is not obliged to subtract at all.

[2] *Ulysses*, The Bodley Head, 1937 edition, p. 470.
[3] *Axel's Castle*, Scribner, 1931, p. 227. See also Philip Toynbee's comment on the same passage, "A Study of James Joyce's *Ulysses*," *Polemic* 7, March 1947, p. 38.

Beside this passage we would place one from *The Family
Reunion*. A choric passage:

> We know various spells and enchantments,
> And minor forms of sorcery,
> Divination and chiromancy,
> Specifics against insomnia,
> Lumbago, and the loss of money.
> But the circle of our understanding
> Is a very restricted area.
> Except for a limited number
> Of strictly practical purposes
> We do not know what we are doing;
> And even, when you think of it,
> We do not know much about thinking.
> What is happening outside of the circle?
> And what is the meaning of happening?
> What ambush lies beyond the heather
> And behind the Standing Stones?[4]

These are not really the words of the choric Aunts and
Uncles, nor are they even self-criticisms imposed on these characters by the dramatist. Rather, the words are critical comments
by the dramatist himself on the values of the amoral world
which Ivy, Gerald, Violet, and Charles represent. There is no
difficulty here; the fact that we, the audience, accept these words
as spoken in chorus by the Aunts and Uncles is due entirely
to the convention of the Chorus itself. The convention is a
licence by which the dramatist tells us, not what these four
limited people think, but what is the essential truth about the
way of life they "collectively" represent. The question of the
precise degree of correspondence between word and feeling is
therefore evaded by dramatic convention.

Elsewhere, no evasion is possible. Consider, for instance, this
passage from the scene between Harry and Mary:

[4] *The Family Reunion*, Faber and Faber, 1939, pp. 132-33.

HARRY: One thing you cannot know:
  The sudden extinction of every alternative,
  The unexpected crash of the iron cataract.
  You do not know what hope is, until you have lost it.
  You only know what it is not to hope:
  You do not know what it is to have hope taken from you,
  Or to fling it away, to join the legion of the hopeless
  Unrecognised by other men, though sometimes by each
    other.

Mary, one of the few characters in *The Family Reunion* capable of taking part in such conversations, replies:

  I know what you mean. That is an experience
  I have not had. Nevertheless, however real,
  However cruel, it may be a deception.

Harry's answer, the crux of his own experience, is also the centre of the problem of language in the play:

      What I see
  May be one dream or another; if there is nothing else
  The most real is what I fear. The bright colour fades
  Together with the unrecapturable emotion,
  The glow upon the world, that never found its object;
  And the eye adjusts itself to a twilight
  Where the dead stone is seen to be batrachian,
  The aphyllous branch ophidian.

Here Harry moves in and out of character, and the weakness of the lines may be described in these terms. Harry's feeling bears *some* relation to a dead stone which is batrachian and to an aphyllous branch which is ophidian, but we cannot believe that the feeling is *like* these words, or that these are the words in which it naturally issues. We have difficulty in acknowledging that the feeling is faithfully served by the tone, weight, and associations of the words. Here, then, one finds that "ventriloquism" which Coleridge saw, with displeasure, in *Sejanus*.[5]

[5] *Coleridge's Miscellaneous Criticism*, edited by T. M. Raysor, Constable, 1936, p. 54.

Joyce and Eliot err in similar ways. We cannot believe that Bloom's fancy has the clarity of the words by which Joyce conveys it. Nothing in *The Family Reunion* persuades us that Harry's feeling is accurately rendered by his words. In this case, furthermore, Eliot makes no attempt to evade the law of probability which he breaks; there are no trances, no special dramatic conventions. It might be argued, rather desperately, that the incongruous lines are Eliot's exposition of the truth about Harry, rather than Harry's expression of his own feelings. But even if we accept this, a serious incongruity remains—a single speech, part of which is the speaker's expression of his feelings, while another part is to be taken as the dramatist's description of the speaker. The audience has no means of knowing at what point the "speaker" is superseded by the dramatist.

If it be argued that the passage quoted is simply an isolated lapse, and that in any event the words are spoken by a character who is mentally unbalanced, we may cite another example, a speech by Agatha:

> There are hours when there seems to be no past or future,
> Only a present moment of pointed light
> When you want to burn. When you stretch out your hand
> To the flames. They only come once,
> Thank God, that kind. Perhaps there is another kind,
> I believe, across a whole Thibet of broken stones
> That lie, fang up, a lifetime's march. I have believed this.

There is nothing to sanction these lines, either in the imposed decorum of the play or in the conversational habits of the society to which Agatha is related. The lines are, if anything, poetry so "pure" as to escape from the play altogether. The same sort of thing happens in *Murder in the Cathedral*.

In *The Family Reunion* more than in any other play Eliot yielded to the temptation to be "poetical," indulging in purely verbal activity at the expense of dramatic relevance and propriety. A final example: in her opening speech Amy says:

O Sun, that was once so warm, O Light that was taken
  for granted
When I was young and strong, and sun and light unsought
  for
And the night unfeared and the day expected
And clocks could be trusted, tomorrow assured
And time would not stop in the dark!

A few minutes later she says:

> I do not want the clock to stop in the dark.
> If you want to know why I never leave Wishwood
> That is the reason. I keep Wishwood alive
> To keep the family alive, to keep them together,
> To keep me alive, and I live to keep them.

It is just possible, in retrospect, to reconcile this clock-fancy
with our conception of Amy as she is presented in the play. But
it is quite incredible that in her last moment of life Amy should
cry out:

> Agatha! Mary! come!
> The clock has stopped in the dark!

Here the poet has intruded, ejecting the dramatist; the poet
could not resist the temptation to recall at this point Amy's
early intimations of mortality by repeating a pregnant image,
despite its incongruity. In *The Family Reunion* Eliot evaded
his favourite virtue, Austerity.

We may conclude this line of enquiry by availing ourselves
of a distinction which Elder Olson formulated some years ago
between Speech as Meaning and Speech as Action. Briefly: what
the poetic character says in a mimetic poem is speech and has
meaning; his saying it is action, an act of persuading, confessing,
commanding, etc. His diction may be accounted for in gram-
matical and lexicographical terms, not so his action. "Pray you,
undo this button" and "The table's full" are profound, not as
statements in themselves full of meaning, but as acts permitting

a great range of implications in that they reveal many aspects of character and situation.[6] When Agatha in *The Family Reunion* expresses her feeling in terms of "a whole Thibet of broken stones/That lie, fang up, a lifetime's march," her words have meaning, but there is nothing in her character or her situation (or in the impact of one on the other) to render the words convincing as an act.

Eliot the poet has laid a heavy hand on *The Family Reunion*. Hugh Kenner has finely observed that the verse of *The Family Reunion* is a dense medium lying in wait for effects of full intensity and damping out anything slighter.[7] One of the results is a certain deliquescence which pervades many of the speeches. Several are insensitively "weighed"; too often one finds oneself saying of even a commonplace remark, "That sounds ponderous, I wonder will it turn out to be significant?" In *The Family Reunion* Eliot failed to write an ideal dramatic verse, that verse which, flexible and pliant, continuously adjusts itself to the slightest variation in intensity or tone. Indeed, trying to account for the peculiarly stolid effect of its verse, we find that instead of a singe flexible language the play contains three distinct kinds of verse, each of which stoutly resist modulation. First, choric verse, almost impersonal, freed from the demands of character and individuality:

> I am afraid of all that has happened, and of all that is to
> come;
> Of the things to come that sit at the door, as if they had
> been there always.
> And the past is about to happen, and the future was long
> since settled.
> And the wings of the future darken the past, the beak and
> claws have desecrated
> History.

[6] Elder Olson, "William Empson, Contemporary Criticism and Poetic Diction," *Modern Philology*, Vol. XLVII, May 1950, p. 229.
[7] "Possum by Gaslight," *Poetry*, October 1954, p. 48.

The second and third kinds may be considered together. On the one hand, there is the verse spoken by the morally sensitive (Harry, Agatha, and Mary). On the other, that spoken by the morally inert (the Aunts and Uncles and, for the most part, Amy):

AGATHA: It is going to be rather painful for Harry
    After eight years and all that has happened
    To come back to Wishwood.
GERALD: Why, painful?
VIOLET: Gerald! you know what Agatha means.
AGATHA: I mean painful, because everything is irrevocable,
    Because the past is irremediable,
    Because the future can only be built
    Upon the real past. Wandering in the tropics
    Or against the painted scene of the Mediterranean,
    Harry must often have remembered Wishwood—
    The nursery tea, the school holiday,
    The daring feats on the old pony,
    And thought to creep back through the little door.
    He will find a new Wishwood. Adaptation is hard.

At this point Amy, seeing only the obvious, makes her inevitable gesture of solidarity. We recall yet again that she has devoted herself to formulae whose desiccation she is too insensitive to realise:

> Nothing is changed, Agatha, at Wishwood.
> Everything is kept as it was when he left it,
> Except the old pony, and the mongrel setter
> Which I had to have destroyed.
> Nothing has been changed. I have seen to that.

Agatha, patiently explicating, fills in the other half of the truth, the part that lurks behind such seemingly innocent words as "happen" and "change":

Yes. I mean that at Wishwood he will find another Harry.
The man who returns will have to meet

The boy who left. Round by the stables,
In the coach-house, in the orchard,
In the plantation, down the corridor
That led to the nursery, round the corner
Of the new wing, he will have to face him—
And it will not be a very *jolly* corner.
When the loop in time comes—and it does not come for
    everybody—
The hidden is revealed, and the spectres show themselves.

Gerald intervenes; he is a younger and heartier version of Amy
on whom Agatha's oblique reference to a story by Henry James
has certainly been wasted:

I don't in the least know what you're talking about.
You seem to be wanting to give us all the hump.
I must say, this isn't cheerful for Amy's birthday
Or for Harry's homecoming. Make him feel at home, I say!
Make him feel that what has happened doesn't matter.
He's taken his medicine, I've no doubt.
Let him marry again and carry on at Wishwood.

The limitation of this verse, and of the language in *The Family Reunion* generally, is that it differentiates not between individuals but merely between groups. Harry, Agatha, and Mary speak the same kind of verse, and within this kind there is a totally inadequate differentiation to represent their separate characters and voices. This applies also to the verse spoken by Ivy, Gerald, Charles, Violet, and Amy: it is a single substance, of which these five partake, Ivy's portion, for instance, being indistinguishable from Violet's.

This limitation pervades the play. The characters inevitably form themselves into two groups (apart from the Chorus). The play is seen to be the imitation of an action by which the leader of a small group of morally sensitive beings frees himself from his own private guilt and from the influence of his mother, leader of a larger group of morally unconscious persons. *The Family Reunion* divides its characters into groups just as radically as does *This Music Crept By Me On the Water,* the difference being that in *The Family Reunion* the division is moral while in Mr. MacLeish's play it is picturesque.

In 1950 a critic assessed *The Family Reunion* as "the most significant of recent English poetic dramas" on the grounds that it showed "that such a drama, in spite of all indications to the contrary, could still deal adequately with the problem of the individual."[8] In the years since this assessment was made, *The Cocktail Party, The Confidential Clerk,* and *The Elder Statesman* have appeared, and it is clear that in these plays Eliot has penetrated more deeply into the nature of the problem. *The Family Reunion* is still, however, the primary document, the natural point of departure for a consideration of the issue and its involvement in Eliot's plays.

Some years ago D. S. Bland investigated the disappearance from modern literature of the individual tragic hero and his replacement by a generalised, typical, or even symbolic hero. In the course of examining the situation he suggested that the characteristic attitude of modern drama is that of Eric in *On the Frontier*:

> Believing it was wrong to kill,
> I went to prison, seeing myself
> As the sane and innocent student
> Aloof, among practical and violent madmen,
> But I was wrong. We cannot choose our world,
> Our life, our class. None are innocent, none.
> Causes of violence lie so deep in all our lives
> It touches every act.

Where none are innocent, Mr. Bland declared, individual error or frailty must count for very little, and where we cannot choose, personality must count for less than conformity.[8]

[8] D. S. Bland, "The Tragic Hero in Modern Literature," *Cambridge Journal*, Vol. III, 4, January 1950, pp. 223, 215.

That similar attitudes are implicit in the modern novel has been established by Albert Guerard. Concentrating his enquiry on Dino Buzzati's *The Tartar Steppe*, John Hawkes's *The Cannibal*, George Orwell's 1984, Ennio Flaiano's *The Short Cut*, and Camus's *The Plague*, Professor Guerard concluded that the modern novel characteristically presents man as having lost his freedom of action. It is within the limits of the smallest conceivable world, he observes, and with all his material reward eaten away by sharks, that Hemingway's fisherman in *The Old Man and the Sea* asserts his human dignity.[9]

In this context Mr. Bland presents *The Family Reunion* as an exception to the rule that modern literature sees individual moral action as either impossible or meaningless. To pursue and to seek are positive, personal acts, even though Harry's freedom, he observes, is the freedom of necessity. To recognize the necessity and to be willing to accept it are the important acts. The significance of *The Family Reunion* consists, accordingly, in the treatment of the situation in such a way that Harry emerges as an individual.[10] It seems probable, however, that this reading of the play exaggerates Harry's individuality and for that reason overlooks some of the most crucial factors in the play.

*The Family Reunion* is generally interpreted as a drama of sin and expiation in which the hero, Harry, moves from guilt through repentance to holiness. John Peter, for instance, comments: "From the negatives of regret, self-mistrust and suffering (Harry's) attitude shifts round to the positives of repentance and the will to expiate his sin."[11] We may regard this movement as corresponding to that of the tragic hero (Becket, for instance) from "purpose" through "passion" to "perception."[12] It largely

[9] Albert Guerard, "The Ivory Tower and the Dust Bowl," *New World Writing*, Summer 1953, p. 356. Compare Stephen Spender's comment: "The modern world is the world where it is impossible for the individual to do either right or wrong." ("Thoughts in an Aeroplane over Europe," *Polemic 8*, p. 59).

[10] Bland, *supra*, p. 223.

[11] John Peter, "The Family Reunion," *Scrutiny*, Vol. XVI, 3, 1949, p. 221.

[12] This formulation, which we owe to Kenneth Burke, was invoked in connexion with *Murder in the Cathedral*.

determines the structure of the play, but it does not account for those parts of the drama which are not directly focussed on Harry's guilt.

There are, in fact, two actions in *The Family Reunion*: a drama of "guilt," which is Harry's private *geste*, and a related action which is wider and symbolic. This second action is represented in the title of the play: the Monchensey family consists of a group, led by Harry, which exhibits moral awareness in the midst of great confusion and misunderstanding, and another group, led by Amy, whose interests are domestic, null, amoral. Harry is an individual quasi-tragic hero only in relation to his private crisis, the "guilt" action: he is a symbolic hero in the conflict of values between the two groups of which the family consists. We are free to emphasise Harry's private action, but not to discount his symbolic conflict with Amy. Individual action is posssible and full of meaning for Harry only because he is driven by divine guidance (the Eumenides) to repudiate and eventually to destroy Amy's world. There is in Harry something of the medieval knight as well as the modern psychiatric "case": he is one of the "elect."

The two actions which we have distinguished are not, indeed, wholly separate; they move together and sometimes cross. There are certain speeches which, touching both, yet bear a closer relation to one. The following lines, for instance, which Harry speaks to the assembled Aunts and Uncles, have only a slight reference to his private crisis and a much more suggestive relation to the conflict of values between his world and Amy's:

> You go on trying to think of each thing separately,
> Making small things important, so that everything
> May be unimportant, a slight deviation
> From some imaginary course that life ought to take,
> That you call normal. What you call the normal
> Is merely the unreal and the unimportant.
> I was like that in a way, so long as I could think
> Even of my own life as an isolated ruin,

A casual bit of waste in an orderly universe.
But it begins to seem just part of some huge disaster,
Some monstrous mistake and aberration
Of all men, of the world, which I cannot put in order.

The two actions are joined, first, by the Eumenides, those figures which have been something of an embarrassment to Eliot
and his producers. Eliot has described them variously, we note,
as "divine instruments," "divine messengers," and again as
"hounds of heaven": their function is to prevent Harry from
evading the spiritual issue or from seeking any way out other
than the way of "purgation and holiness."[13] Hence they are a
link between the two actions, for in grasping the way of purgation and holiness Harry simultaneously rejects the amoral mode
of life so stolidly represented by Amy. At this point the two
actions merge. The culminating speech is Harry's; determined
to "follow the bright angels" he says to Amy:

> And now I know
> That my business is not to run away, but to
>     pursue,
> Not to avoid being found, but to seek.
> I would not have chosen this way, had there been
>     any other!
> It is at once the hardest thing, and the only
>     thing possible.
> Now they will lead me. I shall be safe with them;
> I am not safe here.

The lines are unmistakably crucial and here the play may be
said to end. The ensuing twenty pages of text present Amy's

[13] Letter to E. Martin Browne, quoted in F. O. Matthiessen, *The
Achievement of T. S. Eliot,* Oxford University Press, second edition,
1947, pp. 167-68. It is perhaps relevant to note that Miss Maud Bodkin
minimises the spiritual significance of the Eumenides: ". . . the Furies
embody the energy of passion fixed in an evil relationship or custom—
the same energy which, released from the fixation and redirected, becomes the sustaining force of a better order of individual and social life"
(*The Quest for Salvation in an Ancient and a Modern Play,* Oxford,
1941, p. 46).

death but nothing essential to the dramatic pattern. When Harry says, "I shall be safe with them;/I am not safe here," he has made the moral choice and has passed through his private crisis. The formal redundancy here is strikingly similar to that exhibited, as we have seen, in the second part of *Murder in the Cathedral*.

Another link between the two actions is the idea of Conscience, or rather the impact on human behaviour of Conscience and Consciousness. In *The Family Reunion* Conscience seems to be the smaller force, probably because at an early stage one can dissolve its powers by diffusing them into a cliché. This is what Charles does, for instance, at the end of a particularly obtuse conversation with Harry:

> But *you* have no reason to reproach yourself.
> Your conscience can be clear.

Harry retorts:

> It goes a good deal deeper
> Than what people call their conscience; it is
>     just the cancer
> That eats away the self . . .
>             . . . It is not my conscience,
> Not my mind, that is diseased, but the world I
>     have to live in.

Stephan Dedalus had proclaimed that he was going forth to forge in the smithy of his soul the uncreated conscience of his race. To create such a conscience is also part of Harry's role (Hamlet-wise) in *The Family Reunion*, though in playing it he needs the larger word, Consciousness. Agatha provides the word and the insight to go with it in the second scene of Part Two:

> It is possible that sin may sin and struggle
> In its dark instinctive birth, to come to consciousness
> And so find expurgation. It is possible
> You are the consciousness of your unhappy family,
> Its bird sent flying through the purgatorial flame.

Harry's consciousness (guaranteed by his recognition of the Eumenides) drives him, as hero in his own private struggle, to holiness. Another part of his role requires that, as symbolic hero, he force the inert world of Wishwood at least to acknowledge the existence of Conscience and Consciousness. In one of her last speeches Amy, type of moral inertia, is driven to confess:

> At my age, I only just begin to apprehend the truth
> About things too late to mend: and that is to be old.
> Nevertheless, I am glad if I can come to know them.

It appears, therefore, that in regard to the problem of the individual in modern literature Harry is a special case. To a certain extent he is an individual, bearing a burden of personal and inherited guilt. To an even greater extent he is a symbol, type of moral awareness; here his special problem is that of the religious man in a secular society.[14] This does not mean that he is a post-nineteenth century hero, a figure isolated, at odds with his whole environment. At this point his association with Agatha and Mary (his "adjuncts") becomes important: these two provide a sympathetic context, a feeling of "belonging," the spiritual counterpart of Amy's mechanical solidarity. Placing them more specifically, they form, with Harry, an analogue of the Christian family in a secular or neutral society. Harry makes his moral choice and takes action, therefore, not as a result of his individual heroic strength; aided by divine guidance, as represented by the Eumenides, he capitalises on the strength of the religious brotherhood of which he is a member.

This emphasis is crucial. Resting with the conventional interpretation of the play as simply an action arising from individual guilt, one is forced into an unsound critical conclusion. John Peter, for example, reading the play in these terms, is compelled to argue that two forces are pulling in opposite directions. On the one hand the theme requires that the "murder" should

---

[14] A better word than "secular" is "neutral," which Eliot used so effectively in *The Idea of a Christian Society*, Faber and Faber, 1939.

be as nebulous as possible. On the other, the ferment of Harry's personal experience requires that the "murder" be a very real and substantial "objective correlative." It cannot, however, be both; and, in effect, Harry becomes, what Eliot would have us believe Hamlet becomes, no more than a mouthpiece for obsession, disturbing and impairing the play.[15]

But this is not so. Bear in mind that the "murder" is only part of the story. Harry's obsession arises from two causes: first, the "murder"; second, his sense of the terrible disrelation between the values to which he would cleave and those of the secular, null Wishwood exemplified by his mother. Harry's return to Wishwood symbolises the experience of the "real" in confronting the "actual," the spiritual in confronting the secular. The pain which results is the "passion" of the tragic rhythm. Separately, neither of these causes would be substantial enough to produce Harry's obsession: together, lending each other depth and extension, they provide an adequate "objective correlative." The search for the decisive flaw in the play must be pursued elsewhere.

One of the most pertinent of Eliot's comments on *The Family Reunion* concerns his use of the Eumenides, which he roundly declares a failure. Since he chose to relate Harry's private crisis to the story of Orestes he could hardly have omitted the Eumenides. Their function in *The Family Reunion* is to act as "divine messengers" and yet to carry no positively Christian associations. They are angels without a Credo, performing the same work as the fragments of Sanscrit in *The Waste Land*.[16] Eliot finds them unsatisfactory because they set the producer of the play an impossible task. There can be no more compelling objection, and yet it is difficult to see how the action of the play

---

[15] Peter, *supra*, p. 230.

[16] Compare Cleanth Brooks, "The Waste Land, Critique of the Myth" *Modern Poetry and the Tradition*, Poetry London, 1948, p. 167: "Consequently, the only method is to work by indirection. The Christian material is at the centre, but the poet never deals with it directly. The theme of resurrection is made on the surface in terms of the fertility rites; the words which the thunder speaks are Sanscrit words."

could be presented at all in their absence. It is not necessary, of course, that they be visible to the audience.

In considering the Eumenides one soon concludes that the play suffers from the sheer weight of its machinery. In addition to the Eumenides there are the Chorus of Aunts and Uncles and the post-Tchekovian bits of lyrical verse which Eliot himself has come to dislike. These are lyrical duets isolated from the rest of the dialogue by being written in short lines with only two stresses per line. They are in a sense, as Eliot observes, "beyond character," and the speakers have to be presented as falling into a trancelike state in order to speak them. But they are far more remote from the necessity of the action than operatic arias: "The member of the audience, if he enjoys this sort of thing, is putting up with a suspension of the action in order to enjoy a poetic fantasia: these passages are really less related to the action than are the choruses in *Murder in the Cathedral*."[17] They are also evidence that Eliot in *The Family Reunion* found his dramatic form narrow and intractable. The material in these trance-duets is carried over from prose fiction, where it could be treated much more convincingly.

Eliot's observations on *The Family Reunion* are perceptive but they stop just short of the most important judgments; or rather they fail to relate their separate strictures on a deeper level. He has declared that the defects in *The Family Reunion* include the use of the Eumenides, the Chorus, and the trance-duets. Add these items together: they make up all the "anti-realistic" factors in the play. At this point one comes on a crucial defect. Structurally, *The Family Reunion* exhibits the "technical form" of a modern realistic play; Eliot maintains this form throughout, but he subjects it to the strain of certain anti-realistic devices. On the one hand he provides a realistic setting and more or less realistic characterisation: these prompt the audience to expect that a certain view of life will accompany the play. John Gassner has noted that the realistic and naturalistic dramas incorporate a certain view of reality, and that the rejection of these

[17] *Selected Prose, supra,* p. 80.

procedures and conventions usually involves an opposing idea of reality. He argues that it is not without reason that the realistic drama came to be identified with a positivist and liberal nineteenth-century world-view and that the post-naturalistic styles were associated with the rejection of this world-view and with a general sense of *fin de siècle* and twentieth-century alienation.[18]

Clearly, the subjection of a realistic dramatic form to the pressure of anti-realistic forces has great possibilities. An imaginative playwright might by such means present a dramatic action of great complexity and tension. He might use this device to challenge the view of reality associated with the realistic drama, subjecting its complacency to doubts, testing it on its own terms. By such means he might achieve something like the subtle effects which, as Professor Empson has shown, the Elizabethans secured by using a double plot.[19] Eliot himself seems to have had something like this as one of his aims in *The Cocktail Party* and *The Confidential Clerk*. To obtain such an effect of inclusiveness and complexity, however, the playwright would have to ensure (as a minimum) that the realistic and anti-realistic forces come to grips. Failing that, there is exposition but no drama. In *The Family Reunion* these forces do not even make a pretense of coming to grips. One group does not control or modify the activity of the other; the two simply stand apart, engendering no queries, no implications. In the case of the Elizabethan double plot we feel that the total effect is greater than the sum of its parts; no corresponding feeling emerges in

[18] "Forms of Modern Drama," *Comparative Literature*, Vol. VII, 2, Spring 1955, p. 130.

[19] In *Some Versions of Pastoral* Professor Empson writes: "It is an easy-going device, often used simply to fill out a play, and has an obvious effect in the Elizabethans of making you feel the play deals with life as a whole . . . this may be why criticism has not taken it seriously when it deserved to be. Just because of this carelessness much can be put into it; to those who miss the connections the thing still seems sensible, and queer connections can be insinuated powerfully and unobtrusively; especially if they fit in with ideas the audience already has at the back of its mind. The old quarrel about tragi-comedy, which dealt with part of the question, shows that the drama in England has always at its best had a certain looseness of structure; one might almost say that the English drama did not outlive the double plot." See Brooks, *supra*, p. 206.

*The Family Reunion.* From the audience's point of view the result is not complexity or inclusiveness but sheer frustration, which means the play is, rhetorically and dramatically, a failure, despite its local merits. The responses evoked by the realistic and anti-realistic factors in the play are simply "apart" and lead merely to emotional confusion. It is hardly necessary to say that the audience's confusion from this source is intensified by that which we have already seen arising from Eliot's defective characterisation.

Holiness and the destruction of Holiness have been the concerns of Eliot's plays since *Sweeney Agonistes.* In *Murder in the Cathedral,* as we have seen, Thomas's martyrdom is enacted within an order of Grace which "transcends the quantity of experience that is not Christian." *The Family Reunion* is a more complex play inasmuch as it gives serious consideration to the quantity of experience that is not Christian. This experience is snubbed, however, as being inadequate, absurd. Near the end of the play Amy asks Harry where he intends going after leaving Wishwood. Harry answers:

> I shall have to learn. That is still unsettled.
> I have not yet had the precise directions.
> Where does one go from a world of insanity?
> Somewhere on the other side of despair.

With the null world of Wishwood still in mind Harry continues:

> John shall be the master.
> All I have is his. No harm can come to him.
> What would destroy me will be life for John,
> I am responsible for him. Why I have this election
> I do not understand. It must have been preparing always,
> And I see it was what I always wanted. Strength demanded
> That seems too much, is just strength enough given.
> I must follow the bright angels.

The significant word is "election." We would place it beside an earlier passage. Wishwood and the inert, amoral world which it represents are to be handed over to John; this is his proper milieu. One recalls Harry's description of his brother:

A minor matter like a concussion
Cannot make very much difference to John.
A brief vacation from the kind of consciousness
That John enjoys, can't make very much difference
To him or to anyone else. If he was ever really conscious,
I should be glad for him to have a breathing spell:
But John's ordinary day isn't much more than breathing.

The naming of John as fit head of the world of Wishwood, when Harry will have abandoned it, completes the rhetorical trend of the play. The amoral world is now identified with the lowest level of consciousness. The word "election" is now seen to imply that for those who are *chosen* to be "awake" and "living on several planes at once," the way of life represented by Wishwood is grossly inadequate. The idea of religious vocation emerges now more clearly than before.

Stated in these terms, the rhetoric of the play seems trite, and it is, not because it is obvious but because it has not been sufficiently refined by the interaction of varied and complex attitudes. We return to the crucial defect of the play (which is reflected in the flawed verse): the attitudes, like the characters, never acquire individuality and merely run together in two simple groups. *The Family Reunion* merely marks a necessary stage in the dramatist's progress from the easy, exclusive ritual of *Murder in the Cathedral* to the much more subtle drama of Holiness in *The Cocktail Party* and *The Confidential Clerk*. It is that kind of play.

# CHAPTER SEVEN. *THE COCKTAIL PARTY*

## I

IN *The Cocktail Party*, as in *The Family Reunion* and *The Waste Land*, Eliot proceeds by indirection; he ensnares his audience. To speak of his work in these terms is to point again to the conditions which govern communication between the contemporary artist and society. The characteristic situation of the modern artist, which—despite boredom and natural misgivings—we continue to describe as "alienation," is particularly relevant to an important problem in modern drama. Professor Fergusson has observed that as theatre-poetry was freed from the limitations of modern realism it lost its public status as a mirror of human nature. Obey's *Noah* and Eliot's *Murder in the Cathedral* throw light upon contemporary experience, but only obliquely or at best "experimentally": the literal moorings are cut and the resulting drama is arbitrary in its own way. Each poetic dramatist discerns his own beautiful, consistent, and intelligible dramatic idea while the formless public, looking the other way, is engrossed in the commercially profitable shadows on the cavewall.[1] In his more recent plays Eliot moves his drama into a position between the audience and the cave-wall, hoping to entice them into drama, into consciousness, and perhaps even into spirituality by offering them something which from a distance looks familiar. The trap is prepared with great subtlety.

The surface of the play exhibits all the features of a comedy of manners; the silly party, the urban setting, the trivial chatter:

JULIA: I've always wanted to go to California. Do tell us what you were doing in California.
CELIA: Making a film.
PETER:                          Trying to make a film.
JULIA: Oh, what film was it? I wonder if I've seen it.[2]

[1] Francis Fergusson, *The Idea of a Theater*, Princeton University Press, 1949, p. 224.
[2] *The Cocktail Party*, Faber and Faber, 1950, pp. 13-14.

*114*

The opening scene is packed with ironic stichomythia of this kind, brought over from *A Game of Chess* and comically flattened for the occasion. The inner rhetoric[3] of the play operates on a "high" comic surface: Lady Klootz, the tigers, monkeys, and decayed mansions help to pacify and control an audience temperamentally suspicious of Holiness. George Orwell has pointed out that many people do not wish to be saints, do not want their lives to have that kind of focus. Eliot could no longer be satisfied to communicate only with the pious audience which attended at Canterbury in 1935.

In 1939 Eliot expressed the view that "we have today a culture which is mainly negative, but which, so far as it is positive, is still Christian."[4] Accordingly, the surface appearance of *The Cocktail Party* is designed to offer no obstacle to the "negative" aspects of our culture; on the other hand, the texture of the play is such that its images, to the extent to which they are "positive," are Christian. A typical passage reads:

JULIA: Celia! I see you've had the same inspiration
 That I had. Edward must be fed.
 He's under such a strain. We must keep his strength up.
 Edward! Don't you realise how lucky you are
 To have *two* Good Samaritans? I never heard of that before.
EDWARD: The man who fell among thieves was luckier than I:
 He was left at an inn.
JULIA:        Edward, how ungrateful.
 What's in that saucepan?
CELIA:        Nobody knows.
EDWARD: It's something that Alex came and prepared for me.
 He *would* do it. Three Good Samaritans.
 I forgot all about it.

---

[3] "By rhetoric is meant: the art of persuasion, properly in the service of dialectic or poetic; improperly, in the service of argument on the pleading of a 'cause'; *in extremis* or in abstraction, the art of persuasion uprooted, flourished for its own sake, with its eye on itself." R. P. Blackmur, "The Lion and the Honeycomb," *Hudson Review*, Vol. III, 4, Winter 1951, p. 487.

[4] *The Idea of a Christian Society*, Faber and Faber, 1939, p. 13.

The images in this passage are either domestic or Christian. The Christian images arise naturally from the situation; the domestic details are so authentic that they support the Christian references without strain. It is easy to understand, therefore, why a secular or neutral audience would accept such a passage, complete with its Christian terms. The same audience would react strongly to the dogmatic and "exclusive" fervour of *The Man Born to be King.*

*The Cocktail Party* is a realistic play, up to a point. Shortly after it was completed, Eliot said that he had intended to create characters whose drawing-room behaviour was generally correct. The most important thing was that people should speak in character.[5] These remarks were designed primarily to enable the playwright to evade the invitation to "explain" his play, and they are accurate only to a limited extent. The truth is that while *The Cocktail Party* contains no Chorus, no Eumenides, and no lyrical duets, the anti-realistic forces which it utilises are deployed with much greater success than in *The Family Reunion.* These forces are necessary because *The Cocktail Party* invokes the "real" world only to the extent required to engage the attention of its audience. Gradually the realisation emerges that while the play uses many of the characteristic features of realistic drama it is not a "slice of life," or a "picture" of any society but rather an "envisagement" of a possible Christian community. The distinction is crucial. For we must alter our bearings: we praise *The Cocktail Party* not by describing it as convincing but by drawing attention to the fluid nature of the responses which it elicits. The play invites us, not to observe an interesting slice of life or to suspend our disbelief, but to *envisage* a society in which the vague humanistic motion of our lives would be changed into something more dynamic, more "real" and simultaneously more Christian. "Motion" becomes "action." Eliot's basic procedure is one by which neutral images are exposed to the danger of picking up a specifically Christian infection. The mood is optative.

[5] *World Review,* November 1949, pp. 20-21.

Perhaps the most convenient way to illustrate this procedure is by examining those images which seem to dominate the text. Fortunately, part of the work has been well done for us by William Arrowsmith, who points out that the main images in the play are those involving sight and blindness, light and dark. He quotes Julia's "I must have left my glasses here, / And I simply can't see a thing without them"; Reilly's "And me bein' the One Eyed Riley"; Celia's "I can see you at last as a human being," followed by Edward's "I'm completely in the dark"; Julia's "You must have learned to look at people, Peter / . . . That is, when you're not concerned with yourself / But just being an eye." There are several other instances including the following little sequence:

JULIA: Well, my dears, I shall see you very soon.
EDWARD: When shall we see you?
JULIA: Did I say you'd see me?[6]

The imagery of vision is undoubtedly of great importance in *The Cocktail Party* and it bears an obvious relation to the theme of spiritual progress. But these images operate still more positively, and to an end of great moment.

Eliot introduces the visual reference quite casually, by cliché:

EDWARD: And what is the use of all your analysis
    If I am to remain always lost in the dark?
UNIDENTIFIED GUEST: There is certainly no purpose in remaining
                            in the dark
    Except long enough to clear from the mind
    The illusion of having ever been in the light.

Clearly, the second reference is sharper than the first. The Unidentified Guest, catching the cliché, holds it, literally, to the light. The pattern is similar to that in which Harry's consciousness, in *The Family Reunion*, reveals that the illusions of Wishwood are no longer tenable. In *The Cocktail Party* we have be-

6 "English Verse Drama II: *The Cocktail Party*," *Hudson Review*, Autumn 1950, p. 413.

gun to be aware of the pattern by the middle of the second act. Gradually, while we are wondering how to interpret it, Eliot unobtrusively leads it in a positively religious direction. A late stage in the process is reached when Julia speaks of Celia to Sir Henry Harcourt-Reilly:

> Oh yes, she will go far. And we know where she is going.
> But what do we know of the terrors of the journey?
> You and I don't know the process by which the human is
> Transhumanised: what do we know
> Of the kind of suffering they must undergo
> On the way of illumination?

The formality of the last phrase is enough to differentiate it even from the imagery of vision which has gone before; we feel that the phrase marks a definite stage in the action. It is at this point that Eliot brings into play the Christian potentialities of the imagery. The source may well be St. John of the Cross, whose writings have influenced Eliot's thought since before *Sweeney Agonistes*. We cite the following passage from *The Illuminative Way*: "This tranquillity and repose in God is not all darkness to the soul, as the dark night is, but rather tranquillity and repose in the divine light and in a new knowledge of God, whereby the mind, most sweetly tranquil, is raised to a divine light."[7] It is characteristic of *The Cocktail Party* that its main images are (a) common and domestic, (b) employed in the *Alcestis* of Euripides, from which Eliot's play is remotely derived, and (c) capable of supporting a heavy spiritual burden, when required, without shelving mundane reference. We note that Eliot uses such words as "atone," "salvation," and "crucifixion" only in the later stages of the play. Their relatively unobtrusive use has been made possible by the continuous activity of the imagery of vision; sometimes employed as simple denotation, at other times it harnesses latent implications of spiritual vision. In this

[7] *The Mystical Doctrine of St. John of the Cross*, Introduction by R. H. J. Steuart, S. J., Sheed and Ward, 1948, p. 159.

respect its function corresponds to that of Conscience and Consciousness in *The Family Reunion*.

Let us revert to Mr. Arrowsmith's conclusions. He asks: if, by metaphor, Edward and Lavinia and, at first, Peter and Celia, are said to be "completely in the dark," what are we to make of Harcourt-Reilly and Julia and Alex? Julia is said to be "very observant," but she cannot, she says, see without her glasses, and one lens is missing: she is, in effect, blind in one eye. In response to her query Harcourt-Reilly sings, "And me bein' the One Eyed Riley." We have, then, three metaphorical conditions: blindness, half-sight, and full vision, exhibited, respectively, by Edward, Julia, and Celia. The meaning of Julia's half-sight is to be found in a proverb: In the kingdom of the blind the one-eyed man is king. The intent of the imagery, then, is: the parable of a moral miracle, the recovery of sight.[8]

There is also a correspondence between the imagery of vision (which causes the "domestic" to issue in the "religious") and the moral condition of Celia (who is changed from "neutral" or blindness to "martyr" or full vision). The significance of the imagery and the movement of the dramatic action may be represented somewhat as follows:

| Condition | At the beginning of the play | At the end |
|---|---|---|
| 1. Full Vision or Beatitude. | . . . | Celia |
| 2. Half-Sight, or the positive, Christian life. | Reilly, Julia, and Alex | Reilly, Julia, Alex, Edward, Lavinia, and, in the near future, Peter |

[8] Arrowsmith, *supra*, footnote 6, pp. 413-14.

| Condition | *At the beginning of the play* | *At the end* |
|---|---|---|
| 3. Total Blindness, or the negative life, corresponding to Wishwood in *The Family Reunion* | Edward, Lavinia, Peter, and Celia | |

On this basis we would describe the play as an imitation of an action of spiritual "guardianship," the kind of action which Eliot outlined in *The Idea of a Christian Society*. There he argued that the Community of Christians is not an organisation but a body of indefinite outline composed of both clergy and laity, of the more conscious, more spiritually and intellectually developed of both. It will be their identity of belief and aspiration, their background of a common system of education and a common culture which will enable them to influence and be influenced by each other, and collectively to form "the conscious mind and conscience of the nation."[9] The association of conscience and consciousness reminds us, after studying *The Family Reunion*, of the similarities between the roles of Harry and Celia.

In *Poetry and Drama* Eliot declared that while he was inclined to go to a Greek dramatist for the theme of *The Cocktail Party* he determined to do so merely as a point of departure, and to conceal the source as much as possible. The source, he revealed, was the *Alcestis* of Euripides. As an instance of his debt to Euripides he cited the Uninvited Guest in *The Cocktail Party*; the eccentric behaviour of this character, his apparently intemperate habits, and his tendency to burst into song, are modelled on the behaviour of Heracles in the *Alcestis*.[10]

The relationship between Heracles and Sir Henry Harcourt-

[9] *The Idea of a Christian Society, supra,* footnote 4, p. 35.
[10] T. S. Eliot, *Selected Prose*, Penguin Books, 1953, p. 83.

Reilly is the only point of contact which Eliot has specified between the two plays. Professor Heilman has elucidated several
other affinities.[11] Few of these are amenable to paraphrase, but
we may bear in mind that Eliot's treatment of his source is characterised by the assignment of a spiritual dimension to physical
facts. On some occasions the relation between the two plays
is quite straightforward: compare, for example, the Servant's

> Noble she is, indeed; but Admetus is blind to that.
> He will see the truth when he has lost her . . .[12]

with Edward's

> And yet I want her back.
> And I *must* get her back, to find out what happened
> During the five years that we've been married.
> I must find out who she is, to find out who I am.

More significantly, the physical death of Alcestis has, as its
counterpart in *The Cocktail Party*, the spiritual death of broken
marriage. Alcestis simply affirms:

> I have chosen that you should live rather than I,
> because I honour you as my husband . . .

The corresponding passage in *The Cocktail Party* presents, in
Lavinia, a much more complex motive:

> I thought that there might be some way out for you
> If I went away. I thought if I died
> To you, I who had been only a ghost to you,
> You might be able to find the road back
> To a time when you were real—for you must
>     have been real
> At some time or other, before you ever knew me:
> Perhaps only when you were a child.

[11] Robert B. Heilman, "*Alcestis* and *The Cocktail Party*," *Comparative Literature*, Vol. v, 2, Spring 1953, p. 106.
[12] *Alcestis and Other Plays*, translated by Philip Vellacott, Penguin
Books, 1953, p. 126.

Even the presentation of Sir Henry Harcourt-Reilly is similarly complicated. In the *Alcestis* Heracles's roistering has ancient sanction. David Paul has pointed out that as a traditional Satyric figure in Greek drama Heracles always appears in a state of Bacchic jollity; in the *Alcestis* this helps to reduce him from a status which would otherwise be too big for the play.[13] Some students of *The Cocktail Party*, recalling the role of Heracles, have presented Sir Henry Harcourt-Reilly as a "whole Christian man,"[14] but this seems a mistake. Indeed, Eliot appears to have planned that this character would overflow every realistic vessel, however large, however "whole." He never allows us to forget the symbolic function of Reilly, Julia, and Alex as Guardians; to keep this in our minds he makes it impossible for us to accept them on realistic terms. Professor Heilman, sensing this point, argues that in the presentation of Reilly Eliot has successfully created an air, if not of the inexplicable, at least of the unexplained, of the quizzically irregular, of the elusive. From the time when Reilly tells Edward that he has started "a train of events / Beyond your control," and Lavinia confesses, "Yet something, or somebody, compelled me to come," we are given continual impressions of mysterious forces in action. Psychiatry takes on a spiritual dimension.[15] Indeed, while the *dramatis personae* do not include the Eumenides, one feels that they are hovering in the wings, driving Celia as they have already driven Harry.

This sense of the elusive, the unexplained, applies not only to Reilly but also to Julia and Alex. Alex serves as the conventional bore but the emphasis on his "guardianship" is so strong that we soon ignore the slight extent to which, on realistic terms, he is credible.[16] Similarly with Julia: Edward calls her "a dread-

[13] David Paul, "Euripides and Mr. Eliot," *Twentieth Century*, Vol. CLII, No. 906, August 1952, p. 175.

[14] Arrowsmith, *supra*, p. 421.

[15] Heilman, *supra*, footnote 11, p. 115.

[16] Heidi Heimann ("A God in Three Disguises," *World Review*, June 1950, pp. 66-69) suggests a perceptive comparison between Eliot's Alex, Cocteau's Heurtebise in *Orphée,* and the stranger who advises Joseph in Thomas Mann's *The Young Joseph.*

ful old woman," and yet we are often warned that she has a degree of perception far beyond our expectations. For example, Alex's "She never misses anything unless she wants to"; Celia's "There isn't much that Julia doesn't know"; Edward's "Julia is certainly observant"; Peter's "You never miss anything"; Alex's "Julia is really a mine of information"; and Lavinia's "Nothing less than the truth could deceive Julia."

Does it not seem, then, that Eliot *wants* his audience to be confused by these three, Reilly, Julia, and Alex?[17] He wants us to feel that in some rather intangible way they stand apart from the realistically credible Edward, Lavinia, Celia, and Peter. This prepares us for their emergence as the spiritual Guardians which they have been from the very beginning. The form is that of "qualitative progression," the "confusion" leading eventually and joyously to clarity.[18]

Julia is, of course, the leader, the power to which Reilly is witness and servant. Her emergence in this role at a late stage in the play, after her early exhibition as the silly old woman of Mayfair, is a comic *tour de force*. Near the end of the play we realise that as director of the plot she is the latest, and not the least interesting, of those stage-managers who have directed dramatic affairs at intervals since Aristophanes. Her place in this rich tradition is secure: she stands beside the hero of *The Acharnians* with Prospero of *The Tempest* and the Duke of *Measure for Measure*.

No simple correlation between *Alcestis* and *The Cocktail Party*, in respect of character or incident, is possible without severe distortion of both plays. Even in the case of Reilly there is strong evidence in favour of Professor Heilman's view that he represents not just Heracles but Heracles-plus-Pheres. Certainly, Pheres's function as truth-teller has been taken over by Reilly: the interview between Reilly and Edward in the first act is the counterpart of Pheres's denunciation of his son over the coffin of Alcestis.

[17] *World Review*, November 1949, pp. 66-69.
[18] Kenneth Burke, *Counterstatement*, California, second edition, Hermes, 1953, pp. 124-25.

One of the most interesting and disturbing relations between the two plays arises in the treatment of Alcestis herself. Eliot, while combining Heracles and Pheres into the single role of Reilly, takes precisely the opposite course in the case of Alcestis, whom he divides into two characters. As the wife who died and was eventually restored to her husband she becomes Lavinia, the life of whose marriage is saved. As the woman who sacrificed herself she becomes Celia, who is finally martyred in Kinkanja. We would speculate somewhat on this division.

In the course of *The Cocktail Party* Reilly says that those who choose the lift of common routine

> Learn to avoid excessive expectation,
> Become tolerant of themselves and others,
> Giving and taking in the usual actions
> What there is to give and take. They do not
>     repine
> And are contented with the morning that separates
> And with the evening that brings together
> For casual talk before the fire
> Two people who know that they do not understand
>     each other,
> Breeding children whom they do not understand
> And who will never understand them.

Lionel Trilling has rebuked Eliot for this passage. There is, he argues, no reference to the pain which is an essential and not an accidental part of the life of the common routine. There is no reference to the principles, the ethical discipline, by which the ordinary life is governed: all is habit. There is no reference to the possibility of either joy or glory. This failure to conceive the actuality of the life of common routine is typical, he maintains, of modern literature since Tolstoi. Eliot's representation of the two "ways" of life, that of the common routine and that of the "terrifying journey" to beatitude, exemplifies how we are drawn to the violence of extremity. We imagine, with nothing in between, the dull not-being of life and the intense not-being of death; but we do not imagine Being, we do not imagine that it can be a joy.[19]

Many students of *The Cocktail Party* have had a similar feeling that the play does scant justice to the virtues which make the routine life possible. But to remain too long with this idea is to run the risk of missing a related but much more crucial point. The real defect of *The Cocktail Party*, a defect of drama and rhetoric, is that it presents the life of the common routine and the way of beatitude as totally discrete.

Professor Fergusson would detect a similar representation in Eliot's plays as early as *Murder in the Cathedral*. In an Introduction to Pascal's *Pensées* Eliot observed: "Capital, for instance, is (Pascal's) analysis of the *three orders*: the order of nature, the order of mind, and the order of charity. These three are *discontinuous*; the higher is not implicit in the lower as in an evolutionary doctrine it would be." This notion, Professor Fergusson remarks, throws light upon *Murder in the Cathedral*. In that play the Chorus is in the order of nature; the Tempters, Priests, and Knights are in the order of the mind; and Thomas is in the order of charity. Only the first two orders are visible to us, unless by Grace; but it is only in the order of charity that Thomas and the form and meaning of the play are finally intelligible. In the play this order is represented by the doctrine which Thomas expounds in the sermon, and also by the abstract scheme of the play: the three orders and the three parts of society. Hence the mechanical feel of the play as a whole. The dramatis personae are as discontinuous from each other and from any common world as the parts of a machine, but they move according to the will of God as that is presented by the theological doctrine. It is an idea of the divine plan, and of human experience as subject to it, which comes from modern idealism: one is reminded of Leibniz's preestablished harmony.

---

[19] Lionel Trilling, *The Opposing Self*, London, Secker and Warburg, 1955, pp. 145-47. Similarly, D. W. Harding (*Kenyon Review*, Vol. XVIII, 3, Summer 1956) refuses to accept Edward and Lavinia as properly representing "the human condition."

In *Murder in the Cathedral*, therefore, the whole realm of experience represented by the *Purgatorio*, the direct sense of moral change and of analogies which make the three orders not completely discontinuous—in short, the appeal to a real world which all may in some sense perceive—is lacking.[20]

The lack is concealed to some extent in *Murder in the Cathedral* by the fact that the play, almost by definition, transcends the everyday world of experience or presents it only in circumscribed conditions. But *The Cocktail Party*, confronting such a world, shows that here Eliot has been unable to make the analogical act, or at least to render it dramatically convincing.

In this context it is important to establish the precise meaning of "analogy." Father William Lynch has proposed a description of its intent and in doing so has taken *The Cocktail Party* as his text. He describes the analogical as that habit of perception which sees that different levels of being are also somehow one and can therefore be associated in the same image, in a single act of perception. And, by contrast, we describe as "manichean" all those habits of perception which dispose levels of being in a relationship of hostility or complete separation. For example, every attitude is manichean which—like Forgael in *The Shadowy Waters*—despises the finite, the limited, the human levels of reality, which does not believe in the limited image as a path to the infinite. *The Cocktail Party* is a case in point; it presents two solutions to two human desires. One woman is sent back to "the monotony and dross of her human love"; the other takes up a divine and contemplative vocation. But, says Father Lynch, the psychiatrist speaks truer than he knows in saying that each is but another form of loneliness. One is tempted to wish that it had been the same woman who had taken up the two vocations in the one act and the one situation. Eliot's breakdown of the matter into two situations and two salvations represents a failure and an evasion.[21]

[20] Fergusson, *supra*, footnote 1, p. 217.
[21] William Lynch, S. J., "Theology and the Imagination," *Thought*, Spring, 1954, pp. 66, 67, and 84.

"Monotony and dross of her human love" is too strong as a description of the relationship between Edward and Lavinia at the end of the play; it is not as bad as that; but the larger point remains.[22] When Eliot divided Alcestis into two separate characters and presented each as representative of a certain way of life, he could hardly avoid writing a manichean play.

It may be argued, of course, that whether the rhetorical tendency of *The Cocktail Party* is manichean or not is critically irrelevant, that the only valid criteria are formal and dramatic. We would argue, however, that the reasons which have been advanced to prove the play manichean are precisely those which cause the play to be, as drama, defective.

Father Lynch in another context has complained that *The Cocktail Party* is "filled with a contempt for reality,"[23] by which he means, we infer, that we are made to feel that the activities of Edward and Lavinia, the life of the common routine, are negligible. There is no doubt, of course, as to the supreme importance of Celia's progress, the "way of illumination," but we feel that the two fables are unrelated, that they are not encompassed by an analogical act which guarantees the value of each. This is true. But if, having considered the Christian objections to this separation, we now concentrate on its purely dramatic issues, we find that the separation results in a gross discontinuity of tone. We feel a serious incongruity between the tone of the Edward-Lavinia story and that of Celia's martyrdom. The contrast between *The Cocktail Party* and *Alcestis* is in-

[22] Compare an earlier statement by Walter Stein ("After the Cocktails," *Essays in Criticism*, Vol. III, 1, January 1953, pp. 90, 94): "The disturbing conclusion emerges that *The Cocktail Party* is (unwittingly) a Manichean play. Its vision is not that of a humane . . . Christianity, but approximates to a radical division of existence into spheres of Nature and Transcendence sharply separated from each other: where the transcendent is not merely approached by way of the disclosure of Nature's essential imperfections, but finally embraced as a—literally—*desperate* alternative to the latter's graceless essence."

See also Malcolm Mackenzie Ross, "Fixed Stars and Living Motion in Poetry," *Thought*, Autumn 1952, pp. 384-85.

[23] William Lynch, S. J., "Confusion in our Theater," *Thought*, Autumn 1951, p. 351.

structive at this point; Professor Heilman has noted that *Alcestis* is, in our terms, romantic comedy, but its distinction lies in its daring flirtation with tragedy.[24] *Alcestis* encompasses this range of tone because its characters are sufficiently large, which means sufficiently complex; the frequent changes of tone are sanctioned by the manysidedness of Admetus, Alcestis, and Heracles. Furthermore, the changes of tone in *Alcestis* do not result in the isolation of any of the characters; none of them is restricted by association with a single tone. In *The Cocktail Party*, on the other hand, Eliot, in addition to dissolving Alcestis into two separate characters, isolates these characters still further by a crude disparity of tone. Lavinia and Celia, and all they represent, are from the beginning of the play separate. Their worlds are thrust apart even farther by the fact that Eliot's treatment of Lavinia's activities is for the most part comic while his presentation of Celia's history is in a tone of high seriousness.

On the whole, the characteristic tone of the episodes involving Lavinia seems just right. Given that the play is a comedy of manners, the tone of these parts is finely adjusted. Professor Wimsatt has observed that the homely, patched-up felicity of Edward and Lavinia, glimpsed as they prepare for the second cocktail party, is beyond cavil convincing and just dramatic enough to be interesting.[25] The real fault occurs, he maintains, in the treatment of Celia's martyrdom. At the pinnacle, in the third act, one part of the double outcome, that of martyrdom, aims at something the opposite of tame and shoots too far wide of the comic into the sensationally gruesome:

> It would seem that she must have been crucified
> Very near an ant-hill.

Something more muted, unheroic, was surely required; perhaps a phalanx of abstractions might have served the purpose best, lines such as the later

[24] Heilman, *supra*, footnote 11, p. 106.
[25] W. K. Wimsatt, Jr., "Eliot's Comedy," *Sewanee Review*, Autumn 1950, p. 667.

>    . . . hunger, damp, exposure,
>    Bowel trouble, and the fear of lions.

The occasion seemed to demand that the specific, the detailed
exhibition of death be avoided. In retrospect the gruesomeness
is to some extent sidetracked when Lavinia explains to Sir
Henry Harcourt-Reilly:

> It came to me, when Alex told about Celia
> And I looked at your face. It seemed to convey to me
> That the way in which she died was not important
> Or the fact that she died because she would not leave
> A few dying natives.

At this point one recalls Harry's "insensitivity" to his brother's
accident in *The Family Reunion*; again, in the wider context
of values which Harry was engaged in imposing, a mere matter
of concussion was, indeed, unimportant. To seize these details
as evidence, on realistic terms, of Harry's cruelty or Reilly's
insensitivity would be absurd. But while one can explain the
incidents in terms of the intellectual and rhetorical patterns of
the plays, the quality of the tone which they involve imposes
itself, regardless of our rationalisation. Similarly, the degree of
explicitness in Alex's report remains an artistic flaw because
the details, however easy to "explain," impress their own quality
on the "feel" of the play. The disparity, in qualitative terms,
between the presentation of the two plots is excessive. The
proper antidote to the Mayfair-plot would surely have involved
the emergence in Mayfair of serious moral concerns. No rhetorical law demanded the crucifixion near an ant-hill.

This brings us to Celia and to her role in the play. In *The
Philosophy of Literary Form* Kenneth Burke writes of the
pattern of the Crucifixion (Christ surrounded by the two
criminals) as "a featuring of Good, with the threat of Evil
about the edges.[26] Considered as a whole the scene is a dia-

---

[26] *The Philosophy of Literary Form*, revised edition, Vintage Books,
1957, p. 40.

lectically contrasting frame that emphasises the goodness by polarity. Similarly, may we not observe, in Celia, a featuring of Good pointed up by a context of mediocrity or worse? Celia's "way of illumination" is the brighter because it shines in a context whose quality is determined not only by Edward and Lavinia but by the recollection of Celia's former self. In this tableau Peter represents the continuous threat of evil. The contrast between the old and the new Celia would surely have been sufficient, without martyrdom, to make the dramatic pattern significant.

Furthermore, Mr. Burke, discussing the word "circumference" as used by William James,[27] notes that the choice of circumference for the *scene* in terms of which a given *act* is to be located will have a corresponding effect upon the interpretation of the act itself. The example he cites is that of the mystic Alyosha and the dissolute Mitya in *The Brothers Karamazov*. The "scene" in both cases was the same, but in Alyosha's case it went with and led to different "acts" because for him it had a different *circumference,* so that all actions were interpreted in greatly different terms. Whereas Mitya hoped to become a new man by simply fleeing the "scene," Alyosha's terms amounted to a migration in a more subtle sense, by a "transcendence" that in effect negated the terms of the scene as Mitya had interpreted it.[28] In the case of *The Cocktail Party* the "scene" for Edward and Lavinia is the same as that for Celia, but the scene-act and therefore the act-agent ratios differ in the two cases because of the wider *circumference of consciousness* adopted eventually by Celia. Celia's "conversion," in fact, con-

[27] Ralph Perry (*The Thought and Character of William James*, II, 711) quotes part of a letter from William James to his father: "Consequently a conception really opposed to pantheism must necessarily refuse to admit any such ratio as this—any such external ratio—so to speak, between them; must deny that each term exists only by virtue of the equation to which it belongs; the Creator must be the all, and the act by which the creature is set over against him has its motive within the creative circumference."

[28] *A Grammar of Motives*, New York, Prentice-Hall, Inc. 1945, pp. 77ff.

sists precisely in her adoption of this wider circumference, whereas Edward and Lavinia merely come to a deeper understanding of their own narrower circumference. Celia's fleeing the scene is therefore redundant, since she had already, in her conversion, extended its circumference and thereby its spiritual and regenerative possibilities.

## II.

In *Poetry and Drama* Eliot declared that in writing *The Cocktail Party* he had laid down the ascetic rule to avoid poetry which could not stand the test of strict dramatic utility. In this respect, he added, he had been so successful that "it is perhaps an open question whether there is any poetry in the play at all."[29] It is clear that by "poetry" in this context Eliot means not *poésie de théâtre* but "the language at those dramatic moments when it reaches intensity."[30]

One of the complaints most frequently directed against *The Cocktail Party* refers to the alleged poverty of the text as poetry; one critic has commented, for instance, on "the meagreness of the verse"[31] and again on its "flaccidity."[32] Clearly, these strictures are based not so much on *The Cocktail Party* itself as on the whole trend of Eliot's theory and practice of verse drama. One cannot help feeling that the critic quoted has not yet faced the conclusions, in regard to poetry and drama, to be derived from the plays of Swinburne or from the "post-Tennysonian, facile, and not unpleasing iambics"[33] of Stephen Phillips. The idea of drama which is implied by such strictures is widely held. We recall that in 1935 Padraic Colum spoke confidently

[29] *Selected Prose, supra,* footnote 10, p. 83.
[30] T. S. Eliot, *The Three Voices of Poetry,* Cambridge University Press, 1953, p. 9.
[31] John Peter, *"Murder in the Cathedral,"* Sewanee Review, Vol. XVII, 1, 1950, p. 65.
[32] John Peter, "Sin and Soda," *Scrutiny,* Vol. XVII, 1, 1950, p. 65.
[33] Ivor Brown, "Can There Be a Revival of Poetic Drama in the Modern Theatre?" *Transactions of the Royal Society of Literature of the United Kingdom,* n.s. Vol. XXIII, 1947, p. 75.

of "that element that is essential if the theatre is not to be trivially entertaining—exalted speech."[34] But on the linguistic factor in verse drama the general trend of Eliot's theory is virtually impregnable. A medium whose success is measured by the quantity of "poetry" or "exalted speech" which it contains would be "intractably poetic"[35] and therefore quite useless for modern verse drama. We would postpone full consideration of the question, however, until a later chapter.

One may begin an examination of the verse of *The Cocktail Party* by considering Eliot's idea of the range of dramatic verse. He has argued that if dramatic verse is to have so wide a range that it can say anything that has to be said, it follows that it will not be "poetry" all the time. It will be "poetry" only when the dramatic situation has reached such a pitch of intensity that poetry becomes the natural utterance, because then it is the only language in which the emotions can be fully expressed.[36]

A characteristic example of "verse" from *The Cocktail Party* is the following speech by Alex:

Áh, || in thát case I knów what I'll do.
Í'm going to give yóu || a little surpríse;
You knów, || I'm rather a fámous cóok.
Í'm going stráight || to your kítchen now
And I shall prepáre you || a níce little dínner
Which you can have alóne. || And thén we'll léave you.
Méanwhile, || you and Péter can go on tálking
And Í shan't distúrb you. ||
EDWARD: My déar Alex.

This is an example of the verse line which Eliot has described, a line of varying length and varying number of syllables with a

[34] *Theatre Arts Anthology*, New York, Theatre Arts Books, Robert M. MacGregor, 1950, p. 51.
[35] Eliot in his introduction (1930) to Johnson's *London* and *The Vanity of Human Wishes* wrote: "The development of blank verse in the hands of Shakespeare and some of his contemporaries was the work of adapting a medium which to begin with was almost intractably poetic, so that it could carry the burdens and exhibit the subtleties of prose . . ."
[36] *Selected Prose, supra*, footnote 10, p. 70.

caesura and three stresses. The caesura and the stresses may come at different places, almost anywhere in the line; the stresses may be close together or well separated by unstressed syllables. The only rule is that there must be one stress on one side of the caesura and two on the other.[37] Accordingly, we have marked the reading of Alex's lines which seems most appropriate; the primary aim is to allow the rhythm to participate as fully as possible in the tone of the lines. With the movement of the stresses, especially in the fifth and sixth lines, Alex emerges as the mellifluous hostess, coy, silly, excessive, straight from Joyce Grenfell.

As an example of "poetry" we offer the following passage from the interview between Celia and Sir Henry Harcourt-Reilly in the second act. Celia says:

                                        I cannot argue.
It's not that I'm afraid of being hurt again:
Nothing again can either hurt or heal.
I have thought at moments that the ecstasy is real
Although those who experience it may have no reality.
For what happened is remembered like a dream
In which one is exalted by intensity of loving
In the spirit, a vibration of delight
Without desire, for desire is fulfilled
In the delight of loving. A state one does not know
When awake. But what, or whom I loved,
Or what in me was loving, I do not know.

[37] Ibid., p. 80. Incidentally, many years ago Bonamy Dobrée suggested (*Histriophone: a Dialogue on Dramatic Diction*, Hogarth Press, 1925) that the normal line in Elizabethan drama was a line of three stresses, as in
            "And ríde in tríumph through Persépolis"
from *Tamburlane*, or in
            "Solíciting for Jústice and revénge"
from *The Spanish Tragedy*, "where the stresses fit themselves easily to the sense." But Professor Dobrée was, I think, mistaken. There are five stresses in each of these lines; the wide variation in the *degree* of stress is a main factor in their beauty and sensitivity. See Yvor Winters's brilliant examination of "When to the Sessions of Sweet Silent Thought," *Hudson Review*, Vol. IV, 3, Autumn 1951, p. 442.

And if that is all meaningless, I want to be cured
Of a craving for something I cannot find
And of the shame of never finding it.
Can you cure me?

The author of *The Love Song of J. Alfred Prufrock* and of *Sweeney Agonistes* could have written that passage at any point in his career. It is fine dramatic verse because it refuses to be separated from the agent who speaks it and the situation in which it is spoken. As far as diction and syntax[38] are concerned it convinces us that it belongs to one speaker and to no one else. It is no contradiction to say, after this, that the words are unmistakably Eliot's, deriving their force from his habitual procedure of building the meaning within such key-words as "real," "reality," "dream," "loving," and "desire." Earlier, in *The Family Reunion*, Eliot had written "poetry" which involved the activity of such key-words, but *The Cocktail Party* is the first of his plays in which the operation of such words is compatible with the nature and situation of the persons who speak them.

If we compare the passages quoted in the light of Eliot's development both as poet and as dramatist, we observe that the main purpose of Eliot's experiments was to enable him to write "verse" rather than "poetry." (We need not quarrel with his homely distinction at the moment, though it is probably little more than a distinction between the Mean and the Grand

---

[38] Professor Wimsatt, *supra*, footnote 25, p. 671, observes that the rhythm of Celia's experience and utterance is characterised by the "And if this" climax of sweet, austere discountenance, toward Edward or toward herself:

"And if this is reality, it is very like a dream"
or again
"And if that is the sort of person you are—
Well, you had better have her."

This would seem to be a matter of syntax. Donald Davie (*Articulate Energy: An Enquiry into the Syntax of English Poetry*, Routledge and Kegan Paul, 1955, p. 76) describes "dramatic syntax" as follows: "Poetic syntax is dramatic when its function is to please us by the fidelity with which it follows the 'form of thought' in some mind other than the poet's, which the poet imagines."

Styles.) For him it was more difficult to write the "verse" spoken by Alex than the "poetry" spoken by Celia. It is necessary to account for this. What Eliot the dramatist needed, and what he pursued for so many years, was a "mean" verse style from which he could, when necessary, rise. In 1933 he spoke of his desire to write poetry which should be essential poetry, "with nothing poetic about it," poetry so naked and transparent that we should not see the poetry, but rather that which we are meant to see *through* the poetry. It would be a kind of poetry so transparent that in reading it we would be intent on what the poem points at, not on the poetry itself.[39] Arnold Stein has suggested an illuminating contrast between Eliot and Milton in this respect. Milton needed as his "norm" a style from which he could easily descend. Because of the nature of his subject and the requirements of epic decorum he needed as his norm the "high" or "grand" style; and he needed, on occasion, to relax graciously from that height. Unlike Eliot, Milton, even when he is quite simple in his language, has no wish to get beyond poetry. He never conceals his Muse.[40]

There is certainly a stage in Eliot's poetry beyond which nothing matters but the world to which the poem points. In Milton there is no such impulse: he has gathered all imaginable worlds into his poem and is content to remain there. Similarly in Wallace Stevens the poem is, for the time being, the entire locus of vision and motive. A slightly different point of view will contrast such writers as Eliot and Stendhal with Milton and Hugo: those who, by programme, conceal their art with those who delight in revealing it; those who prefer that their Muse should remain out of sight with those who joyfully exhibit her. Our emphasis is, of course, purely descriptive, not qualitative.

Perhaps because of this trend in Eliot's experiments the most

[39] Part of an unpublished letter first printed in F. O. Matthiessen's *The Achievement of T. S. Eliot*, Oxford University Press, 1947 edition, p. 90. Eliot's fondness for a "bare" style is to be compared with Coleridge's praise of the "neutral" style of Chaucer's *Troilus and Criseyde* and Herbert's *Virtue* (*Biographia Literaria*, Shawcross edition, ii, 70).

[40] Arnold Stein, *Answerable Style*, University of Minnesota Press, 1953, pp. 132-134.

successful passages in *The Cocktail Party*—judged for the moment simply as "speech"—are the "verse" passages. The norm of the play in this respect is fine virile speech, clean and "easy," from which the smoke and shadow of *The Family Reunion* have been very largely eliminated. The verse is so pliant that, as Professor Wimsatt has observed, it makes possible the little joke tied in at the end of the phrase as if without effort:

> Finding your life becoming cosier and cosier,
> Without the consistent critic, the patient misunderstander.

or the sinister incompleteness of:

> Mr. Peter Quilpe
> Was a frequent guest . . .

or the flattened summation, far echo of *Prufrock* or *Gerontion*:

> Each way means loneliness—and communion.
> Both ways avoid the final desolation
> Of solitude in the phantasmal world
> Of imagination, shuffling memories and desires.

We are reminded that the presiding virtues of the play are chasteness, restraint, terseness, and precision.[41]

Very occasionally in *The Cocktail Party* Eliot loses control of his "poetry." In this passage, for instance, in which Edward cries out to Lavinia:

> O God, O God, if I could return to yesterday
> Before I thought that I had made a decision.
> What devil left the door on the latch
> For these doubts to enter? And then you came back, you
> The angel of destruction—just as I felt sure.
> In a moment, at your touch, there is nothing but ruin.
> O God, what have I done? The python. The octopus.
> Must I become after all what you would make me?

This exhibits again, as we have seen in *The Family Reunion*, the tendency of Eliot the poet to break loose from the restraints

---

[41] Wimsatt, *supra*, footnote 25, pp. 669-70.

of the dramatic context. The description of Lavinia as "angel of destruction" is brilliantly ironical, but it is the poet's irony, not Edward's. Such double-talk occurs much less frequently in *The Cocktail Party* than in *The Family Reunion* and, as a result, the rhetoric of the later play is much firmer. Where it persists, however, it accounts for a certain feeling of insecurity which merges into that larger unsteadiness of tone which we have already observed. *The Cocktail Party*, in its entirety, does not quite hold fast.

In *Murder in the Cathedral* the question of a viable alternative to sanctity did not seriously arise to confront either Thomas or the audience: the order of Grace determined the conditions of the drama. In turn, *The Family Reunion* recognised a mundane alternative, sneering at it, however, assigning it to the stupid brother John. *The Cocktail Party* is a more ample play because it at least gives serious representation (in the comic mode, admittedly) to a way of life other than than which issues in beatitude or martyrdom. The implications of the play's "argument" have pleased no one, but it is important in Eliot's development as the first play to make some appeal to "a real world which all may in some sense perceive."[42] It points to a more successful play, *The Confidential Clerk*.

[42] Fergusson, *supra*, footnote 1, p. 217.

THERE are certain words which do not apply to Eliot's later writings, least of all to *The Confidential Clerk*. These words include dense, shrill, plangent, "poetical." And the words which indicate one's response to these works are cool, urbane, transparent, strong, "easy," chaste. Thinking of this play we recall Marianne Moore's poem *Propriety* and her tribute to

> a tuned reticence with rigour
> from strength at the source.[1]

The details here support each other and we may borrow them to describe *The Confidential Clerk*. The reticence of the play is clear, and perhaps its manner is sufficiently gracious to prevent our finding the reticence niggardly or arid. But we would emphasise the rigour of the play and the strength which is undoubtedly the source of this rigour, because several critics have asserted that the verbal richness and density of *Murder in the Cathedral* have been, in the meantime, dissipated. William Becker, for instance, has referred to "the very anaemic dramatism"[2] of *The Confidential Clerk;* Saul Bellow finds that the play is pervaded by "a sort of emotional albinism."[3] And so on.

To understand these judgments fully, one would need to understand their authors. But at all events it is clear that these critics sponsor an idea of drama as "heat, light, and sound,"[4] exemplified by Tamburlane's martial threats. One should hesitate to adopt this Redskin view; it is too exclusive, too reluctant to concede that there may be more than one kind of dramatic excellence. Eliot himself has had occasion to ask: what is dra-

---

[1] *Collected Poems*, New York, Macmillan, 1952, p. 148.

[2] "Broadway: Classics and Imports," *Hudson Review*, Summer 1954, p. 269.

[3] "Pleasures and Pains of Playgoing," *Partisan Review*, May-June 1954, p. 313.

[4] J. C. Trewin (*We'll Hear a Play*, Carroll and Nicholson, 1949, p. 90) writes of Laurie Lee's *Peasants' Priest* that "it wants heat and light and sound, the trinity without which a poet's play must inevitably collapse."

matic? Answering: if one were saturated in the Japanese Noh, in Bhasa and Kalidasa, in Aeschylus, Sophocles and Euripides, Aristophanes and Menander, in the popular medieval plays of Europe, in Lope de Vega and Calderon, as well as the great English and French drama, and if one were equally sensitive to them all, would one not hesitate to decide that one form is more dramatic than another?[5] Or one *quality* of speech?

Many years ago John Crowe Ransom remarked, in an essay on Eliot's work up to *Murder in the Cathedral*, that by old standards *sostenuto* was the one signal lack in Eliot's equipment. That is, his strongest effects were obtained not by sustaining the tone but by juxtaposing incongruous notes, by brilliant discords.[6] This has become a commonplace in critical writings on Eliot's work but we would question its validity in the light of *The Confidential Clerk*. Eliot no longer lacks *sostenuto*. Indeed it is precisely by sustaining the chosen tone and insinuating minor variations that his special effects are now obtained. There is no place in *The Confidential Clerk* for the brilliant, garish thrusts which characterise *Sweeney Agonistes* or *Burbank with a Baedeker*:

> Money in furs. The boatman smiles,
>
> Princess Volupine extends
>    A meagre, blue-nailed, phthisic hand
> To climb the waterstair. Lights, lights,
>    She entertains Sir Ferdinand
> Klein. . . .[7]

In *Four Quartets* Eliot continued to explore the resources of post-symbolist poetry, but there is no trace of that poetic in *The Cocktail Party*, *The Confidential Clerk*, or *The Elder Statesman*. Indeed it lapsed with *Sweeney Agonistes*. The later plays are concerned, broadly speaking, to exploit the serious resources

[5] *Seneca in Elizabethan Translation* (1927); *Selected Essays*, Faber and Faber, 1934, p. 75.
[6] *The World's Body*, Scribner, 1938, p. 167.
[7] *Collected Poems*, Faber and Faber, 1936, p. 41.

of farce or of the "comedy of manners"; in form, diction, and syntax they are much closer to those traditions than to the procedures of Laforgue, Baudelaire, Valery, or the Pound of *Mauberley*.

*Sostenuto*: Eliot's unsympathetic critics have alleged that what is sustained in the later plays is a very feeble thing indeed, and certainly not "poetry." We would argue, however, using *The Cocktail Party* and the recent plays as evidence, that Eliot's dramatic writing since *Murder in the Cathedral* has been consistently directed toward a greater range of expressiveness, greater precision, and, above all, a finer adjustment of verbal weight. The fact that this has involved his concentration on a more chaste "norm" of expression should not prevent our appreciating the nature of that achievement.

One often meets the assertion that the verse in *The Confidential Clerk* merely repeats a kind of success already attained in *The Cocktail Party*, that Eliot in *The Confidential Clerk* "has been satisfied to reaffirm his mastery of ground already won."[8] But this is inaccurate. Indeed *The Confidential Clerk* is quite new inasmuch as for the first time in Eliot's plays one finds dramatic verse which preserves its integrity *from first to last*. There are no "lapses." At no point in that play does one feel, as, frequently, in *The Family Reunion* and, occasionally, in *The Cocktail Party*, that several lines in becoming "poetry" have severed contact with the agent who speaks them and have slipped from the play into verbal autonomy. Furthermore, in *The Confidential Clerk* Eliot has achieved this fusion of "character" and speech, without strain, over a range of expression which, as Hugh Kenner has observed, is surprisingly wide; from cultivated joshing:

KAGHAN: I've just given her lunch. The problem with Lucasta
    Is how to keep her fed between meals.
LUCASTA: B, you're a beast. I've a very small appetite
    But the point is, that I'm penniless . . .

[8] *The Times*, 27 August 1953.

to the ardours of a disappointed creator:

SIR CLAUDE: . . . To be among such things,
 If it is an escape, is escape into living,
 Escape from a sordid world into a pure one.
 Sculpture and painting—I have some good things—
 But they haven't this . . . remoteness I have always longed
  for.
 I want a world where the form is the reality,
 Of which the substantial is only a shadow.
 It's strange. I have never talked of this to anyone.
 Never until now.[9]

*The Confidential Clerk* contains none of the following: set-speeches, poetic arias, characters who speak "poetry" without supporting, at those moments, a necessary role in the play. Indeed it would be possible to illustrate the strength of the play in terms of these and other instances of dramatic control. But we would concentrate on another quality, larger and more positive. For this purpose it is necessary to quote a fairly long passage from the text. Toward the end of the first act Sir Claude Mulhammer speaks to his new confidential clerk Colby Simpkins:

My father—your grandfather—built up this business
Starting from nothing. It was *his* passion.
He loved it with the same devotion
That I gave to clay, and what could be done with it—
What I hoped I could do with it. I thought I despised him
When I was young. And yet I was in awe of him.
I was wrong, in both. I loathed this occupation
Until I began to feel my power in it.
The life changed me, as it is changing you:
It begins as a kind of make-believe
And the make-believing makes it real.
That's not the whole story. My father knew I hated it:
That was a grief to him. He knew, I am sure,
That I cherished for a long time a secret reproach:

<hr>

 9 Hugh Kenner, "Possum by Gaslight," *Poetry*, October 1954, pp. 48-49.

But after his death, and then it was too late,
I knew that he was right. And all my life
I have been atoning. To a dead father,
Who had always been right. I never understood him.
I was too young. And when I was mature enough
To understand him, he was not there.

Colby, confronting in Sir Claude's experience a problem close to
his own, presses for more evidence:

You've still not explained why you came to think
That your father had been right.

Sir Claude answers directly:

Because I came to see
That I should never have become a first-rate potter.
I didn't have it in me. It's strange, isn't it,
That a man should have a consuming passion
To do something for which he lacks the capacity?
Could a man be said to have a vocation
To be a second-rate potter? To be, at best,
A competent copier, possessed by the craving
To create, when one is wholly uncreative?
I don't think so. For I came to see
That I had always known, at the secret moments,
That I didn't have it in me! There are occasions
When I am transported—a different person,
Transfigured in the vision of some marvellous creation,
And I feel what the man must have felt when he made it.
But nothing *I* made ever gave me that contentment—
That state of utter exhaustion and peace
Which comes in dying to give something life . . .
I intend that you shall have a good piano. The best.
And when you are alone at your piano, in the evening,
I believe you will go through the private door
Into the real world, as I do, sometimes.

Colby, finding that Sir Claude's syntax is beginning to establish relations and meaning for his own situation, closes the gap between them:

> Indeed, I have felt, while you've been talking,
> That it's my own feelings you have expressed,
> Although the medium is different. I know
> I should never have become a great organist,
> As I aspired to be. I'm not an executant;
> I'm only a shadow of the great composers!
> Always, when I play to myself,
> I hear the music I should like to have written,
> As the composer heard it when it came to him;
> But when I played before other people
> I was always conscious that what *they* heard
> Was not what I hear when I play to myself.
> What I hear is a great musician's music,
> What they hear is an inferior rendering.
> So I've given up trying to play to other people: . . .

This is an imitation of an action of human perception, a moment in which two people, offering comparisons from a familiar medium, come close to mutual understanding. The relation between the language and that of distinguished modern conversation is at least sufficiently close to be convincing: at no point do we lose confidence in this relation. (Dr. Leavis has recently gloated over an imagined review, by D. H. Lawrence, of *The Cocktail Party*; the point is well taken, especially as much of Eliot's writing on Lawrence has been indefensible. But we would hope that Lawrence's essay on *The Confidential Clerk* would exhibit respect for the "chastity" and reticence of the text, and—in addition—the recognition that such qualities are not "merely literary.") Furthermore, the passage exhibits two fine skills: one, which Eliot possessed from the beginning of his career, the ability to make meaning rise from within the words themselves, almost autonomously; to set words in action as if creating their own meaning. There is something of this in

> It begins as a kind of make-believe
> And the make-believing makes it real

and again in

> That state of utter exhaustion and peace
> Which comes in dying to give something life . . . ,

where words, having entered on a pattern, press toward its formal "perfection," at which point (but not before) the meaning is complete.

The second skill is one which such poets as Chaucer, Wyatt, Donne, Williams, and Pound possessed, it seems, by nature, but which Eliot acquired only after many years of error—the ability to suggest a human voice saying things. The human voice vibrates in practically everything Pound writes, in *Women of Trachis*, in the *Cantos*,[10] in the translations:

> So he won't talk to me when we meet?
> Terrible!
>      I still can eat.
> So clever he won't even come to dinner;
> Well, beds are soft,
>         and I'm no thinner.[11]

Here the primary feeling is of a girl in firm and innocent possession of what she wants to say: the skill involved is similar to that exhibited in *The Confidential Clerk*:

> I intend that you shall have a good piano. The best.
> And when you are alone at your piano, in the evening,
> I believe . . .

The second speech by Sir Claude which we have cited is remarkably sensitive to the slightest variation in tone or pressure: moving from "verse" to "poetry" and back again several times

---

[10] This applies also to the post-Pisan Cantos. See *Section: Rockdrill,* Faber and Faber, 1957.

[11] *Songs of Cheng, No. XII, The Classic Anthology Defined by Confucius,* Faber and Faber, 1955, p. 41.

without any feeling of discontinuity; clinging to its context, to *this* speaker in *this* situation. The skill is one which enthusiasts for verse drama have often envied in *The Apple Cart* and in much of Congreve. That *The Confidential Clerk* in this respect sustains such comparisons is proof that verse drama has recovered a considerable amount of ground in the past twenty years.

Nearly thirty years ago M. Cocteau referred to the theatre as "un gros véhicule de poésie," and lamented "Hélas! il oblige à des réussites immédiates." His advice was: "Le seul moyen d'obtenir un résultat sera donc de créer un malentendu a la faveur duquel plusieurs publics puissent simultanément trouver leur compte (Shakèspeare, Molière). . . ." In another connexion, though in the same spirit, he offered a generalisation: "Une bonne chose ne peut réussir parce qu'elle est bonne, mais elle porte toujours en elle assez de mauvais pour s'accrocher à quelques esprits et prendre ainsi racine à la longue."[12]

Eliot's recent experiments in verse drama have shown a corresponding sense of the practical. Like Cocteau he has decided not to play the role of the intransigent purist, the Stephen Dedalus of modern drama. In *The Cocktail Party* and again in *The Confidential Clerk* and *The Elder Statesman* he has shown himself ready to go more than halfway to meet his audience. In *The Confidential Clerk* to a greater extent than in *The Cocktail Party* he offers his audience an expanse of comic material in which the "meaning," or the moral rhetoric, is concealed more deeply than ever below the surface—so much so that the meanings which have been unearthed sound as if each critic has been studying a different text:

[12] *Le Rappel a l'Ordre*, Paris, Editions Stock, 1948, pp. 229 and 211. On the other hand, Sir Herbert Read (*The True Voice of Feeling*, Faber and Faber, 1953, pp. 147-48) quotes the "study that tree" lines from Yeats's *Purgatory* and comments: "This is the diction, the poetic diction of *King Lear* and *The Tempest*: a universal diction not bound to time or a temporal audience. It would not, perhaps, be acceptable on Broadway or Shaftesbury Avenue; but is that public . . . to stand between drama and poetry?"

*Francis Fergusson*: "I think he is talking about Providence, which is believed to answer our prayers or our wishes, in the course of a lifetime, according to the wisdom of God: sometimes denying us what we wish for, for our correction: sometimes giving us our wishes to show how wrong they were; and in rare cases (when the wish coincides with God's plan) actually fulfilling the heart's desire."[13]

*Hugh Kenner: "The Confidential Clerk*, another play about choice being reconciled with necessity. . . . Unfortunately, the Victorian complications of the revelation-scene tend to put forward in too simple-hearted a way the proposition that who you are depends on who your parents were."[14]

*Harold Hobson*: "We are, (Eliot) implies, a bastard generation that has lost its faith; can we substitute, for what we have no longer, a trust in something else, in art, for example, and cause it, unsatisfactory as it is, to be a refuge through the sheer force of make-believe? Who are our parents, and whither do we come? And what, at that, is parentage itself? These questions, which are the play's essence, are . . ."[15]

*The dramatic critic of "The Times"*: ". . . a consistent pattern runs faintly through all the discussions, whether they are serio-comic or serious. Sir Claude and Colby alike share the belief that heredity is part of the design of life to which men who do not happen to be geniuses must conform."[16]

*Anthony Hartley*: ". . . the real subject of the play: self-knowledge . . . Colby Simpkins's search for a father and the resulting farcical revelations symbolise this coming to terms with one's permanent self."[17]

*Russell Kirk*: ". . . its principal theme: the prison of Self. . . . From Sir Claude to Mrs. Guzzard, they are men and women of kindly natures, honest inclination and generous hearts. But, being human, they are heir to all the imperfections of the spirit

[13] *Sewanee Review*, Vol. LXVII, 1954, p. 477.
[14] *Poetry*, October 1954, pp. 53-54.
[15] *Sunday Times*, 30 August 1953.
[16] *The Times*, 27 August 1953.
[17] *The Spectator*, 26 March 1954.

and the flesh; thus they cannot escape the rootlessness of their time, nor the sense of talents run to waste, nor the prison of Self. They do not know themselves or the nature of being."[18]

*Saul Bellow*: "If Mr. Eliot says, as I think he does, that our earthly fathers and mothers do not matter so much . . ."[19]

*Richard Findlater*: ". . . a tragicomedy of choice . . . all of his characters choose their destiny in the moment of crisis."[20]

*Henry Hewes*: ". . . there is the implication that only truly religious people and men of genius can find some unity in life, that the rest of us have at best to live in two worlds, each a kind of make-believe."[21]

*William Arrowsmith*: ". . . a drawing-room drama of conversion and transfiguration whose key terms are conscious and unconscious Christian conspiracy, the putting-on of the new Adam, the adoption of God, and the intimation of the Incarnation."[22]

Of these interpretations only Mr. Bellow's strikes me as being wide of the mark. Furthermore, there is some justification for suggesting affinities between *The Confidential Clerk* and works as various as the *Ion* of Euripides, Menander's *Epitrepontes, The Importance of Being Earnest, H.M.S. Pinafore, The Comedy of Errors, The Government Inspector, The Wild Duck* and *Great Expectations*. But in examining such matters in relation to the determining motive of *The Confidential Clerk* we should not ignore a work which "corresponds" to that play in much more significant respects: *The Cocktail Party. Poetry and Drama* showed that Eliot has tended to write a new play by correcting the faults of the preceding one. If he were to rewrite *The Cocktail Party*, keeping more or less the same preoccupations but presenting them in a different light, extending the humour to the farcical and drawing Celia's story more closely into the organization of the comedy, he would arrive at a play very like

[18] *The Month*, October 1953, p. 225.
[19] *Partisan Review*, Vol. xxi, 3, May-June 1954, p. 315.
[20] *Twentieth Century*, October 1953, p. 312.
[21] *Saturday Review*, 12 September 1953, p. 45.
[22] *Hudson Review*, Summer 1954, p. 292.

*The Confidential Clerk.* These are the terms in which we would relate the two plays.

It is generally agreed that *The Confidential Clerk* is serious farce; the basic situation of foundlings and castaways is the surface of the play. Bonamy Dobrée has observed that as an amusing comedy erected on a farcical situation *The Confidential Clerk* holds one's attention from the beginning.[23] But farce in the play has another dimension; it is not merely a bone thrown to the mob to keep them quiet while the playwright converses with the elite. Above all, it serves to control the tone of the play, making boisterous appearances whenever the plot threatens to become too serious. In the revelation scene, for instance, a moment of farce suddenly forces a comic perspective on a discussion which sounds austere and portentous:

EGGERSON: Lady Elizabeth, before her marriage
 Had a child . . .
LADY ELIZABETH:        A son.
EGGERSON:            Had a son
 Whom she could not, in the circumstances, acknowledge.
 That happens not infrequently, Mrs. Guzzard.
MRS. GUZZARD: So I am aware. I have known it to happen.
EGGERSON:—Who was taken charge of by the father.
 That is to say, placed out to be cared for
 Till further notice by a foster-mother.
 Unfortunately, the father died suddenly . . .
LADY ELIZABETH: He was run over. By a rhinoceros
 In Tanganyika . . .

This is the simplest level on which the play operates. Whether or not we find the farce amusing[24] no critical difficulties arise until we consider the serious aspects of the play, the parts which

---

[23] *"The Confidential Clerk," Sewanee Review,* Vol. LXII, 1954, p. 118.
[24] Saul Bellow finds "little laughter" in it. Harold Hobson describes the play as "a tower of absurdity which will strike as funny anyone whose sense of humour is developed even far enough to be diverted by the spectacle of Mr. Robertson Hare losing his trousers."

Noel Coward could *not* have written. Here the situation would seem to be somewhat as follows. In *The Cocktail Party* there were two worlds, the secular or neutral and the spiritual. Eliot named them unambiguously, the "common routine" and the "way of illumination." The presentation of those worlds, it will be recalled, involved Eliot in the false tone of Celia's martyrdom and the resultant disruption of the play. In *The Confidential Clerk* there are again two worlds, but on this occasion no difficulty of tone or of doctrine arises, because instead of naming these worlds "secular" and "spiritual" Eliot presents them as "Commerce" and "Art." This is a fine tactical move. Instead of tustling with his audience over thorny spiritual ground Eliot meets them in the inoffensive region which the play calls Art. Thus he ingratiates himself with his audience by introducing them into two worlds both of which they either know or can imagine; no doctrinal suspicions are aroused. The world of Art, unlike the world of Martyrdom and Beatitude, is at one and the same time "special" enough to embody the higher reaches of aspiration and yet within the imaginative range of a secular audience.

And yet the change—in dialectical terms—is more apparent than real. Eliot has not, in fact, shifted ground: his two worlds are still the same. (Eliot has invariably known—better than his critics—what he has been up to.) The "common routine" of the secular life is thinly disguised in *The Confidential Clerk* as the world of Commerce ("the City," Sir Claude, B. Kaghan). The spiritual life is presented in terms of Art. There are no martyrs. Colby takes Celia's place in a less spectacular but more convincing role.

There is no difficulty in accepting a correspondence between the secular life and the life of Commerce. It remains to show, then, that in *The Confidential Clerk* art (Colby's music and Sir Claude's ceramics) is a symbol of spiritual vision.

The second act of *The Confidential Clerk* opens with a fine scene in which Colby and Lucasta examine their world: it corresponds to the discussion between Harry and Mary in *The Family Reunion*. (Eliot's plays have a moment in which the sheep are distinguished from the goats by their possession of consciousness and perception: this is it.) Lucasta feels that Colby's life has a dimension which is lacking in her own:

> But you've something else, that I haven't got:
> Something of which the music is a . . . symbol.
> I really would like to understand music,
> Not in order to be able to talk about it,
> But . . . partly, to enjoy it . . . and because of what
>     it stands for.
> You know, I'm a little jealous of your music!
> When I see it as a means of contact with a world
> More real than any *I've* ever lived in.

The last words warn us to give the speech more than its face value: recalling Sir Claude's earlier conversation with Colby:

> And when you are alone at your piano, in the evening,
> I believe you will go through the private door
> Into the real world, as I do, sometimes.

We should feel, then, in Lucasta's words, that the dimension "of which the music is a symbol" is a spiritual reality. In context this is the only kind of meaning which accords with the emphasis on a "*real* world." It will be recalled that this word reverberates through *The Confidential Clerk* like the word "understand" in *The Family Reunion*. At the very least such words operate on the periphery of a world of spiritual vision. In an earlier conversation Sir Claude discussed with Colby the relation between the worlds of matter and spirit:

> You shall play to yourself. As for me,
> I keep my pieces in a private room.
> It isn't that I don't want anyone to see them!
> But when I am alone, and look at one thing long enough,
> I sometimes have that sense of identification

With the maker, of which I spoke—an agonising ecstasy
Which makes life bearable. It's all I have.
I suppose it takes the place of religion:
Just as my wife's investigations
Into what she calls the life of the spirit
Are a kind of substitute for religion.
I dare say truly religious people—
I've never known any—can find some unity.
Then there are also the men of genius.
There are others, it seems to me, who have at best to live
In two worlds—each a kind of make-believe.
That's you and me . . .

Unity and make-believe are also the key terms in the corresponding passage in which Colby discusses his "private garden" with Lucasta:

What I mean is, my garden's no less unreal to me
Than the world outside it. If you have two lives
Which have nothing whatever to do with each other—
Well, they're both unreal. But for Eggerson
His garden is a part of one single world.

Lucasta asks, "But what do you want?" Colby replies:

Not to be alone there.
If I were religious, God would walk in my garden
And that would make the world outside it real
And acceptable, I think.

These are the terms through which the central motive of *The Confidential Clerk* emerges. Colby becomes a "truly religious" man, without martyrdom. God, walking in this man's garden, makes his two worlds contiguous and therefore real. This is the kind of "unity" which Colby achieves. At the end of the play Sir Claude has not attained this: his two worlds, being disparate, are unreal. But, like Edward in *The Cocktail Party*, he finds, as palliative, a new and promising relationship with his wife. A paraphrase of the play's moral rhetoric would say: God must walk in our private garden of the spirit if the garden is to be real and if that reality is to extend to the world outside the garden. If God walks in our garden we shall achieve that "unity" which we seek:

> But for Eggerson
> His garden is a part of one single world.

Colby's attainment of "unity" coincides with his renunciation of the world of Commerce which Sir Claude represents, but his "illumination" is not acquired, as in *The Cocktail Party*, by rejecting the entire circumstantial world: Colby remains part of that world, benignly, as organist in the parish church at Joshua Park. In this context Eggerson's suggestion, which William Becker has found "astonishing and somewhat irrelevant,"[25] is only the gathering together of those spiritual implications which have been crowding in on each other during the progress of the play:

> I don't see you spending a lifetime as an organist.
> I think you'll come to find you've another vocation.
> We worked together every day, you know,
> For quite a little time, and I've watched you
> pretty closely.
> Mr. Simpkins! You'll be thinking of reading for orders.
> And you'll still have your music.

At this point all the analogies in the play meet and are harmonised: Colby's music, Eggerson's garden, the ideas of "unity," "make-believe," "one single world," "the real world," and the serio-farcical theme of paternity:

COLBY: . . . But now I know who was my father
> I must follow my father—so that I may come to know him.

If Eggerson's is perchance a rose garden we renew contact at this point with a symbol of exaltation which Eliot has often used before, notably in *The Family Reunion*.

[25] William Becker, *supra*, footnote 2, p. 270.

The possibility of Holiness, the relation between the secular life and the "way of illumination," the precarious and glorious possibility of winning through to "one single world"—*The Cocktail Party* and *The Confidential Clerk* are concerned with such problems, under different guises. It is not surprising, therefore, that the motives of these and earlier plays are presented through characters who exhibit striking similarities. Colby, for example, shares with Celia, Harry, and Thomas Becket the faculty of "consciousness," of spiritual perception; he is the one who *sees*, type of the hero in Eliot's world. Eggerson is the Julia of *The Confidential Clerk*, God's agent in the action. Professor Fergusson has suggested that Eggerson has been God's confidential clerk, more than Sir Claude's, from the beginning, and that Colby will now succeed to that position, gradually working his way up until he becomes confidential clerk to his Father in Heaven.[26] Sir Claude and Lady Elizabeth correspond, of course, to Edward and Lavinia in *The Cocktail Party*: the "happy ending" is promise of a happier beginning in a new relationship. The list is incomplete, but it suffices to remind us that Eliot's plays are variations on the idea of Holiness, its perversion, and its possibility in the modern world. The later plays attempt to represent the emergence, in wider and more challenging contexts, of a quality of sanctity corresponding to Thomas's in *Murder in the Cathedral*. They are dramatic versions of problems which are objects of meditation in *Ash Wednesday* and *Four Quartets*.

*The Confidential Clerk* is a much more successful play than *The Cocktail Party*. Think of the integrity of tone in *The Confidential Clerk*, which the earlier play lacked. It will be recalled that the most serious flaw in *The Cocktail Party* was the failure to bring into harmonious relation the two actions and the two worlds represented. This defect has been completely eliminated in *The Confidential Clerk*. In this play the two worlds impinge: although different, they are presented as being not completely discontinuous; they acknowledge the reality of a common, cir-

[26] Francis Fergusson, *supra*, footnote 13, p. 477.

cumstantial world. It is important to emphasise this consideration because at least one critic of repute, William Arrowsmith, has argued that the play shows "a gnostic denial of the reality of the world." He maintains that Colby is an inadequate presentation of the incipiently perfect Christian life. It is just because the positive Christian in Colby has been negatively defined as the denial of the world, he argues, that Colby is interesting neither as a Christian nor a man. All that his Christianity comes to is renunciation of worldly love, father, and vocation. He maintains, finally, that it is this doctrine of negative transcendence, steadily denying dignity or reality to the illusions of the world which the play is intended to transfigure, that impoverishes its human characters and makes their conversion a hollow ritual.[27] These comments on *The Confidential Clerk* are probably remnants of the critic's distaste for *The Cocktail Party*; the philosophical case against Eliot had far more cogency in the case of the earlier play. The clue to *The Confidential Clerk* is indeed *The Cocktail Party,* both in its similarities and, no less, in its differences.

Indeed, pausing to consider the two plays again in association, one realises that *The Confidential Clerk* is in fact a *critique* of the moral rhetoric of *The Cocktail Party*. The theme of *The Cocktail Party* is restated, but with a difference which not only redeems it as doctrine but strengthens it as drama. It is unnecessary to present the doctrine as either prior or secondary to the drama; one is happy to find that a more humane presentation of existence and a more harmonious dramatic unity are now available in the same play.

It remains, then, to discuss the point which Eliot reached with *The Confidential Clerk,* for it is clear that this play completed a stage of inquiry in a sense which does not apply to, say, *The Family Reunion*. We would also take this opportunity of illustrating the relation between theory and practice in Eliot's later work as dramatist.

[27] William Arrowsmith, *supra,* footnote 22, pp. 293-94.

*The Human Voice*

In *The Music of Poetry* (1942) Eliot, discussing the defects of nineteenth-century verse plays, suggested that even if the poets had possessed greater natural gifts for the theatre, or had toiled to learn their trade, their plays would have been just as ineffective, unless their theatrical talent and experience had shown them the necessity for a different kind of versification. These plays are lifeless, he argued, not primarily because they lack plot or suspense or because their characters are imperfectly realised, but because their rhythm of speech is something that we cannot associate with any human being except a verse speaker.[28] Hence Eliot's insistence on the difference between dramatic and all other kinds of verse.

There can be no doubt that the verse of *The Confidential Clerk* is quite different from that of Eliot's own poems. Some of the finest passages in those poems strike one as being almost anonymous; they do not depend on a relation to an individual voice or personality. Here is a passage from *Little Gidding* which sounds as if it came from an Ionesco chair:

> Ash on an old man's sleeve
> Is all the ash the burnt roses leave.
> Dust in the air suspended
> Marks the place where a story ended.
> Dust inbreathed was a house—
> The wall, the wainscot and the mouse.
> The death of hope and despair,
> This is the death of air.
>
> There are flood and drouth
> Over the eyes and in the mouth.
> Dead water and dead sand
> Contending for the upper hand.
> The parched eviscerate soil

[28] *Selected Prose*, Penguin Books, 1953, pp. 61-62.

> Gapes at the vanity of toil,
> Laughs without mirth.
> This is the death of earth.[29]

*The Confidential Clerk* is the first of Eliot's plays in which no trace of anonymous or autonomous verse appears. The relation between the following words, for instance, and Eggerson's speaking them could hardly be more intimate:

> Don't say that, Sir Claude,
> It's true, I haven't much nowadays to bring me;
> But Mrs. E. wishes I'd come up oftener!
> Isn't that like the ladies! She used to complain
> At my being up in London five or six days a week:
> But now she says: "You're becoming such a countryman!
> You're losing touch with public affairs!"
> The fact is, she misses the contact with London,
> Though she doesn't admit it. She misses my news
> When I came home in the evening. And the late edition
> Of the papers that I picked up at Liverpool Street.

## The Example of Shakespeare

In *Poetry and Drama* (1950) Eliot declared that the self-education of a poet writing for the theatre required a long period of disciplining his poetry and putting it, so to speak, on a very thin diet in order to adapt it to the needs of the stage. Later, however, he might find, if and when the understanding of theatrical technique had become second nature, that he could make more liberal use of poetry and take greater liberties with colloquial speech. He based this belief on Shakespeare's progress and on a study of Shakespeare's language in his later plays.[30]

Eliot had offered evidence for this view some eight years earlier. In *The Music of Poetry* he argued that the development of Shakespeare's verse could be roughly divided into two phases. During the first, Shakespeare was slowly adapting his form to

[29] *Four Quartets*, Faber and Faber, 1944, p. 37.
[30] *Selected Prose, supra*, footnote 28, p. 84.

colloquial speech; this stage culminated in *Antony and Cleopatra*. Having reached this point he began to elaborate his style. In the first period the poet who had begun with *Venus and Adonis* but who had already, in *Love's Labour's Lost*, seen what he had to do, moved from artificiality to simplicity, from stiffness to suppleness. The later plays move from simplicity toward elaboration. In this phase Shakespeare was occupied with the second task of the poet, that of experimenting to see how elaborate, how complicated, the music could be made without losing touch with colloquial speech, and without his characters ceasing to be human beings. This, according to Eliot, is the poet of *Cymbeline*, *The Winter's Tale, Pericles*, and *The Tempest*.[31]

*The Family Reunion* is Eliot's *Love's Labour's Lost; The Confidential Clerk* is his *Antony and Cleopatra*. This is the end of the first stage in a quasi-Shakespearean progression. It is important to bear in mind that there is nothing at all mechanical in Eliot's adhesion to this Shakespearean example in versification, because it consorts perfectly with his idea of the development of twentieth-century non-dramatic poetry. In his 1947 lecture on Milton, Eliot declared that poetry should help, not only to refine the language of the time, but to prevent it from changing too rapidly. He argued that the current danger was that the language would change too quickly and therefore deteriorate. The proper course would be that the poetry of the immediate and foreseeable future would discover new and more elaborate patterns of a diction now established.[32]

This ideal is consistent with Eliot's experiments in dramatic verse. *The Waste Land* and *The Confidential Clerk*, so different in many respects, are alike in this, that each work represents the end of a certain stage in experiment and the point of departure for new work in the same mode. The later impulse is conservative.

[31] *Ibid.*, pp. 63-64.     [32] *Ibid.*, p. 148.

# CHAPTER NINE. *THE ELDER STATESMAN*: ELIOT IN FAIR COLONUS

ELIOT's plays strive toward the condition of prayer. In a period in which public or communal prayer has declined, he is tricking his theatre-audiences into an analogue of worship. Thus the opening scene of *The Cocktail Party* is a representation of—from a religious point of view—oaths and blasphemies (politely translated) which by the dramatist's dialectic will be made over into prayers: the prayers are enacted in Celia's death and in Alex's report of that death. Being of our own irreligious or neutral time, we perpetrate such oaths and blasphemies, and Eliot takes us as we are before attempting to make us over in his own prayerful image. He has to begin somewhere: "If people believe *eight*, I can recommend *nine*; I can do so by the manipulation of their *eightish* assumptions; I need not justify my *nine* by arguing for *one*."[1] These are not Eliot's words, but no matter: they serve. Eliot's later plays begin with eight oaths, politely disguised, and end with nine prayers.

This transformation is achieved by gentle indirection, not by apocalyptic admonitions: these plays are not jeremiads. Eliot may feel as strongly as Increase Mather, but we have forced him to con a different style. He achieves his prayers nonetheless. The first act of *The Elder Statesman* has a few beguiling moments of thin young love, but it is essentially a malign fiesta: bitter, sophisticated, with a gray wit. It is a concentration of Wyndham Lewis's horror in the more familiar medium of guilt, deception, and emptiness. It is the waste sad time in which the ghosts of *The Hollow Men* are more palpable than Lambert who brings in the tea. The "oaths" in *The Elder Statesman* are spoken by the ghosts from Lord Claverton's past, the sinister forces which he has carried within himself for many years.

[1] Kenneth Burke, *The Philosophy of Literary Form*, New York, new edition, Vintage Books, 1957, p. 309.

Eliot calls them Federico Gomez and Mrs. Carghill. They command a language which he long ago perfected for such purposes: "The laughter in the doorway, the snicker in the corridor, the sudden silence in the smoking-room." Lord Claverton himself spends most of the first two acts mouthing "oaths": putting up a righteous façade against the bland Gomez, playing a world-weary part to fend off Mrs. Carghill, gesticulating as a maligned father in the face of a son who has repudiated his inheritance.

Thus the beginning. And the end is a litany of love intoned for us—as hierophants—by Charles and Monica. These two are our stylists, "saying the right thing," finishing off the play with an essay in practical love now no longer thin but rich and mellow. Thus the play, changing oaths to prayers, is an uncovering, a pulling back the curtains, a breaking up of the pieces to put them together again in new configurations. It is a substitution of new and deeper pieties, deeper because Lord Claverton, in exorcising the prudent devil which has "guided" him for many years, frees himself from the spectres and emerges "into something like reality."

There is a motto for all this; it is a-going-back-to-the-beginning, a new beginning in a different spirit. The false gods are rejected and we go back to the point at which—impiously—we went astray. One of the most moving speeches in *The Elder Statesman* comes at the end of the second act when Lord Claverton, watching his severed son Michael go arm-in-arm with Mrs. Carghill and Federico Gomez, sees that there is no escape from one's self; and, seeing this, he sees that he must go back to the beginning, and his son must do likewise. Michael and he must now "go to school together" to learn the meaning of things, and he wonders, "Is it too late for me, Monica?" This gesture is carried down into the detail of several speeches: it is a process of constant revision and correction—as children at school—in the pursuit of truth and reality. Thus when Monica refers to her father "thinking of nothing," he revises the remark to "contemplating nothingness."

Everyone has seen that *The Elder Statesman* bears a certain relation to *Oedipus at Colonus*: the relation is both structural and qualitative. *Oedipus at Colonus* provides the "shape" of the new play, some of its most important relationships, and a model for its tone. At the centre of both plays there is the father-daughter relationship, testifying to possibilities that will be realised—prayerfully—at the end of the play. These possibilities, insofar as they express themselves in terms of sexual love, involve the substitution of Charles Hemington for the second sister Ismene: Monica is a gracious, if pallid, reflection of Antigone. Michael-Polynices is the common ground through which the protagonist and the antagonist principles come to grips; the "translation" into modern terms is in his case entirely convincing. There is no Teirisias in Eliot's play, because Lord Claverton in his role as self-critic, the silent observer who when forced speaks out, gathers up this role unto himself as Oedipus. Since the context in which the action of *The Elder Statesman* is imitated is not very important, there is no need of a Theseus; and since the gods are to be invoked—if at all—only obliquely and apologetically, there is no need of a Creon. These omissions speak for themselves.

The tone of *The Elder Statesman* cannot be described as if it were something static. As the play moves from oaths to prayers it "spits from the mouth the withered apple-seed" and yearns toward the autumnal mellowness of the great beech-tree at Badgley Court. There is a place for gray, bitter wit, but it would be a breach of decorum here in the late afternoon near the beech-tree which is in the place-without-a-name at fair Colonus. Perhaps it is also under the larches of Paradise. In any event Eliot has been graciously loyal to the Sophocles of *Oedipus at Colonus*; he has not bruised the late fruit, nor has he hurt the moving spirit of consolation—Boethian also—in which Oedipus proceeds on his last journey. *The Elder Statesman* is one of the few modern plays which move with distinction in the realm of Perception.

In this respect the play is an extension of *The Family Re-*

*union*, just as *The Confidential Clerk* is a revised version of *The Cocktail Party*. In this new version of *The Family Reunion* the issues of the early play are reconsidered in a fresh attempt to accost that guilt-ridden experience which has been in the shadows of Eliot's world since before *The Hollow Men*. There may seem to be little connexion between Harry Monchensey and Richard Claverton, but if we seek an early figuring of the elder statesman do we not find it in Harry's father, the man who hands on a smoky inheritance to his son? It is as if Eliot were to bring Harry's father out of the shadows into the world of human relationships, giving him another chance to redeem himself. In his earlier world "there was no ecstasy"; the elder Monchensey lived with his wife in a lonely country house learning the meaning of loneliness. It is a fitting context for the awful privacy of Lord Claverton, imprisoned in guilt and deception: "only fear of the emptiness before me." These may not be one and the same person but they are more than mere participants in the same black world; they share the same figure in the carpet. The difference is that where the elder Monchensey was doomed to the spectral existence of a "presence" behind Harry's guilt-ridden life, in the new play he has been granted a second chance to liberate himself from the human wheel. When we speak of the "humanity" of the new play this is what we mean; that it offers a second chance which we had been given no reason to expect.

And of course *The Elder Statesman* is a more humane play than *The Family Reunion*, more humane, indeed, than any of its predecessors. There are no longer any aunts and uncles whom we can use as scapegoats, burdening them with our guilt and resentment before we cast them off the rocks. There is no longer a John Monchensey to whom we can bequeath a rancid world, thereby exhibiting our own fine taste. Lord Claverton and his Monica do not opt out of the human world in their pursuit of latter-day felicity; there is in the new play no urge to deny the integrity of the human world, or to sell it short. It is a measure of the play's humanity that it preserves the finite world intact—

*161*

through Charles and Monica—more generously than *The Cocktail Party* or even *The Confidential Clerk*, and that it endorses no inevitable dichotomy between our everyday world and the world of our most strenuous aspirations. Edward and Lavinia from *The Cocktail Party* have now been given a second chance; as Charles and Monica they find at Badgley Court a richer love than they were granted in their London flat. Perhaps Julia was to blame: she was a severe moralist:

> Everyone makes a choice, of one kind or another,
> And then must take the consequences. Celia chose
> A way of which the consequence was crucifixion;
> Peter Quilpe chose a way that takes him to Boltwell;
> And now the consequence of the Chamberlaynes' choice
> Is a cocktail party. They must be ready for it.
> Their guests may be arriving at any moment.

But Sir Henry Harcourt-Reilly was a little more yielding:

> You will have to live with these memories and make them
> Into something new. Only by acceptance
> Of the past will you alter its meaning.

and Edward interpreted this as saying "that every moment is a fresh beginning." But Edward was not granted the illumination of knowing the meaning of love. He could not have glowed in the insight as Charles does when he says to Monica:

> And no future life is even conceivable
> In which we should not be conscious of each other
> And conscious of our loving. . . .

The love of Charles and Monica is, among other things, a mellow critique of the love of Edward and Lavinia, just as it "defines" the love which Colby and Lucasta sketched in *The Confidential Clerk*.

At the centre of all this is Lord Claverton's vision of his world. This is the determining focus of the play; we can understand it best, perhaps, if we chart its development, bearing in mind its earlier manifestations.

The Ur-hero in Eliot's previous plays was the religious man defining himself in a secular society. It was part of Eliot's dialectic—and part of the thin humanity of the earlier plays—to load the dice too heavily in the hero's favour. Not content to exalt his hero as a man of outstanding integrity, Eliot made the mistake of regarding as the Enemy not only the avowedly irreligious factors in the quotidian world but that world itself, in its entirety, in all its manifestations. Everything went into the same bin. In the plays up to *The Cocktail Party* the *scene* itself was endowed with malignant motives. Hence the tendency of those plays to denigrate the finite and to associate the hero's aspirations with some esoteric Essence which demanded, as a prerequisite, that the finite world of Matter and Body be sloughed off. But Lord Claverton's role is new in at least one important respect. It is not a case of a hero, a man of Conscience and Consciousness, confronting a hostile *scene*—and then destroying it or transcending it—but such a man confronting *himself*. The dialectic of *The Elder Statesman* is strikingly personal and internal. The place of the scapegoat *scene* is now taken by those factors of cowardice, meanness, and emptiness which Lord Claverton sees in himself: he does not put the blame on Society, or on Matter, or Body, or Nature, or on any other capitalised malignity. He does not say, as Harry said in *The Family Reunion*:

> It is not my conscience,
> Not my mind, that is diseased, but the world I have to
> live in.

That was an easy way out, at least provisionally, but it is not available to Lord Claverton; to get to his great beech-tree he must cut his way through his own deception.

This involves an act of moral choice: an unfashionable procedure in modern drama, including Eliot's own. Bearing in mind the ambiguous representation of such an act in *The*

*Family Reunion* we should now acknowledge that *The Elder Statesman*, penetrating similar experience, commits itself firmly to the possibility of an individual moral act. There comes a certain stage in *The Elder Statesman* at which Lord Claverton, like Harry Monchensey, decides not to run away from his spectres; but Claverton's decision, unlike Harry's, issues un-ambiguously from his own resources as an individual moral being. The new play asserts, as clearly as anyone could wish and much more clearly than he might have expected, that Man has the power of moral choice, that he holds this power by virtue of his existence and dignity as a human being, that the exercise of this power is a matter of incalculable moment. When Monica urges her father to escape from those obnoxious famil-iars Federico Gomez and Mrs. Carghill, he corrects her advice, warning her that there is no escaping one's self. This act of moral choice leads not to the conventional "happy ending"— or to that only superficially—but to the radical extension of the circumference of insight within which Lord Claverton sees his world. And in this new, wider circle there is a mellower place even for such "failures" as that of his relations with his son. Michael's flight to San Marco represents the enormous risk attendant upon an individual act of moral choice, but the risk is accepted graciously and incorporated into the new circle of interpretation.

The key-word is Love: not indeed a new word even in the spare landscape of Eliot's plays, but until now a word used only with a certain embarrassment. *The Elder Statesman* offers the word with full, grave commitment as the Meaning of Meanings. Eliot could have found the word already with a rich meaning in *Oedipus at Colonus*, seizing it now as the definitive term, not so much correcting what had gone before as acknowledging a more humane direction. Conscience, Consciousness, Under-standing; and now Love. And since this is the wisest as well as the wittiest of Eliot's plays, the nature of Love is defined not by a context of limp "good deeds" but by a genuinely won illumination, a flowering of insight into the relation between reality and responsibility. Eliot's new testament is endorsed by Love as the Term of Terms within which all lesser terms find speech.

The words spoken in *The Elder Statesman* are neither diffident nor ostentatious: benign, more relaxed than those of *The Confidential Clerk*, and more beautiful in their partnerships. And it is significant that along with the more humane version of experience represented in *The Elder Statesman* there is a greater trust in the possibility of verbal communication. (This is offered at least as a pious hope, and the gentleman's agreement still holds: there are certain topics, certain names, which the dramatist has undertaken not to mention, on pain of "excommunication"). There is a feeling in the new play that if our words could only be supported by Love they need not break under any burden thereafter. In *The Family Reunion* Harry's psychosis was intensified by the failure, the collapse, of verbal communication. Agatha encouraged him to speak in his own language without stopping to debate whether it might be too far beyond the understanding of his audience; and he made the effort, without much assistance from syntax:

The sudden solitude in a crowded desert
In a thick smoke, many creatures moving
Without direction, for no direction
Leads anywhere but round and round in that vapour—
Without purpose, and without principle of conduct
In flickering intervals of light and darkness;
The partial anaesthesia of suffering without feeling
And partial observation of one's own automatism
While the slow stain sinks deeper through the skin
Tainting the flesh and discolouring the bone—

But he fell back from this awful privacy of insight:

This is what matters, but it is unspeakable,
Untranslatable: I talk in general terms
Because the particular has no language. . . .

Lord Claverton is more fortunate: with Love supporting him he finds the words for the confessional act which he performs in the presence of Monica and Charles. Hence we chart the following terms in the same nexus: Love, Speech, Communication, Understanding, Illumination, Consciousness. Monica encompasses this entire world of possibility when she refers to "Love within which all other love finds speech": at this stage she has recognised, with Charles, that the felicity of one's private world exists not as a secret place blocked off from the public world but as the consciousness of "love unchanging" in the integrity of the public world. The garden of Monica and Charles—to speak of it in terms of *The Confidential Clerk*—is a part of one single world. It is a glowing image. Lord Claverton's terms are an autumnal translation of this insight: he speaks of "the peace that ensues upon contrition," and "the illumination of seeing what love is"; again, "I have been brushed by the wing of Heaven." This is luminous speech and there are luminous acts, too, as when Lord Claverton says to his severed son, "I shall never repudiate you, though you have repudiated me."

In *The Elder Statesman* Eliot has stuck to his guns: he has been scrupulously loyal to those insights which he has been exploring since *The Family Reunion*. To some the new play has seemed an "ironic melodrama," perhaps a sequel to *The Strange Boarders of Palace Crescent*, but this is to mistake the *genre*. Keeping before his mind the development of Shakespeare's later plays, Eliot has written in *The Elder Statesman* an "ideal comedy"—the term is Northrop Frye's[2]—gently drawing forth, from an ambiguous situation, an image of communal order. The mood is optative rather than indicative, and what the play envisages is not merely individual felicity but an idea of social harmony of which the Claverton family—in its new circumference of insight—represents a beautiful instance. Eliot's problem—or so we conceive it—was to compose a modern

[2] Northrop Frye, "A Conspectus of Dramatic Genres," *Kenyon Review*, Vol. XIII, 4, Autumn 1951, pp. 543-62.

equivalent of *The Tempest* or of *Oedipus at Colonus*—each would serve—while keeping adequately close to the "realistic" expectations of his audience. Perhaps the solution emerged somewhat as follows: starting with Lord Claverton's psychosis, Eliot broke it down into its two conflicting parts—the "negative" or sinister part, which he divided between Gomez and Mrs. Carghill, and the "positive," upward-striving part, which he reflected in Monica and her Charles. Michael the erring son provided the battleground. Lambert the butler was added to make the Claverton home more substantial. Mrs. Piggott was added for several reasons: to insinuate the play's contact with a world outside its windows, a world which knowing nothing of Lord Claverton's problems was nevertheless implicated in them; to offer comic relief in those moments in which the situation might have "gone soft"; above all, by providing a local, innocuous dissatisfaction, to modulate between the much more sinister distresses represented by Gomez and Mrs. Carghill. These are sound rhetorical reasons.

Eliot we have already recognised as a skilful rhetorician, and we may cite *The Elder Statesman* as a case in point. When a Mrs. Piggott is needed, Eliot is quick to sense the lack and to remedy it. But in one respect—and that a serious one—he has erred: he has been niggardly in providing *The Elder Statesman* with the climax for which it cries out. We have already emphasised the significance of Lord Claverton's moral act: the entire play depends on it; but it comes too easily. We are asked to acknowledge the soul-stirrings, the agonising torments which Lord Claverton suffers, but we are shown little theatrical evidence of their existence: a craggy, pained face; a few wise, sad words; nothing more. Contrition here seems an easy thing, hardly an act at all, but it can hardly be so. Likewise, confession: it is as if the fears, the misgivings, and the shame were suffered off-stage; Lord Claverton enters, resigned, to tell his story to a gentle daughter. No wonder, then, that we remember as the climax of the play the moment in which Michael cries out to his father, "What is my inheritance?" True, the moment is highly charged, at once poignant and chilling, but it should be no more than a prefiguring of Lord Claverton's own pained appraisal. It may be that Eliot was reluctant to risk injuring the tone of his play by charging it here with the laments of a disconsolate chimera; *The Family Reunion* was a more ample *genre* for this kind of thing. But even in "ideal comedy" a man does not tear himself apart without our hearing the noise.

This is the most serious defect in *The Elder Statesman* and it injures the play as theatre-poetry. The central relationships, particularly the relationship between Lord Claverton and his daughter, would be much more convincing if Lord Claverton were shown in agonised recognition of his own emptiness. Monica's answering love would then seem a rich fulfilment rather than an unearned increment. Mrs. Carghill and Federico Gomez would seem more palpable servants of Satan. And the process of spiritual regeneration would seem a truly heroic endeavour.

Perhaps the fault lies in Monica's role. Gentle, and "qualitatively" apt, yes, but she makes very little contribution to the play. In one scene in particular she fails us entirely. Eliot was perhaps foolhardy in having Lord Claverton confess his sins *twice* (once to us, then to Monica), but he might have negotiated the hazard if he had ensured that the second confession would be *a new thing*, a new phase in the central relationship. If Monica had received the confession with something more intense or more individual than the elaborate recitation of *It's-alright,-daddy,-I-love-you-more-than-ever*, the scene might have been saved. As it is, it merely repeats what we already know, and it has nothing new to enact in the father-daughter relationship.

## CHAPTER TEN. ELIOT'S VERSE LINE

KENNETH LEE PIKE has shown that in sequences of spoken English the lapse of time between any two primary stresses tends to be the same, regardless of the number of syllables or the "junctures" between them.[1] That is, by contrast with Spanish, which is syllable-timed, English is stress-timed, or isochronic. Such isochronism is produced not only by accelerating and crushing together the syllables between primary stresses but also by increasing or decreasing the pauses which may follow the three terminal junctures.[2] Eliot has recognised this habit of the language in his choice of a verse line for the later plays. This line, we have already seen, varies in length and in the number of syllables; it has a caesura and three stresses. The caesura and the stresses may come at different places, almost anywhere in the line. The stresses may be close together or well separated by unstressed syllables, the only rule being that there must be one stress on one side of the caesura and two on the other.[3] Tonal variations in the lines are therefore obtained either by varying the number of syllables between primary stresses or by increasing or reducing the pauses between the syllables. A case in point from a speech by Colby:

> Álways, || when I pláy to mysélf,
> I hear the músic || I should líke to have wrítten,
> As the compóser héard it || when it cáme to him . . .

The main variation exhibited in these lines arises from the separation of the two primary stresses on "compóser" and

---

[1] Kenneth Lee Pike, *Phonetics: A Critical Analysis of Phonetic Theory and a Technique for the Practical Description of Sounds*, Michigan University Publications, Vol. XXI, 1943. Linguists define a juncture as that particular configuration of pause and pitch by which the voice connects linguistic units to each other or to silence. Four are differentiated in English. See Seymour Chatman, "Robert Frost's 'Mowing': An Inquiry into Prosodic Structure," *Kenyon Review*, Summer 1956, p. 422ff.

[2] Harold Whitehall, "From Linguistics to Criticism," *Kenyon Review*, Autumn 1951 and Summer 1956, pp. 418-19.

[3] *Selected Prose*, Penguin Books, 1953, p. 80.

"héard" by only a single syllable, in contrast to the other stresses which are separated by two, three, or four syllables. This effect is intensified by the "falling juncture" on the final syllable of "composer."

Before examining some passages from Eliot's later plays we would point out that there is nothing in his theory to prevent him from using in his plays a line as traditional as the iambic pentametre. While a pentametre contains, by definition, five stresses, these are not all primary. Indeed, if one scans a "normal" iambic pentametre according to the system of four-level stresses outlined by George L. Trager and Henry L. Smith,[4] one finds that the number of primary stresses is unlikely to exceed three. We have then three or, occasionally, four syllables of primary stress with isochronic stretches of more weakly stressed syllables between them:[5]

Thĕ cúrfèw tôlls thĕ knéll òf pârtĭng dáy.

It is quite proper, of course, to refer to such a line as a pentametre. Technically, the line is accentual-syllabic with five stresses; in speech only three of these are primary. A similar line could therefore fit into Eliot's accentual pattern, if necessary. (The point is a bit tenuous, I admit; especially as Eliot has no real intention of using any line which would recall blank verse, however remotely.)

In experimenting toward the line which he has now adopted Eliot seems to have been mainly concerned to ensure that the peaks of attention indicated variously by the syntax, by the rhetoric, and by the metre should coincide. This arises from several considerations. First, he wants to avoid forming in the theatre-audience any special frame of mind such as attends on the experience of listening to a poetry-recital. Second, since the beginning of his career Eliot has been engrossed with the relation between Tradition and the spoken language. In *The Social Function of Poetry* he conceived of language, the spoken

---

[4] Battenburg Press, 1951, Studies in Linguistics, Occasional Papers 3.
[5] Whitehall, *supra*, footnote 2, p. 419.

language, as the vehicle of one's tradition, and its guardian. Furthermore, he argued that the feelings of the most refined and complex individuals have something in common with those of the crudest and least educated, which they do not share with persons of their own level of culture who speak another language. In order to maintain contact, as poet, with this element which is common to the feelings of a race, the poet should therefore take the language as he finds it, the spoken tongue with its characteristic "shapes" and rhythms. This is necessary, Eliot argued, for the preservation and extension of feeling, since the language of people in everyday usage is the language which names feelings and attitudes.[6]

These ideas determined the context in which Eliot referred to "the law that poetry must not stray too far from the ordinary everyday language which we use and hear." Whether poetry is accentual or syllabic, rhymed or rhymeless, "formal" or "free," it cannot afford, he argued, to lose contact with the changing language of common intercourse.[7] This does not mean that poetry should be exactly the same speech that the poet speaks and hears. Conversation and good prose or verse are not identical, but the poet should take his bearings from the habits of speech with which he is most familiar. If a poet's literary models tend to strengthen this relation between his verse and current habits of speech, so much the better. Discussing the influence on Pound's early poems of Browning, Yeats, Swinburne, and Morris, Eliot declared that these influences were all good, for they combined to insist upon the importance of *verse as speech,* while from his more antiquarian studies Pound was learning the importance of *verse as song.*[8] Finally Eliot observed that the

---

[6] T. S. Eliot, "The Social Function of Poetry," *Adelphi,* July-September 1945, reprinted in Robert W. Stallman, *Critiques and Essays in Criticism: 1920-1948,* New York, The Ronald Press, 1949, pp. 112-14. See also Mr. Eliot's Introduction to Paul Valery, *The Art of Poetry,* Pantheon Books, 1958.

[7] T. S. Eliot, *The Music of Poetry,* Glasgow University Publications, Jackson, 1942, pp. 13, 16, 17.

[8] T. S. Eliot, Introduction to *Ezra Pound: Selected Poems,* Faber and Gwyer, 1928, p. ix.

dependence of verse upon speech was much more direct in dramatic poetry than in any other.[9]

In pursuing these aims Eliot has sacrificed others. For example, one of the characteristics of his verse line is that its accentual nature avoids any conflict, such as we find with great expressiveness in the blank verse of Shakespeare and of Milton, between a *theoretic* metrical pattern and an *actual* pattern of rendered sound. Such conflicts and their expressive resources are available only where the metrical norm exists as a putative, regular pattern: when this happens, departures from the norm, and acts of violence within it, become momentous. Paul Valery was particularly sensitive to such clashes: "Verse. The vague idea, the intention, the many-imaged impulsion breaking on the regular forms, on the invincible defenses of conventional prosody, engenders new things and unexpected figures. There are astonishing consequences from this shock of the will and of feeling against the insensibility of conventions."[10] There are several lines in *The Cocktail Party* which, while exemplifying the arrangement of caesura and three stresses which Eliot has described, could, in themselves, be read as iambic pentametres. In some cases the variations are precisely those sanctioned by traditional usage

Ĕscápe frŏm ă sórdĭd wórld íntŏ ă púre ŏne . . .

but no iambic pentametre norm has been established in the play. Consequently, Eliot's verse line cannot utilise the "promotions" or "suppressions"[11] of the stress levels of normal speech possible by means of the pressure of an established metrical pattern.

As partial compensation Eliot has secured one advantage. Ignoring the number of technically unstressed syllables, he has left scope, in performance, for the most sensitive adjustment of the voice to the rhetorical weight of the syllables. In a performance of *The Confidential Clerk* the actor playing Colby would speak the line

[9] *The Music of Poetry, supra,* footnote 7, p. 20.
[10] "Rhythm and Metre," *Hudson Review,* Winter 1950, p. 542.
[11] *Chatman, supra,* footnote 1, p. 424.

It cán't be done by íssuing invitátions

more sensitively by placing primary stresses as shown and by speaking the words according to their rhetorical emphases than by having in mind a blank verse pattern, however flexible:

Ĭt cán't bĕ dóne bў íssŭing ínvĭtátĭons.

There is another advantage inasmuch as Eliot's verse line is not sufficiently positive in its characteristics to be "typed." Certain verse forms are enriched but also to some extent limited by their special skills.[12] We have already remarked that the poetic couplet is too "perfect" for certain purposes. Hamlet, ranging swiftly into the crevices of his feeling, would find the couplet too calm in its perfection, too "strong," tending toward a degree of poise far beyond that of his mind at such moments. It is possible, of course, to thwart such a bias in a metrical form, and the experiments of Dryden in *MacFlecknoe*, Pope in *Arbuthnot*, and Churchill in *The Candidate* show what can be achieved. But the bias remains, leaping to reveal itself if and when virtuosity flags. Eliot's verse line has the advantages and the disadvantages of being "free"; it is in keeping with his recent poetic which, as we have seen, requires as its norm a level from which when necessary it can rise.

The sources of this verse line have been named much too positively. Sir Herbert Read has asserted that the system of versification which Eliot has worked out differs in no important respect from the "sprung rhythm" of Hopkins. If there is a difference, he thinks, it lies in the use of the caesura.[13] But this is too restrictive. Sprung rhythm—Professor Winters has described it—occurs when two stresses come together by means other than the normal inversion of a foot. It occurs freely in accentual metre and in syllabic metre; it may also occur as a variant in standard English meter as a result of the dropping of an unaccented syllable with the resultant creation of a monosyllabic foot, or as a result of the equally heavy accentuation of both syllables

[12] "Action as Rational," *Hudson Review*, Summer 1948, p. 201.
[13] *The True Voice of Feeling*, Faber and Faber, 1953, p. 63.

of a foot.[14] However, the occasions in *The Confidential Clerk* on which two stresses come together are few; they are certainly not determining factors in the verse, as they are in that of Hopkins. An instance occurs in the following speech by Colby

> They would just have to come. And I should not
>         see them coming.
> I should not hear the opening of the gate.
> They would simply . . . be there suddenly,
> Unexpectedly . . .

where in the third line the context and the organisation of the verse suggest a reading as follows:

> They would símply . . . be thére súddenly.

To associate this with Hopkins, however, is misleading. It is much more important to recognise that the isochronic bias of the language, imposing a rhetorical pause after "there," ensures that each of the words bears necessary emphasis, and that the lines retain contact with recognisable habits of speech.

There is more justification for citing Pound's *Cantos* as a possible source for Eliot's verse line. This passage, for instance, from the early Canto XIII:

> And Kung said, and wrote on the bo leaves:
>         "If a man have not order within him
> He can not spread order about him;
> And if a man have not order within him
> His family will not act with due order;
>         And if the prince have not order within him
> He can not put order in his dominions."
> And Kung gave the words "order"
> And "brotherly deference"
> And said nothing of the "life after death."
> And he said
>                 "Anyone can run to excesses,

---

[14] "Gerard Manley Hopkins," *Hudson Review*, Vol. I, 4, Winter 1949, p. 462.

It is easy to shoot past the mark,
It is hard to stand firm in the middle."
And they said: "If a man commit murder
   Should his father protect him, and hide him?"
And Kung said:
        "He should hide him."[15]

This is typical of the structures of sound in the early Cantos.
Pound's variations are innumerable, but his norm is a line of
indefinite number of syllables and three stresses. This is also
the norm in Eliot's plays since *The Family Reunion*:

   Oh yes, Mr. Kaghan is very good company.
   He makes me laugh sometimes. I don't laugh easily.
   Quite a humorist, he is. In fact, Mrs. E.
   Sometimes says to me: "Eggerson, why can't you
      make me laugh
   The way B. Kaghan did?" She's only met him once;
   But do you know, he began addressing her as Muriel—
   Within the first ten minutes! I was horrified.
   But she actually liked it. Muriel *is* her name.
   He has a way with the ladies, you know.
   But with Lady Elizabeth he wasn't so successful.
   She once referred to him as "undistinguished"; . . .

The long, swinging line of three stresses is Eliot's norm in re-
laxation, used for "verse" rather than for "poetry." When a high
degree of intensity is reached the pattern changes unobtrusively;
the rhythm is "tightened" by reducing the number of syllables
between the three primary stresses:

           You don't understand
   That when one has lived without parents, as a child,
   There's a gáp that néver can be filled. Néver.

It is hard to estimate the extent to which Eliot is indebted to
Pound or to anyone else for the verse line of the later plays.

[15] *The Cantos of Ezra Pound*, Faber and Faber, 1954, p. 63.

Certainly this trend obeys the spirit of Pound's early advice to "compose in the sequence of the musical phrase, not in sequence of a metronome."[16] But Pound was not the first to use such terms. In 1802 J. Sibbald argued that the rhythm of poems composed before about 1540 "appears uniformly to have been regulated according to that measure which in music is called common time." In poems of the sixteenth century and later, the verse was regulated by triple time. "In the former, a short note is never found single, or placed between two long ones. In the latter, the case is precisely the reverse; the motion of the syllables, in point of uniformity, resembling that of a pendulum; while that of the ancient or Saxon rhythm may be said to resemble the beating of a drum, in various or irregular numbers of strokes, but in common time." Accordingly Sibbald argued that ancient English versification depended on quantity, "by which is meant the length of time employed in reciting the line," without any other regard to the number of syllables than that the longest line should not contain more than twice the number of the shortest corresponding line, and that both the longest and shortest should be capable of being recited within the same portion of common time, "which portion must either be one compleat bar, or two." Again: Sibbald observed, examining the metrics of Chaucer and of Gawin Douglas's translation of the *Aeneid*, that in ancient versification the number of syllables in the lines varied frequently. Furthermore, he noted that the syllables did not follow in order "according to the modern rhythm of a short and a long syllable alternately; or of a long and two short repeated": "The measure seems rather to be regulated by the division of the time required for recitation of the line, into portions like musical phrases; not necessarily equal in the number of syllables, but requiring an equal period of time for their pronunciation."[17] Accordingly Sibbald, using musical notation,

16 Ezra Pound, *A Retrospect*, 1918; *Literary Essays*, Faber and Faber, 1954, p. 3.
17 *Chronicle of Scottish Poetry from the Thirteenth Century to the Union of the Crowns, to which is added a Glossary by J. Sibbald*, Edinburgh, Stewart, 1802, IV, lii, lv, xlvi. My attention was drawn to this

set out each of the opening lines from the Prologue to the *Canterbury Tales* in two bars of four crotchets, or their equivalent in quavers. Likewise with the first lines of Douglas's *Aeneid*.

The verse of Eliot's later plays and that of Pound's Cantos share several characteristics: the use of rhetorical rather than metrical stresses; the habit of disregarding the number of syllables between stresses; the use, on occasion, of two stresses in juxtaposition. Both poets have been engrossed with the habits of a *spoken* language. Of Eliot's verse in the recent plays, as of Pound's and Chaucer's, one may say that "it is the movement of a highly developed English speech."[18] We recall Valery's reference to "the 'magnetism' of the voice."[19]

The success of Eliot's verse line does not mean that it is the only line which is available to the modern verse dramatist. Even the clanging couplets of *Happy as Larry* are valid for that special case of "planned incongruity." But Eliot has shown in *The Confidential Clerk* that a line of three stresses, rhetorically determined, is suitable for a verse play which takes its bearings from modern habits of speech. It would be foolish to stake a higher claim. An expressionist or a "folksy" verse play would probably have little use for Eliot's verse line. With this reservation in mind we would agree, however, with Professor Dobrée that the verse of *The Confidential Clerk* is "beautiful stage speech," and perhaps also "the most perfect theatre measure since Congreve."[20]

But there is a difficulty. Many students of Eliot's later plays are disappointed because—or so I suppose—the verse does not sound at all like that of Elizabethan drama. And that is still, for most of us, the only conceivable "way" for an English poet to write in the theatre. But we are wrong: there are other ways.

---

remarkable book by Mr. Noel Stock. See his essay "Some Notes on Old Scots and Melodic Line in Verse," *Shenandoah*, Vol. VI, 2, Spring 1955, p. 28.

[18] J. G. Southworth, *Verses of Cadence*, Oxford, Blackwell, 1954, p. 91.
[19] *supra*, footnote 10, p. 541.
[20] *"The Confidential Clerk," Sewanee Review*, Vol. LXII, 1954, p. 127.

Indeed the issue cannot be restricted to the theatre. Hugh Kenner has argued very persuasively[21] that whereas the modern English poet has at hand a language rich in "majestic imprecision and incantation," a language from the magnetic field of Shakespeare and the Elizabethan dramatists, the modern American poet— a poet like William Carlos Williams or Marianne Moore—owns a younger language, with expressive resources going back no farther than Jefferson, a language which is not haunted by Shakespeare or Donne. Or, as in Pound's case, a language which takes its foreign extensions directly, not refracted through Shakespeare and Marlowe. This gives no scope for jeering: it is unnecessary as well as ungracious to claim that one language is "better" than the other. And there are several modern American poems to which the distinction does not apply: John Berryman's *Homage to Mistress Bradstreet*, for instance, manoeuvres itself, through Hopkins, into configurations "English" rather than "American." But it is still a valid generalization that those modern American poets who have acknowledged their complex fate as Americans tend to use the language in ways which seem wilfully thin to many English readers. Such readers expect their poets to use a language freighted with Latin, with Shakespeare, with Seneca, with Italian; but the American poet would feel embarrassed, like a tourist, if he were to try for such effects. Besides, he has a virile language of his own.

Suppose we concede the point, and then look again at Eliot's development in his plays. Is it not clear that, deliberately or not, Eliot has been developing his language, since *The Cocktail Party*, on "American" rather than on "English" lines? These plays do not use the language as a sounding-board to signal news in depth: they use it as a means of transport, to get from one point to another, swiftly and with a certain winning grace. Eliot has been sensitive to this use of language for many years now: this is shown in his taste for the poems of Marianne Moore, though in praising those poems he was not then pre-

[21] "Words in the Dark," *Essays by Divers Hands*, Royal Society of Literature, n.s., Vol. XXIX, Oxford University Press, 1958, pp. 113-23.

pared to drive his preferences very hard. But he recognised that Miss Moore's way of using the language was a force which helped to maintain the strength and subtlety of speech, helped to preserve the quality of feeling in our time. That Eliot attributed to Miss Moore a high place in this crucial endeavour is evidence we cannot ignore. It is also relevant that he praised her for saturating her mind in the perfections of prose, "in its precision rather than its purple."[22] There have been few such poets, and we have perhaps been sluggish in responding to them.

We need not press the point. But it explains why an Empsonian search for buried treasure will find far more nuggets in *Sweeney Agonistes* than in *The Confidential Clerk*; and it is a more accurate explanation than the common assertion that the later play is simply impoverished. The same situation arises also in reading the *Cantos* and *Paterson*: surely the most devoted Empsonian must feel that for these poems his way of reading is off the point. The "genius" of the language in these poems reveals itself in lithe transitions, clean surfaces, the brisk direction of energy from point to point, rather than in tentacular roots or thrilling auras of imprecision. It would be a gracious accomplishment if we could respond fittingly to the exertions of both languages. If we can't, if we remain inert in the face of *Paterson I* or Miss Moore's *Pangolin*, we are likely to miss similar effects in *The Confidential Clerk*.

[22] Introduction *to Selected Poems of Marianne Moore*, Faber and Faber, 1935, p. 7.

# CHAPTER ELEVEN. CHRISTOPHER FRY'S
# THEATRE OF WORDS

THAT Christopher Fry has acquired some reputation as a dramatist on the strength of such plays as *Venus Observed* and *The
Lady's Not for Burning* is one of the more disquieting facts
about the contemporary theater. We had assumed that Marius
Bewley's penetrating account of Mr. Fry's plays up to *A Sleep of
Prisoners* (1951)[1] would have settled the "climate" of any
future study. Not so, however. In the same year Derek Stanford
published an elaborate "appreciation" of Mr. Fry's work and, in
1954, followed up with a second work of similar intent.[2] Robert
Gittings, while preparing a book on Keats, described Mr. Fry as
"an original major poetic talent."[3] Confronted with these facts
we may reasonably propose to bring forward more evidence. To
give Mr. Fry his due we propose to give particular attention to
his best play, *The Dark is Light Enough* (1954).

Mr. Fry's pronouncements on poetry, reality, and verse drama
have been unsatisfactory. His most representative statement is
that "what we *call* reality is a false god, the dull eye of custom."[4]
The echo from Wordsworth is interesting, but it leads to the
dubious equation of Prose with Verisimilitude, and of Poetry
with Truth. There is no end to the prose possibilities, Mr. Fry
says, to the expression of this actual appearance of life: "And
if you accept my proposition that reality is altogether different
from our stale view of it, we can say that poetry is the language
of reality." The argument is charmingly simple: appearance,
reality; actual, real; fact, miracle; prose, poetry. The same conception operates again in Mr. Fry's discussion of *The Lady's*

---

[1] "The Verse of Christopher Fry," *Scrutiny*, June 1951.
[2] *Christopher Fry: An Appreciation*, Peter Nevill, 1951; *Christopher
Fry*, Longmans, Green and Co., 1954.
[3] "Christopher Fry: A Rejoinder," *World Review*, July 1952, p. 57.
[4] "Why Verse?" *World Theatre*, Vol. IV, 4, Autumn 1955, p. 52. Also
"Poetry in the Theatre," *Saturday Review of Literature*, 21 March 1953,
p. 18.

*Not for Burning*. He set out, he declared, to write a play that
would be first cousin to an artificial comedy. But he could see
no reason, writing such a comedy, why he should not treat of
the world as he saw it, a world in which "we are all poised on
the edge of eternity," a world which has "deep and shadows of
mystery," in which God is "anything but a sleeping partner."
Why, Mr. Fry asks, should I use poetry instead of plain prose?
Answer: "Well, if we have to be born into a world as wildly
unprosaic as this one is, what else can be done, if we mean to
be realistic?"[5] The tone is hearty but evasive; the proposed insight has a characteristic way of slipping through one's fingers.
But the most revealing factor is the stark opposition between
"poetry" and "plain prose." We are back again with the
Georgian verse dramatists, with Phillips, Flecker, and Bottomley, as if *Sweeney Agonistes*, the *Pisan Cantos*, and Yeats's
Crazy Jane poems were still unwritten.

Mr. Fry's theory leads to his practice, to a passage like this
from *The Lady's Not for Burning* (the speaker is Jennet):

> Twilight, double, treble, in and out!
> If I try to find my way I bark my brains
> On shadows sharp as rocks where half a day
> Ago was a wild soft world, a world of warm
> Straw, whispering every now and then
> With rats, but possible, possible, not this,
> This where I'm lost. The morning came, and left
> The sunlight on my step like any normal
> Tradesman . . .[6]

Of this one may say, as L. C. Knights has said of Restoration
wit, that the verbal pattern is quite unrelated to an individual
mode of perceiving, that the words "have an air of preening
themselves on their acute discriminations."[7] But there is an
essential difference. Much of Restoration wit, unrelated as it is

---

[5] *World Review*, June 1949, p. 18.
[6] Oxford University Press, 1949, pp. 49-50.
[7] *Explorations*, Chatto and Windus, 1946, pp. 136, 145.

to genuine modes of perception, is related at least to patterns of standardised superficiality, in speech and manners, which were certainly potential and probably actual in the typical theatre-audience of the period. Mr. Fry can make no such claim. He has not even as much of a framework of values and speech as, say, Firbank had, or Beerbohm, who could point to *something* at large in contemporary society to which their mannered writings could be referred. Mr. Fry's comedies up to *The Dark is Light Enough* can point to nothing apart from their tenuous and precious selves: that is why their style is, pervadingly, self-regarding. In the passage quoted Mr. Fry handles the words as if they were specially favoured exhibits from a rarefied vocabulary, which he need only place in a pretty position to engender "style." We have learned from poems like W. R. Rodgers' *Europa* that the English language if merely given its head produces "style" of this quality.

The real defect in Mr. Fry's language in the early plays is that it is so determined to be distinctive that it cannot accommodate its revelations or its jokes. In *The Firstborn* Moses visits his sister Miriam, who says

> I am very well; I have nothing to offer you
> To drink . . .

and then

> You will find it very tiresome after five or six minutes.
> I repeat myself unendurably, like the Creation.

The simile is Mr. Fry's, not Miriam's, an increment of superficial insight which would be culpable even if it were not superficial, forced on us because of Mr. Fry's indiscriminate expense of language. What suffers here and elsewhere in Mr. Fry's early plays is the integrity of the drama as drama. In those plays the wanton prancing of words reveals in Mr. Fry not only poor economy but a grave lack of those motives which urge a writer to conserve language. We have in mind discrimination, discipline, the ideas of order and decorum, a sense of the relation between a writer's responsibility to words and his responsibility to things; or, in a wider context, the urge to find relationships, thence order, thence value, in experience. Indeed, the main difficulty in dealing with Mr. Fry's early plays is that one often has the feeling that as dramatist he has little to say and therefore little to take seriously. If this is even partly true, to accuse him of verbal flippancy is to point to a really fundamental triviality.

Mr. Fry assumes that in exploring and recreating life in terms of the theatre "we should use language as fully charged and as pliant as we can make it." "Fully charged" is ambiguous, tricky ground for discussion. Perhaps it would be more profitable to examine its application in a few passages from *Venus Observed*. First, a passage about Perpetua's homecoming:

DUKE: Our stability is a matter
    For surprise.
REEDBECK: I feel the terrible truth of that.
    Even now, for example, when I see my Perpetua
    Sitting like a girl on a swing on an Easter Monday
    Under a Wedgwood sky, I can feel my heart—
PERPETUA: That's just what it's like, a girl on a swing.
REEDBECK:                    My heart
    Knocking most anxiously against the future,
    As though afraid to be alone with the present time:
    Ready, really, for almost any disaster
    Rather than this unsteady tight-rope of joy
    I'm walking on now.[8]

Later in the play Hilda describes her husband:

    . . . Once he had worn away the sheen
    Of his quite becoming boyhood, which made me fancy him,
    There was nothing to be seen in Roderic
    For mile after mile after mile, except
    A few sheeplike thoughts nibbling through the pages
    Of a shiny weekly, any number of dead pheasants,

[8] Oxford University Press, 1950, p. 27.

Partridges, pigeons, jays, and hares,
An occasional signpost of extreme prejudice
Marked "No Thoroughfare," and the flat horizon
Which is not so much an horizon
As a straight ruled line beyond which one doesn't look.

Here one admires the perseverance with which Mr. Fry has driven the "landscape" metaphor, and the lines are amusing. In context, however, one feels that these words have little to do with Hilda; that if she finds her husband petty she does not do so in these verbal terms. The neat verbal pattern, amusing in itself, is autonomous, bearing only a nominal relation to the speaker's feeling. It follows, then, that the feeling itself remains largely inarticulate; we have to guess its precise nature, convinced that the words are to a large extent misleading.

Now the final passage. Rosabel has burnt down the Duke's observatory:

DUKE: Your fire was too small, Rosabel, though enough
    To singe my butler into ecstasy,
    And smoke tears into eyes unaccustomed to them,
    Mine, I mean. So much I delighted in
    Is now all of ash, like a dove's breast feathers
    Drifting dismally about the garden.
ROSABEL: Time and I both know how to bring
    Good things to a bad end, all
    In the course of love. No wonder
    "God be with you" has become "Good-bye,"
    And every day that wishes our welfare says
    Farewell. To-night will go past, as a swan
    Will pass like a recurring dream
    On the light sleep of the lake,
    And I shall be smoothed away in the wake of the swan;
    But I can never return what I've lost you, or lose
    What I gave, though the long steadiness of time
    May long to make us well.

*184*

This is very good. Its languid, *fin de siècle* tone defines the mood precisely, and the transition from the brittle wit of the Duke's first words to the later wistfulness is beautifully managed. But look at the lines together with the two passages just quoted: all the characters talk alike, their verbal poses are predictable. On the one hand the organisation of the play asks us to interest ourselves in the behaviour of a number of characters (a duke, his son, his agent, his former mistresses) in certain situations; the terms of the play suggest that "character" or "personality" are important. But character-differentiation is the very thing that is blunted by the language of the play. The differences between the various characters are practically eliminated by the verbal postures which they share. Self-conscious metaphor is but the most recurrent of these, and is indeed a temptation which Mr. Fry in his early plays was quite unable to resist.

The assumptions on which these strictures are based are, first, that the language of a play should be answerable to the play's decorum, which is closely related to its structure. Second, that if the language becomes autonomous at any point the decorum of the play should be such as to support this autonomy for a special dramatic purpose. For example, the decorum of *Troilus and Cressida* is amenable to certain purely rhetorical speeches by Achilles which are temporarily unattached to "character."[9] Finally, that if we can complain of a dramatist, as Virginia Woolf complained of Arnold Bennett, that he is trying to make us imagine for him, the dramatist is to that extent at fault.

Is it possible, then, to justify the language of *The Lady's Not for Burning, A Phoenix Too Frequent*, and *Venus Observed*? The only enthusiastic study of these plays which deserves to be taken seriously is William Arrowsmith's *Notes on English Verse Drama*. But why does this fine critic endorse the absurd comparison of Mr. Fry's style with that of Marlowe? There is, he maintains, the same verbal impatience, the laddering of effects

[9] See William Empson, *Some Versions of Pastoral*, Chatto and Windus, second impression, 1950, p. 37ff.

toward an overall tonal roof, and the exuberance and extravagance of the autonomous language which is only an extension of the theme itself. It is this very identity of language and theme in Mr. Fry's three early comedies, he argues, which has misled the critics, made them doubt the existence of a controlling theme or attitude, and then proceed to pillory Mr. Fry for mere verbal vanity.[10] Mr. Fry's theme and attitude, however, are clear enough. Anyone can see that in these plays Life-as-Norm is shamed in the eyes of Life-as-Miracle. The theme is potentially comic, but for reasons which we shall examine Mr. Fry slips too easily on his theme into mere whimsy. He constantly throws ironical glances at "actuality," but his own attitudes are carefully protected from similar shocks. His basic procedure is to place a spokesman in the centre of a play and let him proclaim that life is an enormous miracle. Thus the Chaplain in *The Lady's Not for Burning*:

> When I think of myself
> I can scarcely believe my senses. But there it is,
> All my friends tell me I actually exist
> And by an act of faith I have come to believe them.

It is "a good thing" to be reminded that life is joyous, fresh, even miraculous, and Mr. Fry's attitudes retain a certain interest except when they lapse into spurious joviality. But having recognised these attitudes we are entitled to argue that the pressure toward exuberance in Mr. Fry's "controlling theme" does not justify the arrangement by which all his characters speak exuberantly, extravagantly, cleverly. In *Venus Observed* Bates, the Duke's footman, rebukes his colleague Reddleman:

> I'd just like to know who give him permission
> To go measuring my soul? I never done.
> I've got it nicely laid away: spotless,
> Wiv lavender.

The defect here, as throughout the plays up to *A Sleep of Prisoners*, is the disrelation between the language and the over-all

10 *Hudson Review*, Vol. III, 1950, p. 208.

theme, on the one hand, and, on the other, the chosen decorum of the play. Instead of the genuine rhetoric of decorum we find the spurious rhetoric of "style."

The word is ambiguous. The author of *The Lady's Not for Burning* seems to think of style in terms of such a writer as Doughty, and he would probably feel that some less hallowed word is appropriate to Swift, even in *A Tale of a Tub*. What Mr. Fry seems particularly to admire is *copia*, but this abundance not only available when needed but continuously pouring into the writing: a grand stylistic pose become habitual. But this issue, relatively straightforward in the case of narrative or expository prose, is tricky in the case of drama, for here the stylistic requirements go very deeply into the decorum of genre. The stylistic "unity" in *Macbeth* is not a mode of speech imposed on the play, or spread over its structure, but unity coming up from between the individual and constantly changing speech-acts of the characters. It is an over-all unity emerging from these responses, not dominating them. There is no unity of this kind in Mr. Fry's early comedies. Instead, one feels in these plays that speeches are determined by the chance of introducing clever remarks rather than by the requirements of the play at that point.

Mr. Fry has described *The Dark is Light Enough* as a "winter comedy." Like *The Devil's Disciple* it is akin to romantic melodrama. The most welcome feature of the play is that it goes a great distance toward the elimination of the verbal eccentricities which impaired the earlier comedies. Indeed there is some evidence here that Mr. Fry's writing may eventually become quite frugal. If the play still misses success it does so because of certain defects arising simultaneously from its structure and from the attitudes which it embodies.

A glance at the language. The following passage shows Mr. Fry's recent writing at its best. Its virtues are at least as important as its defects. The virtues are new: the defects are ingrained in Mr. Fry's style and are likely to persist. The lines are

*187*

spoken by the Countess, at a point when, as Mr. Fry has remarked, the situation has reduced everyone to silence:

> How shall we manage, with time at a standstill?
> We can't go back to where nothing has been said;
> And no heart is served, caught in a moment
> Which has frozen. Since no words will set us free—
> Not at least now, until we can persuade
> Our thought to move—
> Music would unground us best
> As a tide in the dark comes to boats at anchor
> And they begin to dance. My father told me
> How he went late one night, a night
> Of some Hungarian anxiety,
> To the Golden Bull at Buda, and there he found
> The President of your House of Deputies
> Alone and dancing in his shirtsleeves
> To the music of the band, himself
> Put far away, bewitched completely
> By the dance's custom; and so it went on,
> While my father drank and talked with friends,
> Three or four hours without a pause:
> This weighty man of seventy, whose whole
> Recognition of the world about him
> During those hours, was when occasionally
> He turned his eyes to the gypsy leader
> And the music changed, out of a comprehension
> As wordless as the music.
> It was dancing that came up out of the earth
> To take the old man's part against anxiety.[11]

It is distinguished; every detail is sanctioned by character and
situation. The delicate pastoral-elegiac tone answers not only
to the internal requirements of the play but to the audience's
desires at that point. The words themselves are the nearest
equivalent of the liberating, comprehensive gesture of spirit

[11] Oxford University Press, 1954.

which is their motive. Indeed, the writing shows no trace of that waste of words in the early comedies which would remind one of *Look Homeward, Angel* except that it lacks Wolfe's genuine energy. In Wolfe we respond to the energy even when the waste is appalling. Mr. Fry's moments of waste in the early plays were, characteristically, static. His exhibitionist gestures involved motion but no action.

To think of other writers in association with Mr. Fry is to realise that his peculiar weakness, even in *The Dark is Light Enough*, is that he writes as if the lessons of Stendhal, Flaubert, Henry James, Eliot, and Ford had eluded him, as if nothing of significance had happened in European literature between Southey and J. C. Squire. Mr. Fry's language has a soft centre, even where Flaubertian bone is urgently required. Its typical effect is not to concentrate feeling and thinking into the word, but to diffuse these activities over a broad verbal area. Indeed there are few writers and fewer dramatists who yield so readily to the lyric temptation. Where ideas are involved Mr. Fry uses them to make verbal show-cases, rather than, like Shaw, to start dialectical battles. Frequently, Mr. Fry's language seems perversely designed to smooth away any conflict inherent in the situation. There is a moment in *The Dark is Light Enough* in which the play cries out for tension of some kind, and a possible source of such tension is in sight. Janik asks:

> Then you have no thought for the downtrodden men,
> The overlong injustice, madam?

The Countess, ever perfect, answers:

> Not
> As they are downtrodden, but as they are men
> I think of them, as they should think of those
> Who oppress them. We gain so little by the change
> When the downtrodden in their turn tread down.
> But then, deserters all, we should all change sides,
> I dare say; and that would be the proper behaviour
> For a changeable world, and no more tiring

Than to go to the extraordinary lengths
Which men will go to, to be identical
Each day . . .

Thence to the recollection of time past:

You teach me to let the world go, Colonel.
I've known this house so long,
Loved it so well
The hours, as they came and went, were my own people.
In obedience, time never failed me, as though
The keys of the year were on my chatelaine.

Finally:

You see how well you have done
To remind me my only privilege
Was to go about a vanishing garden.

Here the conflict of values, from which a genuine dramatic sequence might have emerged, is introduced merely to support yet another lyric-elegiac song. Drama escapes into lyric via courtesy and reminiscence. This characteristic sequence from the potentially dynamic to the static would seem inevitable in view of Mr. Fry's ideas of poetry and of drama.

The Countess is, of course, the outstanding exhibit in *The Dark is Light Enough*, a ceremonial and pacifist version of Aunt Agatha in *The Family Reunion*. Everyone has seen that from her first charming entry in the play she is quite perfect and therefore incapable of development: a beautiful and touching *dea ex machina* making lives by "divine non-interference." Certainly she is the most attractive and substantial pacifist in the modern theatre, but this fact conceals the most serious flaw in the structure of the play. In *The Dark is Light Enough* the Aristotelian tables are overturned: the movement of the play is designed primarily to illustrate the Countess's moral beauty; the fable is a mere vehicle for the exhibition of her character. Hence the play, so interesting to read, is lifeless even in a competent performance: it lies prone on the stage and in the remembering mind. The character of the Countess is there, palpable, fully formed, and we can do nothing but watch the portrait, admire its dispassionate charm, and witness its self-expression in altering the character of Richard Gettner. One comes away from a performance of the play wondering why it benefits so little from performance, and realising that the proper genre for this material and for Mr. Fry's attitude to it is the lyric short-story or nouvelle. Fundamentally, what Mr. Fry lacks is a histrionic sense, a feeling for those actions which demand enactment, not description, and which will prove intractable if deprived of the theatre.

We mentioned the relation between *The Dark is Light Enough* and romantic melodrama, a relation of character and incident. But the tone of the play is somewhat different. It is significant that Mr. Fry's progression, evident in *The Dark is Light Enough*, toward a more disciplined and frugal style is accompanied by a developing tone which is more akin to "comédie larmoyante" than to any other dramatic genre. The play is comedy in the sense that it is designed "not to condemn evil, but to ridicule a lack of self-knowledge":[12] war is presented not as an evil but as the symbol of our defective sense of Being. The tone of the play, however—what emerges from the languid skirmishing of values, pacifist and belligerent—is strikingly *larmoyant*. The local witticisms cannot alter Mr. Fry's sentimental direction.

Indeed the "wit" in this play is subordinate at all times to the sentimentality. Toward the end Richard asks the Countess:

> And I'm the cause
> Of this illness, I suppose.

She answers:

> The arithmetic
> Of cause and effect I've never understood.
> How many beans make five is an immense

[12] Northrop Frye, "The Argument of Comedy," *English Institute Essays*, 1948, edited by D. A. Robertson Jr., Columbia University Press, 1949, p. 61.

Question, depending on how many
Preliminary beans preceded them.

One is relieved that the reply is not lachrymose, but it merely
delays, without dispelling, the tender-pathetic tone which the
pacifist moral has inflicted on the entire play. We have in *The
Dark is Light Enough* an example of the tension (undramatic,
alas) between local "wit" and a deep impulse in the play to dissolve the whole situation in tender sighs. One had foreseen that
this winter-comedy would end with the Countess's quiet death.
Richard's last speech as he watches the dead Countess is but
the culmination of that *larmoyant* tone which dominates the
play:

You're dead, Rosmarin. Understand that.
What is there to stay for? You never showed
Any expectations of me when you were alive,
Why should you now?
This isn't how I meant that you should love me!

He closes the window and comes back to her and speaks curtly:

Very well, very well.

He stands beside her:

Be with me.

To conclude: Mr. Fry's language at present is such that whatever dramatic impact is latent in his invented situations has a reasonable chance of coming through. The words are no longer obstacles: in fact, they are acquiring a certain degree of transpar-
ence. On the other hand Mr. Fry seems to share the widespread
disbelief in the possibility of Aristotelian "action," and to take
the wrong way out by merely illustrating qualities in repose.
When these chosen qualities are humane, precarious, and pacifist, a heavily sentimental tone is unavoidable. It is very difficult
to say whether these factors are causes or effects of the slackness noticeable in Mr. Fry's histrionic sense. That they all go
together, however, suggests that his permanent contribution to
the theatre is likely to be slight. He is hardly as interesting as
William Inge.

# CHAPTER TWELVE. THE MOOD PLAY IN VERSE:
## STEVENS, EBERHART, AND MAC LEISH

WILLIAM BECKER has noted, with regret, that a new set of formal dramatic values is being established in the American theatre. The values are largely negative. They imply a reduction of the medium and not, for the most part, a reduction to fundamentals, but to a preoccupation with the most subsidiary and peripheral of dramatic values, the "mood." The mood play is the first really identifiable new genre to emerge within the last twenty years. It deserves study, even though it is unmistakably a sign of decadence.[1]

The mood play has not until now been commercially produced. It is clear, however, that such plays as Tennessee Williams's *The Glass Menagerie* and Horton Foote's *The Trip to Bountiful* are closely related to those verse plays, such as Wallace Stevens's *Three Travellers Watch a Sunrise*, which were published in *Poetry* in the Twenties and performed once or twice by the Provincetown Players. The essential differences between such verse plays and the recent mood play are that the recent examples are much longer, the verse has been replaced by sophisticated prose, and the number of characters has been increased.

*Three Travellers Watch a Sunrise*[2] brings together an Italian girl named Anna (whose lover has hanged himself), two Negroes, and three Chinese. Nothing happens; highly charged words are spoken. The Chinese, inevitably, contribute philosophical maxims; the Negroes, inevitably, remind us of human suffering. They all speak like the earliest poems of Mr. Stevens, the poet who had not yet written *The Rock*. In particular, the characters handle a symbolism of colour which is pretentious and naïve. At one point, for instance, the third Chinese, seeing the hanged man, says:

[1] William Becker, "The New American Play," *Hudson Review*, Vol. VI, 4, Winter 1954, p. 578.

[2] *Poetry*, July 1916, pp. 163-79.

Red is not only
The color of blood
Or                          (*indicating the body*)
Of a man's eyes
Or                          (*pointedly*)
Of a girl's . . .
Sunrise is multiplied
Like the earth on which it shines,
By the eyes that open on it,
Even dead eyes,
As red is multiplied by the leaves of the trees.

Here as elsewhere in *Three Travellers Watch a Sunrise* the grossly overworked symbolism bears only a minimal relation to dramatic action and depends for its justification solely on its effect in establishing a rarefied atmosphere or mood. It is perhaps harsh to emphasise Mr. Stevens's failure to appreciate in 1916 the factors which Mr. Eliot was just beginning to grasp in 1935: such as the difference between drama and lyric, the relation of speech to character, the difference between dramatic and other kinds of verse, and the fact that a play does not become poetic by merely absolving itself from the restrictions of realism. *Three Travellers Watch a Sunrise* may be "explained" as the result of Mr. Stevens's inordinately pious reading of Yeats's poems up to *The Green Helmet*. In itself it exhibits to a striking degree the preciosity of the "poetic" drama of the Twenties.[3]

Richard Eberhart's *The Apparition*[4] is a mood play of stronger texture than *Three Travellers Watch a Sunrise*. The following passage is representative:

JOHN: What did you come in here for?
Didn't you think it would be dangerous?

[3] For a more sympathetic account of this play see William Van O'Connor, *The Shaping Spirit: A Study of Wallace Stevens*, Chicago, Henry Regnery, 1950, p. 34ff.
[4] *Poetry*, March 1951, pp. 311-21. The play was performed in Cambridge, Mass., in February 1951.

GIRL: Who cares for danger? Do you think I am a fool?
I'm bored. I've been bored since eight o'clock.
I was at a party downstairs in the diningroom.
My boy friend bores me to death. I can't escape him.
He's always taking me out to dinners and dancing.
JOHN: Would you like a little more to drink?
GIRL: Well, maybe.
JOHN:                  Take it easy, now, take it easy.
GIRL: I just couldn't stand it another minute.
I said to myself, I'm going to take the elevator
And go to the thirteenth floor. Then I'll get out,
Turn to the right, walk down three rooms,
Knock on the door three times, and see what happens.

At least the situation is credible. Also, in establishing the mood of nervous frustration, the dramatist has contrived that the flat, jerky rhythms of the dialogue function toward that end. A significant defect in the writing, clearly revealed by contrast with *Sweeney Agonistes*, is that the dramatist arranges to have the girl *talk about* her boredom rather than exhibit it in act and speech. Nevertheless, *The Apparition* is an unpretentious little play which, on the whole, justifies itself.

The third example of a mood play in verse which we would examine is Archibald MacLeish's *This Music Crept By Me On the Water*.[5] The scene is the Antilles: a garden above the sea, evening, palm trees, an elegant house owned by wealthy Americans. The mood is a special kind of exaltation, fulfilled when Peter and Elizabeth, stirred by a particularly beautiful moment on the island, communicate to each other a vision of happiness. The epiphany is spoiled and the play ends.

It is a simple play, based on the dubious idea that "the blinding instant" is of supreme importance. The play moves from Peter's

> All my life I've lived tomorrow
> Waiting for my life to come:

[5] First published in *Botteghe Oscure*, Vol. XI, 1953, then by Harvard University Press, 1954.

Promises to come true tomorrow,
Journeys to begin tomorrow,
Mornings in the sun tomorrow,
Books read, words written,
All tomorrow. Cities visited,
Even this fever of the sleepless heart
Slept away tomorrow . . . all of it. . . .

to Elizabeth's

Happiness was always now.
Happiness is real—the only
Real reality that any of us
Ever have glimpses of. The rest—
The hurt, the misery,—all vanishes.
Only the blinding instant left us.

Elizabeth is the heroine of the play and of Mr. MacLeish's entire world. Her special powers are not those of action or of conscience and consciousness, as in Eliot's Harry and Celia. Rather, she is the one who *feels*, who listens to the sea and the night, often out of reach of human discourse. She loves the island and its people. Above all, she responds instinctively to the "quality" of the here-and-now:

ELIZABETH: Not the least like natives, Oliver.
  *They* have no time to lose. They live
  Now. Not late, not soon, but now.
  They can't lose now. They live there.
OLIVER:                               Only the
  Trees have found that fabulous country.
ELIZABETH: Every paradise is laid in it.
  Here and now must meet each other
  Like the two impossible rivers joining
  Just where Jerusalem begins
  No matter which Jerusalem.
OLIVER: The unattainable, unvisited now
  That's never here when we are.

*196*

ELIZABETH:                    No!

(*violently*)

    Now and here together in one gulp

    To burn the heart out with its happiness!

CHUCK: Elizabeth!

ELIZABETH:                    I'm sorry,

OLIVER:                        Why be sorry?

    Only those who've been there know it.

ALICE: And most of them won't tell.

ELIZABETH:                    Sorry

    Because I've never been there, then.

OLIVER: I wish your guests were now . . . *and* here.

    Are you quite sure you asked them, darling?

This is finely managed. Elizabeth's emotional climax grows from the trivial conversation which precedes it and moves down again to the commonplace by way of Oliver's quibble. Here, for once, when the purple passage comes, we are not required to dissolve the connexions with situation and character which the dialogue up to this point has established. Besides, the thing is purple not only to us (outside the play) but to Chuck and the others (inside). The passage compels us to make room, therefore, in our conception of Elizabeth, for the passionate and the explosive. This is proper enough. In *The Family Reunion*, as we have seen, some speeches issue in highly charged statements for which no preparation has been made. As a result it is impossible to fit them into any coherent idea of the speaker. At such points the play temporarily stops, the speaker ceases to exist, and we are left listening to a fragment of unattached poetry. Pure Poetry, if anything.

This happens occasionally in *This Music Crept By Me on the Water*. Two passages present themselves, both spoken by Oliver, the Englishman anxious for his dinner. When Chuck says

    What Elizabeth means—the books latched onto them,
    Rousseau's Noble Savage was an Arawak . . .

Oliver answers:

Ah, that explains it all! Columbus,
Seeing those laughing, splashing Indians
Naked as jays and beautiful as children
Knew at once what latitudes he sailed in.
The place was Paradise! That settled it!
Had he no eyes at all for reefs
Or shark fins or the green volcanoes
Lurking in this smile of trees?

This is a breach of decorum, not because "literary" phrases
are automatically suspect, but because nothing in the preceding
dialogue has given us even a hint that Oliver is the kind of person who might speak of "this smile of trees": Oliver, up to this
point the dry, realistic Englishmen. Mr. MacLeish's uncertainty in this regard has serious effects on the play. In Oliver's
case it frustrates the impact of such a passage as the following:

OLIVER: People who all their lives have lived
　　Pursuing happiness, pursuing something
　　More or farther off or brighter?
　　In Paradise there's nothing more.
　　Everything that will be, is.
ELIZABETH: Is, and is everything!
OLIVER: 　　　　　　　　　　　They'd go mad.
　　We all would—all of us. We're all the same:
　　We live by what's still left to live for:
　　Something in another life,
　　Another love, another country,
　　Even in another world,
　　At least some other day. In Paradise
　　Everything is here, is this:
　　The ordinary heart can't bear it.
　　Suffering, yes: suffering we endure.
　　But happiness! Happiness is long ago
　　Or far away or not yet come to.
　　Only a child or those like children,
　　Meeting happiness in a summer's door

*198*

Can take it by the hand and run with it.
The rest walk past it and remember.

Most of this passage is fine dramatic verse, verse which traces
the developing pattern of the character. For example, in

Suffering, yes: suffering we endure
But happiness! Happiness is long ago
Or far away or . . .

we hear a distinct voice, with individual emphasis. On the other
hand, the lines

Meeting happiness in a summer's door
Can 'take it by the hand and run with it.

are another point at which the play stops. The phrase "in a summer's door" is not uninteresting, but the mode in which it
operates is not that of dramatic verse. When we hear the phrase
spoken by Oliver we may enjoy it in itself as interesting *diction*
but we cannot believe that Oliver would have used it.

In this connexion we would for the moment oversimplify by
arguing that if a character in a play performs an act, this act,
however surprising at that point, should be felt to be consistent
with whatever "quality" has already been established for the
agent. Whatever is explicit should be felt as consonant with an
implicit quality in the agent: the actual, as consonant with the
inherently potential. This does not do away with surprise. We
may apprehend a set of qualities in an agent without being able
to anticipate the precise act by which he will "materialise" these
qualities in a particular situation. But when this act has been
performed we should be able to respond to its fitness. The
ventriloquism of "in a summer's door" disturbs the continuity
and therefore the coherence of the play.

Perhaps the principle involved may be illustrated by comparing a phrase in Dylan Thomas's poem *Love in the Asylum*:

A stranger has come
To share my room in the house not right in the head,

*199*

## STEVENS, EBERHART, MACLEISH

### A girl mad as birds

Bolting the night of the door with her arm her plume . . .[6]

In itself the phrase "Bolting the night of the door" is an interesting use of language, but it involves a breach of decorum just as serious as that of "in a summer's door." The reason is that a quasi-dramatic situation is necessarily established as soon as the speaker, addressing his imagined reader, says "A stranger has come / To share my room. . . ." The "I" who speaks the opening words in the poem is from that moment a putative dramatic character, and his "acts" must therefore be sanctioned just as rigorously as those of an agent in a play. Nothing in the "quality" of the speaker sanctions the act by which he uses the phrase "Bolting the night of the door." *This Music Crept By Me on the Water* is seriously impaired by such gestures on the part of the poet. It is unnecessary to list them; they generally take the form of strained metaphor. A case in point is Peter's

> We cling so to the skirts of suffering
> Like children to their mothers . . .

We have indicated that the desired mood in *This Music Crept By Me on the Water* is exaltation. This mood, in varying degrees of intensity, affects nine of the characters in the play. The tenth is Harry Keogh. One part of Keogh's function is to express, and thence to liberate, our unconscious antagonism to the hot-house exaltation of such characters as Elizabeth and Peter. In the following passage, for example, in which Helen Halsey talks about her husband as he stares at the moon:

HELEN: I wish he'd looked at me like that:
    Just once.
SALLY:               Like what?
HELEN:                        Oh, like a man . . .
    Who sees the whole of his desire.

[6] Dylan Thomas, *Collected Poems 1934-1952*, Dent, 1952, p. 108.

HALSEY: You don't know what you're saying, Helen.
HELEN: A man who saw his whole desire,
   Near as the world was in that moon,
   Might get it.
OLIVER: Yes. And where would he be?
ELIZABETH: Here.
OLIVER: Or his desire?
ELIZABETH: Here.
KEOGH: They're tight as mountain ticks, the lot of them.

Up to a point this is, of course, quasi-comic relief. But beyond that point Keogh's function in this situation is to liberate the ironic element in the audience's response to the preceding sequence. But the liberation is allowed, rhetorically, only "under controlled conditions," since Keogh, obviously a barbarian, in expressing *our* feelings at this point, forces us to recognise (shamefacedly) the "barbarous" ingredient in our response to the play. Or he forces us to regard such ironic resistance as in this instance barbarous. The net effect is that we dissociate ourselves from this motive, yield it up, reinstating ourselves on the side of Mr. MacLeish's angels. Similarly in *Hamlet* Shakespeare brings into the open ("freely," it seems) the audience's possible boredom with the Player's passionate speech about Pyrrhus, by having Polonius express *his* boredom. But again the sequence is "controlled": Polonius is wittily tripped up by Hamlet. Laughing *with* Hamlet at the boorish Polonius, we change sides, dissociating ourselves from Polonius and from his complaint. We are now "cathartically" happy to continue, all irony, for the time being, spent.

Returning: Keogh is type of the insensitive man, hearty and crude. One of the most important reasons for his presence in the play is that he represents the completely extrovert, unfeeling way of life which is rejected so violently by Elizabeth and Peter in their moment of epiphany. In loud opposition to such epiphanies

PETER: Why does it take so long to know?
   We tell our miserable creeping hearts
   Men aren't made for happiness.
ELIZABETH:                                    The world is.
PETER: I never knew it till tonight.
ELIZABETH: This world is. And we two in it.
PETER: Answerable to the loveliness of our lives:
   To nothing else.
ELIZABETH: To nothing else . . .
stand Keogh's
         Watching these goddam goofy idiots
         Gawk by the water while the moon
         Came up and gawked at them, for Chri' sake!
and again
         The beauty of the night!
         Imagine that! At his age! Stuck there
         Staring at the island in the moon
         As though he'd never seen it till that moment!

Readers of Mr. MacLeish's poems will anticipate that Keogh
is firmly rejected, not only by Elizabeth and Peter, but by the
rhetorical bias of the play. Elizabeth is the heroine, Keogh the
vulgar oaf. The indications are unmistakable. Keogh talks like
Harry Brock in *Born Yesterday*, shows no interest in the moon,
is concerned only with the next drink and a quiet, ordinary life.
Indeed, generically, he is, like Yeats's Aibric, the "merely"
rational man whom romantic poets conspire to repudiate.
Elizabeth, on the other hand, is exactly the kind of person whom
Mr. MacLeish envisages as the reader of his poems. She trusts
in the sun on the leaves, her life quickens at the touch of the
wind, her senses are constantly tingling. Reed Whittemore has
noted that the images to which Mr. MacLeish is most attracted,
and from which he expects the richest fruits, are images from
nature: the moon, trees, leaves, stars, wind, surf, sunlight, and
earth. The themes which pervade all the phases of his poetry
are essentially pastoral, implying that life is richest and best in

its elemental forms.[7] *This Music Crept By Me on the Water* is an act of reverence toward such forms. The island, the moon, the wind, the "here" and the "now," Happiness, "the blinding instant," Elizabeth and Peter, are its determining agents. The pervading mood of the play arises from those circumstances in which a person of utmost sensitivity feels the impact of elemental forms. The Enemy, extreme sophistication, lurks behind the veranda, ready to intrude on such moments, and eventually to destroy them.

There is no real motive in *This Music Crept By Me on the Water*. Instead, a mood of exaltation is established, to which most of the characters respond, one, however, continuing to remain insensitively uncommitted. The sensitive are blessed, the crude one is rejected, circumstances combine to thwart the sensitive, and life reverts to an inert and undistinguished norm. It is clear that the play is closely in touch with the pastoral impulse in Mr. MacLeish's poetry, and that the type of drama engendered by that mode is in this case strikingly naïve. Cleanth Brooks has indicated[8] the lack of dramatic tension in much of Mr. MacLeish's poetry and the effect of this on the early verse play *Panic*. Recognition of this defect may have urged Mr. MacLeish toward the mood play, but the defect remains just as serious in the new context. In *This Music Crept By Me on the Water* there is no sign of that poise, that ability to entertain discordant elements and judgments, which is as necessary in drama as in thought. The lack of this power accounts for the thinness of the drama and the *simpliste* nature of the rhetoric. It is surely possible to remain unimpressed by the moon, the wind, and tropical islands, as Harry Keogh's behaviour shows. It is also possible to be deeply stirred by these things and by what they symbolise, as Elizabeth is, and even to be changed permanently by their impact. Faced with these attitudes Mr. MacLeish merely rejects the one and exalts the other. His

[7] Reed Whittemore, "MacLeish and Democratic Pastoral," *Sewanee Review*, Vol. LXI, 1953, p. 702.

[8] Cleanth Brooks, *Modern Poetry and the Tradition*, London, Poetry London, 1948, p. 123.

ultimate judgments are reached too quickly and too easily. His poems and plays suggest that the ability to handle complex material or to create poetic or dramatic forms adequate to such a task is not one of his gifts.

The most successful parts of *This Music Crept By Me on the Water* are the single-line conversations:

ELIZABETH: No one can speak for Ann.
ALICE:                                         Not even
     Ann.
OLIVER (*to Alice*): You know her?
ALICE:                                         Yes, she's beautiful.
ELIZABETH: She's everything a woman should be.
ALICE: There's nothing Ann can't do . . .
OLIVER:                                         But? . .
ELIZABETH:                               Feel.
ALICE: Or know she feels at least.
ELIZABETH:                    Or show it.

One exults at the economy of this passage. (Ann is clearly not a pastoral heroine; Mr. MacLeish's goddesses are seldom competent but they always "feel.") The single-line conversation protects Mr. MacLeish from that kind of "style" which so often tempts him.

Our point of departure was William Becker's note on the mood play as a new and regrettable genre. Briefly, Mr. Becker objected to the mood play on the grounds that it as far as possible dispenses with plot, failing to appreciate its unique formal and expressive value; that it abstracts from the complete dramatic organism two functional elements—mood evocation and character portraiture—and pursues these elements for their own sakes. These arguments are persuasive and they are strengthened, in Mr. Becker's presentation, by association with Aristotle's *Poetics*: "But most important of all is the structure of the incidents. For Tragedy is an imitation, not of men, but of an action and of life, and life consists in action, and its end is a mode of action, not a quality."[9]

The plays by Wallace Stevens, Richard Eberhart, and Archibald MacLeish which we have discussed are open, in varying degrees, to all the objections proposed by an Aristotelian view of drama. In addition, they seem to work on the assumption that their "poetic" quality will be more readily visible by means of character and mood than by significant dramatic action. Perhaps the most serious charge which can be made against them, the most serious because it includes all the others, is that they do not stand to gain anything by theatrical performance. Each of them was written for performance, but none of them utilises the resources peculiar to the stage. None of them convinces us that it needs a theatre or that it achieves a degree or quality of expression beyond the reach of a poem or a novel. To be specific: *This Music Crept By Me on the Water* does not persuade us that it achieves a range of expression different in quality or degree from that of Katherine Mansfield's story *A Dill Pickle*. Indeed, a study of the three plays suggests that, whatever their individual and incidental merits, they set out to do something that could be done far more successfully by the techniques of fiction.

It has been suggested[10] that there are certain kinds of experience which drama is unable to handle: experiences so strictly internal that they could not be apprehended by the observer of one's behaviour, experiences which could not be adequately represented by any succession of visible acts. Experiences of this order, which issue not in public or external acts but in new states of an individual's sensibility, lend themselves to expression by lyric or by narrative prose but not by drama. It is possible to argue that the mood play (issuing, ultimately, from Maeterlinck) and the symposium play (from Plato) are

[9] Aristotle, *Poetics*, translated by S. H. Butcher, Macmillan, second edition, 1898, p. 27 (VI, 9ff.). Becker, *supra*, footnote 1, p. 587.

[10] John Crowe Ransom, "The Aesthetics of *Finnegans Wake*," *Kenyon Review*, Vol. I, 1939, pp. 424-28.

attempts to circumvent this limitation. Symposium plays, which consist of nothing but talk, arise not only from a desire to utilise the conflict latent in argument, but from the impulse to bring the most internal acts within the scope of drama. The first step, naturally, is to place those acts within the form and scene, the "semblance" of drama. Such plays rarely succeed in objectifying the innermost experiences. Even *In Good King Charles's Golden Days*, which is a distinguished example of the genre, succeeds only inasmuch as one is interested in listening to fine conversation; one does not feel that the conversations reveal experiences till then private or internal.

The assumption on which such plays are based is that experiences, however internal, may issue at least in speech. One thinks of the soliloquy. But the soliloquy is a convention by which an agent at certain crucial moments reveals the condition of his "psyche." The revelation is conceivable only because of what has preceded it. The idea on which the mood play is based is that experiences, when they have become extremely rarefied and internal, may be rendered only through "moods." The characteristic play in this genre selects a single quality of experience and thereafter seeks to render its equivalent in terms of character and "scene." It is like landscape-painting. Clearly, if one were to examine such a play in terms of act, agent, scene, agency, and purpose, one would find only two of these relevant, agent and scene.

The implications of the mood play are far-reaching and, as yet, imperfectly understood. Sir Herbert Read, for instance, in a recent examination of Eliot's *Poetry and Drama*, concluded that "the future may have in store for us a form of poetic drama that imitates not so much modes of action as states of sensibility."[11] The sensibility play and the mood play are identical, an attempt to make an extended lyric do the work of drama.

One must be careful at this point, however. We have already

[11] Herbert Read, *The True Voice of Feeling*, Faber and Faber, 1953, p. 150.

had cause to emphasise that there is more than one kind of drama. Since drama arose to provide a strong focus for the feelings of a community, it has developed in many directions. But if we hold in mind as many of these developments as we know and can grasp, we are justified in arguing that the drama which concerns itself with states of sensibility rather than with modes of action will merely transfer lyric poetry to the stage.

In this context, therefore, it is pleasant to find Mr. MacLeish, in his new play *J.B.*, virtually repudiating the aesthetic of the mood play, and returning to a version of drama ultimately Aristotelian, or at least to a kind of drama which endorses Aristotelian terms. *J.B.*, enacting the story of Job in modern conditions, is formally an heroic romance: which means, to begin with, that more resonant issues are involved than in *This Music Crept By Me on the Water*; also, that more of the basic expressive resources of drama are engaged. The new play invites description as the imitation of an action.

What, then, is imitated? Strictly speaking, as Francis Fergusson has argued,[12] Aristotle seems to use the word "praxis" to mean a movement of the will in the light of the mind: it is a "purpose" involving a high rational element. Dante uses the corresponding term "moto spiral" to mean something more inclusive, referring to all modes of the spirit's life, not only those determined by conscious purpose. Yet Dante's meaning moves graciously in an Aristotelian context. So does *J.B.*: J.B.'s fictive life, like Job's, is clarified by his determining motive, to assert the justice of God in the face of sensory evidence to the contrary. The propulsive force is Faith or Piety; the action of the play is a movement of J.B.'s will in this strong light. This is what is imitated: a determining force, a gesture giving shape and meaning to an entire life.

The plot—the sequence of events which, in its total unity, stands for the action—is drawn closely from the Book of Job. *J.B.* also exhibits something very like the "rhythm" of the plot of Job, its habit of moving in cycles of disasters, pointed up

[12] *The Human Image*, New York, Anchor Books, 1957, p. 115ff.

by such refrains as "I only am escaped alone to tell thee." The rhythm of the plot of *J.B.* is the formal counterpart of this; it moves in sequences of local disasters, accepted by J.B., rejected by his wife Sarah, and eventually accepted by both in the final epiphany:

> Blow on the coal of the heart.
> The candles in churches are out.
> The lights have gone out in the sky.
> Blow on the coal of the heart
> And we'll see by and by. . . .
> > We'll see where we are.
> The wit won't burn and the wet soul smoulders.
> Blow on the coal of the heart and we'll know . . .
> We'll know. . . .[13]

In terms of "character" Mr. MacLeish has softened the stark outline of Job, locating J.B.'s heroism in the degree to which he is "sensitive," rather than "conscious." This is one of the points of dialectical contact between *J.B.* and *This Music Crept By Me on the Water*: J.B., a hearty version of Elizabeth, is Mr. Mac-Leish's new culture-hero. Sarah testifies to his version of the heroic:

> . . . He lies there watching
> Long before I see the light—
> Can't bear to miss a minute of it:
> Sun at morning, moon at night,
> The last red apple, the first peas!
> I've never seen the dish he wouldn't
> Taste and relish and want more of:
> People either!

What is described here is J.B. in his role as pastoral "witness," supplying a "feeling" perspective—from the resources of a Marvellian garden—within which the recalcitrant, the complex, may be controlled. And, it is implied, this is deeply involved in that other version of the heroic by which J.B. holds out

[13] *J.B.*, Boston, Houghton Mifflin Co., 1958, p. 153.

against the enticement of an easy moral critique of God, the critique enforced by Sarah and by Nickles:

J.B.:                                          The Lord

    Giveth. . . . Say it.

SARAH:                                    The Lord giveth.

J.B.: The Lord taketh away . . .

SARAH:                                         Takes!

    Kills! Kills! Kills! Kills!

This is a strong, simple conflict in terms of character. As an heroic romance *J.B.* has little traffic with "character" in a modern sense, only with an Aristotelian idea of character as the moral forces at work through a person's acts. The play is rich in this kind of character, rich as a morality play is rich, rich as Cummings's *Santa Claus* is rich. It operates in terms of sharply opposed moral perspectives—which is again piously Aristotelian.

The new play is also rich in the quality which Aristotle calls "dianoia," which we may take to mean the ability to keep up large-scale movements of thought. We are apt to think of this part of the play as being sustained mainly by Mr. Zuss and Nickles, since they are the professional critics, each representing a way of life, an insight comprehensive however partial. But it would be inaccurate to infer that J.B.'s function in this regard is merely to provide, by enactment, material—substance—for the critical battles of Mr. Zuss and Nickles. J.B. has his own powers of argument, his own amateur eloquence:

                                    He was wrong.

It isn't luck when God is good to you.

It's something more. It's like those dizzy

Daft old lads who dowse for water.

They feel the alder twig twist down

And know they've got it and they have:

They've got it. Blast the ledge and water

Gushes at you. And they knew.

*209*

It wasn't luck. They knew. They felt the
Gush go shuddering through their shoulders, huge
As some mysterious certainty of opulence.
They couldn't hold it. I can't hold it.

J.B. is no "thinker," but these words in this order are a handsome recitation of his feeling at that moment. One never has the uncomfortable impression in this play that the speakers are too clever by half, too wise—as if they, in the middle of the event, were saying what they might possibly be able to say only after the event. The speakers possess nothing more than a reasonable amount of insight—just enough to be convincing— and a reasonable amount of skill in the speaking.

When it comes to the question of diction—Aristotle's "lexis" —Mr. MacLeish's play is satisfying within the limits of decorum. The style is often "high," but only when the dramatic occasion makes this demand, and it is consistently restrained to the limits of the mind which is speaking. This is enough, however, to sustain language which is lithe and sinewy:

> My
> Sin! Teach me my sin! My wickedness!
> Surely iniquity that suffers
> Judgment like mine cannot be secret.
> Mine is no childish fault, no nastiness
> Concealed behind a bathroom door,
> No sin a prurient virtue practices
> Licking the silence from its lips
> Like sugar afterwards. Mine is flagrant,
> Worthy of death, of many deaths,
> Of shame, loss, hurt, indignities
> Such as these! Such as these!
> Speak of the sin I must have sinned
> To suffer what you see me suffer.

This language closely imitates a movement of the psyche; the declamations, however expansive, are tied to a local occasion and are therefore close enough to the ground to "actualise" the

*210*

childish faults and to render the "quality" of prurient virtue. It is evidence of the precision of this writing that the hurled abstractions culminate not in a larger-than-ever declamation but in the severe formality of

> Speak of the sin I must have sinned
> To suffer what you see me suffer.

The severity makes this *formally* a satisfying climax, where the situation is felt to call for nothing more strident than a simple pointing-to-the-facts.

Of *J.B.* as dramatic verse: Aristotle was rather niggardly about the metres, but the verse dramatist cannot afford to be, and the modern practitioner has perhaps made up for the lack by being, if anything, too busy about them. Mr. MacLeish's verse in *J.B.* is a line of four rhetorical stresses, amenable to the behaviour of speech and recognisably *verse*:

> Of course he sickens you,
> He trusts the will of God and loves—
> Loves a woman who must sometime, somewhere,
> Later, sooner, leave him; fixes
> All his hopes on little children
> One night's fever or a running dog
> Could kill between the dark and day;
> Plants his work, his enterprise, his labor,
> Here where every planted thing
> Fails in its time but still he plants it. . . .

This is honest verse: it evades the blandishments of blank verse, yields up its expressive resources, trusting in its own looser organization. The verse pattern is just sufficiently *there* to provide one kind of continuity to endorse the kinds available from other sources.

We hardly know what to make of the "spectacle," but we feel it to be more important than Aristotle implied. Perhaps the most useful meaning we can assign to spectacle in this context is that of the pure theatrical image, the visual image

*211*

as it acts over and above the words spoken, or the scene itself insofar as it is strikingly engaged in the rhetoric, moment by moment. In *Antony and Cleopatra*, for instance, it is particularly appropriate that Antony, who speaks of running to his death as a bridegroom to a lover's bed, should try to kill himself in Cleopatra's palace. The scene itself, the spectacle, is—to use Kenneth Burke's term—a fit container for the act. Or again when Antony calls upon Eros to unbuckle his breastplate, there is a pure theatrical image of surrender to the "battery" of Cleopatra's death. In *J.B.* there is Sarah, in the resolution of the play, sitting on the doorsill, a broken twig in her hand; J.B. kneeling naked in the rubble; Nickles doubled up with sound-less laughter when J.B. says "God will not punish without cause"; the First Messenger taking a flash-photograph of Sarah as he tells her

> Four kids in a car. They're dead.
> Two were yours. Your son. Your daughter.

And more. Modern drama can show more striking scenic images than anything in *J.B.*: the inhabitants of the dustbins in *Fin de Partie*; Mother Courage dragging her cart; the symbolic birds in Aymé's *Les Oiseaux de Lune*; but there is a fine propriety in the scenic element in Mr. MacLeish's play—that is enough.

I have perhaps said enough to indicate that *J.B.* is a substantial play, far more so than *This Music Crept By Me on the Water*, and not at all a mood play. As a *genre* the mood play strikes me as the theatrical version of pure poetry, an attempt to relieve the poem of all association with the stuff of philosophy or politics or ethics or sociology, retaining only the "pure gold." The whole endeavour today seems unbearably precious: we distrust this version of the ineffable more than most. It is per-haps sufficient, in "placing" the mood play, to say that the current examples would fit comfortably enough in George Moore's notorious anthology.

# CHAPTER THIRTEEN. EZRA POUND AND
## *WOMEN OF TRACHIS*

Women of Trachis[1] is a play by Ezra Pound based on the *Trachiniae* of Sophocles. We do not propose here to enquire into Pound's treatment of his original, apart from noting that he has described the work not as a translation but as a "version" of the *Trachiniae*. Several scholars have already commented on the play as translation.[2] We propose therefore to concern ourselves mainly with the text as dramatic verse, recognising that this is a marginal consideration.

Mr. Eliot in a brief note on *Women of Trachis* declared "with complete assurance" that the poet had lost none of his skill. Pound's handling of the verse, especially in the choruses of the play, seemed to Mr. Eliot masterly: "his ear is as faultless as ever."[3] Such praise is quite justified. We would cite the passage in which the Nurse announces that Daysair (Deianira) is dead:

(*Enter Nurse*)

KHOROS: Look,
> look at the old woman's face. Something awful,
> it's all twisted up.

NURSE: Children, children,
> no end to the troubles from sending that present to Herakles.

KHOROS: More, you mean more?

NURSE: She's gone . . . . . . Daysair,
> The last road of all roads
> . . . . . . . without walking.

KHOROS: What! Dead?

NURSE: That's all. You heard me.

KHOROS: You mean the poor girl is dead?

NURSE: Yes, for the second time. Yes.

---

[1] First published in the *Hudson Review*, Vol. VI, 4, Winter 1954.

[2] See the contributions of C. M. Bowra, F. R. Earp, Richmond Lattimore, and Frederic Peachy to the *Pound Newsletter 5*, University of California, January 1955.

[3] *Ibid.*, p. 3.

The two speaking voices are beautifully modulated to "fit" character and situation. To describe the passage as *efficient* is to draw attention to its economy and its integrity as drama. The announcement of Daysair's death is made with just that degree of suspense necessary to render it theatrically effective. The suspense, if intensified beyond that point, would impose on the incident a degree of emotional priority which properly belongs to the scene of Herakles's death. Furthermore, it is part of Pound's skill in this passage that he controls the impact of the announcement by simultaneously drawing attention slightly away from the death itself toward the Nurse who relates it. When we hear the words we are compelled to respond variously to their meaning and to the Nurse's tone in saying them:

>               That's all. You heard me . . .

and then:

>               Yes, for the second time. Yes . . .

That is, our awareness of the Nurse's tone, in itself, is just sufficient to modulate the climax of her announcement.

There are several comparable examples in *Women of Trachis* of rhythm operating to refine the statement. Near the beginning of the play Daysair sees the messenger Likhas approaching; she calls out:

>          Yes, my dear girls, I make out the crowd
>          and finally and at last and at leisure
>          the herald, to be received,
>                                   and,
>          if his news is good,
>                         welcomed.

Likhas answers:

>          That it is, Milady,
>                              and worth hearing,
>          and paying for.

Daysair asks: "Is Herakles alive?" Likhas replies:

>          Sound in wind and limb, mind and body.

Here, in Daysair's first words, the rhythm directs and controls
the tone: the confident climax, prepared by the alliterative fullness of the second line, in "herald"; the easy vigour of the detached "and" in the fourth. The energy in Likhas's reply is of a
different order, arch, bumptious, aware of its own value; hence
the flourish in

> That it is, Milady
>
> > and worth hearing,
> and paying for . . . ,

and the touch of excess in

> Sound in wind and limb, mind and body.

The skill which we hope to isolate in such passages is that
of utilising the resources of verse so as to render with utmost
precision the slightest change in feeling or attitude. Indeed, if
verse drama has a "theoretical" justification, it is *here*, in this
particular kind of expressiveness.

In the choral odes of *Women of Trachis,* as previously in
the *Pisan Cantos,* Pound shows himself to be the most accom-
plished master of versification in twentieth-century English
poetry. We are not the first to say this: to illustrate it we must
quote one of the choruses in full. When Hyllos has accused
Daysair of causing his father's death, Daysair leaves the stage
without a word: the Khoros then speaks:

KHOROS (*low cello merely sustaining the voice*):

> OYEZ:                                         (*str. 1*)
> Things foretold and forecast:
> Toil and Moil.
> God's Son from turmoil shall
> —When twelve seed-crops be past—
> be loosed with the last,
> > his own.
> Twining together, godword found good,
> Spoken of old,
> > as the wind blew, truth's in the flood.

We and his brood see in swift combine,
   here and at last that:
Amid the dead is no servitude
   nor do they labour.
*(controbassi and drums muffled)*
   LO, beneath deadly cloud            *(Ant. 1)*
Fate and the Centaur's curse, black venom spread,
Dank Hydra's blood
Boils now through every vein, goad after goad
from spotted snake to pierce the holy side,
nor shall he last to see a new day's light,
Black shaggy night descends
                         as Nessus bade.
   WHAT MOURNFUL case           *(str. 2)*
            who feared great ills to come,
New haste in mating threatening her home,
Who hark'd to reason in a foreign voice
Entangling her in ravage out of choice.
Tears green the cheek with bright dews pouring down
Who mourns apart, alone
Oncoming swiftness in o'erlowering fate
To show what wreck is nested in deceit.
   LET the tears flow.              *(Ant. 2)*
   Ne'er had bright Herakles in his shining
Need of pity till now
   whom fell disease burns out.
How swift on Oechal's height
   to take a bride.
Black pointed shaft that shielded her in flight,
Attest
That
Kupris stood by and never said a word,
Who now flares here the contriver
manifest . . .
and indifferent.

This is not an example, such as we frequently encounter in Eliot, of language discovering, during its activity, reserves of meaning and significance till then unperceived. Rather, it is an outstanding instance of language being refined and moulded to the shape of a human voice and an individual tone. In the passage

> Tears green the cheek with bright dews pouring down:
> Who mourns apart, alone
> Oncoming swiftness in o'erlowering fate
> To show what wreck is nested in deceit . . .

the pathos of the first three lines (the "grand" style refreshed), encouraged and at the same time controlled by the internal rhymes, culminates in the ironic comment of "nested" in the last. In turn, this astringent note continues in the background, concealed by the "bright Herakles" lines, until it is heard again in a final judgment:

> Black pointed shaft that shielded her in flight,
> Attest
> That
> Kupris stood by and never said a word,
> Who now flares here the contriver
> manifest . . .
> and indifferent.

The precision of statement here is characteristic of *Women of Trachis*. The severity of the first three lines and the strongly marked rhythm, forcing the issue, throw the weight of the indictment on *Kupris*. In turn, the deliberate flatness of

> Kupris stood by and never said a word

sharpens our response to the bitter tone of the last three lines. The statement is Augustan not only in its moral indignation but in its precision: it is even "plotted" like a couplet.

It is reasonable to describe such effects in terms of rhetorical finesse, though Pound himself (and, I imagine, Henry James) would prefer to regard them as depending for their force on their place in the "scenario." In *Make It New* Pound declared that neither prose nor drama could attain poetic intensity save by "construction," almost by "scenario"—that is, by so arranging the circumstance that some perfectly simple speech, perception, dogmatic statement, appears in abnormal vigour. As cases in point he cited: the moment in *L'Education* in which Frederic notices Mme. Arnoux's shoe-laces as she comes down the stair; in Turgenev, the quotation of a Russian proverb about the "heart of another"; or "Nothing but death is irrevocable" toward the end of *Nichée de Gentilshommes*.[4] These incidents derive their force not from their intrinsic interest or profundity but (in our own terms now) from the almost magical propriety with which they satisfy a desire in the reader at that point and play their part in the composition as a whole. The depressed casualness of

> Kupris stood by and never said a word

coming, as it does, in the midst of language which is Johnsonian in its "height," exhibits the operation, on a high level, of rhetorical precision or "scenario." From a slightly different point of view it is an example of "formal excellence," a large-scale power carried down into the writing of a short passage of verse. Indeed, we are tempted to offer this passage as illustration, in miniature, of Pound's brilliant versification and of the mutual coherence exhibited by the various elements in the play. Just as the elements of the play cohere to form an instance of "poésie de théâtre," so also the various tones of the words in the passage form, as an analogue of plot, a complex and unified statement. It is significant that the terms in which one describes the large-scale qualities of "poésie de théâtre," such as coherence, economy, and integrity of structure, are precisely those evoked by a typical passage of verse in *Women of Trachis*. The exaltation of "scenario" which one finds in Aristotle, Henry

---

[4] Ezra Pound, *Make It New*, Faber and Faber, 1934, p. 289.

James, Pound, and Cocteau is exemplified with distinction in the passage under consideration.

Perhaps the most convenient way to describe the verse of *Women of Trachis* is to show in what respects it differs from several earlier verse-translations of the *Trachiniae*. We may begin with a characteristic passage from the translation by Browning's disciple, Robert Whitelaw:

CHORUS: Mischief we needs must fear: but fortune still
    Rules the event; esteem not forecast more.
DEIANIRA: Forecast, of courage ministrant, is none—
    Of hope no help, when men have counselled ill.
CHORUS: When men have stumbled all unwittingly,
    Anger has pity—as 'twere fit you found.
DEIANIRA: So talks no partner of the evil deed,
    But one upon whose heart no burden weighs.
CHORUS: Silence from further speech of this were best.
    Or will you speak to your own son? for here
    He comes, who went erewhile to seek his sire.[5]

Next, a more recent translation of the same passage by Professor Storr:

CHORUS: 'Tis true dread perils threaten; yet 'twere well
    To cherish hope till the event be known.
DEIANIRA: They who have counselled ill cannot admit
    One ray of hope to fortify their soul.
CHORUS: Men will not look severely on an act
    Unwittingly committed, as was thine.
DEIANIRA: With a good conscience one might urge this plea
    Which ill becomes a partner in the crime.
CHORUS: 'Twere better to refrain from further speech,
    Unless thou wouldst address thy son; for he
    Who went to seek his father is at hand.[6]

Finally, Pound's version:

[5] Rivingtons, 1883, pp. 285-86.
[6] Loeb edition, Heinemann, 1913, II, 315.

CHORUS: Don't give up yet.
   There's danger. But it mayn't necessarily happen.
DEIANIRA: There's no hope for those who have done wrong.
CHORUS: But if you didn't mean it, they won't
   blame you as much as all that.
DEIANIRA: Talk that way if you're not involved,
   not if you've got the weight of it on you.
CHORUS: Better wait to hear what your son's got to say.
   There he is to tell you, himself;
   he went to look for his father.

Clearly, Pound's version bears a relation to human speech which neither Whitelaw's nor Storr's has even approached; of the three, Pound's is the only one which we could imagine anyone speaking. The pervading affinities of the earlier versions are to previous literatures:

   Forecast, of courage ministrant, is none—
   Of hope no help, when men have counselled ill . . .

and again

      'Twere better to refrain from further speech,
      Unless thou wouldst address thy son . . .

Pound's, on the other hand, takes its bearings directly from speech. In this connexion, and in order more precisely to understand Pound's idea of translation, we recall his observation that Pope's *Iliad* has the merit "of translating Homer into *something*."[7] In this respect *Women of Trachis* is similar in style to those fragments of translation which Pound offered his readers many years ago when commenting on Browning's version of Aeschylus.[8]

The verse of *Women of Trachis*, then, is primarily designed to sound authentic when spoken. Pound sought to approach Sophocles's text directly, evading as far as possible the temptation to look at the words through the eyes of Milton or Browning

---

[7] Pound, *supra*, footnote 4, p. 126.
[8] *Translators of Greek, Make It New, supra*, footnote 4, Chapter iv.

or Landor. Denis Goacher, who played the part of Hyllos in a broadcast performance of the play some years ago, has observed that throughout the text "cadence and hiatus indicate the 'tone' and stress for the actor." Pound's success, Mr. Goacher declares, is twofold: he has seen how a play works and, in certain passages such as the speech beginning

> Hoist him up, fellows
> And for me a great tolerance
>     matching the gods' great unreason,

he has written verse of an ingenious intonation and allusive beauty that has not been heard in English drama for a long time.[9]

*Women of Trachis* is, of course, a special case. At first sight it may appear that Pound has achieved in this play the kind of dramatic verse which eluded Eliot until *The Confidential Clerk*. Not so. *Women of Trachis* is a fine achievement, but it is a specially limited case in a sense which does not apply to *The Confidential Clerk*. The language of *The Confidential Clerk* is available to an English verse dramatist as a model for a play dealing with a contemporary theme. A dramatist searching for such a model would find little assistance in *Women of Trachis*. The case is complicated, first, by Sophocles's part in the work, which accounts for the detailed organisation of the play and therefore for most of its "poetry." Second, the student of *Women of Trachis* must confront a considerable amount of American idiom, quite foreign to English ears, which Pound has employed in several parts of the dialogue.

However, Pound has shown in *Women of Trachis* that an effective "version" of a classical play can be written in modern speech, provided the language is fresh and lithe. He has also made it possible to argue that this is the best way to recover, for the present generation, the idea of drama as "poetry in the

[9] Denis Goacher, "Modern Poetic Drama," *The Listener*, 16 December 1954, pp. 1067-68. Mr. Goacher comments further on *Women of Trachis* in his essay, "A Visit to Ezra Pound," *Nimbus*, Spring 1957.

medium of action." It seems likely, however, that a verse dramatist who wished to write on a contemporary issue would gain
less assistance from *Women of Trachis* than from *The Confidential Clerk*

# CHAPTER FOURTEEN. RICHARD EBERHART:
## *THE VISIONARY FARMS*

■■■■■■■■■■■■■■■■■

*The Visionary Farms*[1] is a *drame à thèse* which owes a great deal to the expressionist tendencies of the early plays of Eugene O'Neill, Thornton Wilder, and Elmer Rice. It is not in any important sense original; it does not enlarge the range of dramatic art; but it provides an opportunity of examining an interesting alliance between modern dramatic verse and those non-representational procedures which have been developed in the theatre in such plays as *The Hairy Ape*. To consider the play from this point of view may be more rewarding than to treat of the affinities between *The Visionary Farms* and such plays as *The Show-Off, Beggar on Horseback,* and *Strange Interlude*.

First the thesis. The theme of *The Visionary Farms* is not "money" but the larger motive of "Progress," which Professor Weaver has described as the "god term" of the present age. By "god term" he means that expression about which all other expressions are ranked as subordinate. Its force imparts to the others their lesser degree of force, and fixes the scale by which degrees of comparison are understood. In the absence of a strong and evenly diffused religion there may, of course, be several terms in competition for this primacy; yet, Professor Weaver argues, if one has to select the term which in our day carries the greatest blessing, and whose antonym carries the greatest rebuke, one will not go far wrong in naming "Progress." It is probably the only term which gives the average American or West European a concept of something larger than himself, which he is

[1] The play was first performed at the Poets' Theatre in Cambridge, Massachusetts, in May 1952. In that form it was published in *New World Writing*, 3, Summer 1953, pp. 63-96. This is the text from which quotations are taken in the present study. For the second production at Seattle, Washington, in May 1953 a further scene was added, "showing what happened to Hurricane Ransome later on." This scene was published in the *Quarterly Review of Literature*.

socially impelled to accept, and for which he is ready to sacrifice.[2]

The context of *The Visionary Farms* is largely determined by such considerations: its "scene" is a climate of feeling in which Progress is cultivated without restraint from any other values. Adam Fahnstock is a self-made man, well-to-do, ambitious, and yet scrupulously honest; he owns thirty-five per cent of Roger Parker's manufacturing business. "Hurricane" Ransome, their manager, is the man who has made their success possible, by means of expansion, efficiency, and speed. Parker's son discovers that Ransome has been embezzling the company's funds for several years and that the enormous expansion of the firm has kept just one step ahead of its creditors. Parker insists on calling in Fahnstock's shares to cover possible bankruptcy. Fahnstock, while his wife is dying, tells his children that his fortunes are destroyed. He begs them not to react with hatred. The play ends with choric observations.

If *The Visionary Farms* is a *drame à thèse* it is such with a difference, for Mr. Eberhart has not presented a realistic enactment of the ruin of a commercial empire in 1919. Rather, he has dramatised his impression of the inevitable conclusion of the cult of Progress. The play, technically related to America in 1919, is visionary in the sense in which one applies the word to such works as *R.U.R.*, *The Trial*, *Brave New World*, and *1984*. (It will be understood that these comparisons are descriptive, not qualitative. Qualitatively, *The Visionary Farms* is nearer to John Hawkes than to Kafka.) For this reason it is inaccurate to describe the play as "a study in fourteen scenes of the collapse of a business empire."[3] *The Visionary Farms* does not study anything. Rather it envisages, in fear and solicitude, and enacts this vision.

The technique by which Mr. Eberhart dramatises his concep-

[2] Richard M. Weaver, "Ultimate Terms in Contemporary Rhetoric," *Perspectives*, 11, Spring 1955, pp. 123, 125. The essay is taken from Professor Weaver's *The Ethics of Rhetoric*, Chicago, Henry Regnery, 1953.

[3] Selden Rodman, "The Poetry of Richard Eberhart," *Perspectives*, 10, Winter 1955, p. 40.

tion includes among its most active features these two: distortion and simplification. The two procedures cooperate in the quasi-expressionistic structure of the play. The characteristic form of distortion is a gesture, not toward the baroque, but toward the rudimentary. If one examines the presentation of character, time, and incident in *The Visionary Farms* one finds that in each case the distortion takes the form of cutting away the circumstantial details which the physical laws impose on normal living. For instance, all the characters in the play are one-dimensional. To describe "Hurricane" Ransome as symbol of Progress-mania is not to give special attention to one feature from a fully rounded character; it is to name the only feature, the only dimension, which is *there*. There is nothing more to him. The audience is not encouraged to see him as a whole man, but rather as a bloodless symbol, logical conclusion of a grotesque cult. He is Man, from whom all levels of existence other than the predatory have been cut away by greed. Here is a typical moment in his one-dimensional life:

RANSOME: Taft, this is a sweltering hot day.
    I want these farms thoroughly modernised.
    How would you like to be one of our cows?
    I have to swat flies even in here.
    They spend half of their energy swishing their tails
    Trying to keep off the flies. I want action.
    I want a master-fan made with six-foot arms,
    Here is a rough sketch.
                Notice the fine points.
    Put plenty of power on it. Blow all the flies
    Into and pen them in this metal corridor,
    Like this. Set up these elements there
    Where they will be automatically asphyxiated.
TAFT: I will try to have it made in a month, sir.
RANSOME: A month! I want it done in a week.
TAFT: I'll try, sir.
RANSOME:         Also, I want an electric fan
    For each cow . . .

For the purposes of the play, anything further along the realistic road would be irrelevant. The treatment of the other characters reveals distortion in precisely the same way. Fahnstock's wife, for instance, has no meaning at all, no existence, except as symbol of the pastoral desire to rest in a modicum of contentment:

> I wanted a comfortable house, just large enough,
> Instead of this enormous mansion . . .

The treatment of time in *The Visionary Farms* exhibits similar distortion. Taft telephones the State University to send down a chicken surgeon; the surgeon arrives within a few seconds. A mere thirteen lines of verse are spoken between the time Ted Parker telephones the police and the arrival of the detective officer. Distortion of this kind has, of course, a dual function. In addition to "interpreting" the action it also evokes in the audience responses quite different from those envisaged by a realistic play. It is an indication that the probable is not to be relied on, that we are in a Kafka-like world.

Similarly, in the treatment of the incidents the technique of distortion sets aside plausibility, causes, and expectations, cutting away all indication of the part played by these forces in human decisions. Existence and behaviour as presented in *The Visionary Farms* show hardly more than a nominal connexion with the rational. Man has thrust himself *down* the scale of existence, throwing away his Reason as he approaches the rudimentary or animal level of behaviour. Motives are so attenuated that they are indistinguishable from the movements of a machine:

SALESMAN: Good day, sir.
RANSOME: Good day. What do you want?
SALESMAN: I have a new eight-cylinder Cadillac outside
    I would like to show you.
RANSOME:                          What colour is it?
SALESMAN: Blue.
RANSOME:         I'll take it . . .

Distortion and simplification—but there is no real distinction between the two. Or, rather, in the most significant parts of the play the two merge to cut away all trace of the complex or the circumstantial. The effect is, of course, cumulative; its success is a matter of loosening the audience's instinctive adherence to those factors in the everyday world which (however precariously) operate in terms of cause and effect, circumstance and probability. This adherence is not totally severed. What remains has the effect of supplying, as it were on the margin, a severely critical and "proper" attitude to the events being enacted. If this is the purpose of the procedure it is successful, notably in the following scene in which Fahnstock and the Parkers confront Ransome with his crime:

RANSOME: Well gentlemen, what can I do for you?
PARKER: Hurricane, this is a very serious matter.
    Do you see these figures here? And these statements?
    They do not agree. It looks like the Company is short.
    How do you account for these discrepancies?

Ransome takes a pad of paper from his left pocket. He takes a pencil from his vest pocket. With meticulous care and seemingly without emotion he writes down a figure on the pad, looks at it intently, and hands it to Mr. Parker:

PARKER: (*reading*) One million, one hundred and eighty seven
    thousand dollars.
    Hurricane, what does this mean?
    What is this figure?
RANSOME: I have embezzled precisely that amount of money
    From the Company during the past eight years.

The world of *The Visionary Farms*, like the presentation of this scene, is "artificial"; it exists only in one's fears for the future. And the reality which it invokes is the persistence of those fears.

The pervading tone of *The Visionary Farms* is satirical, but the satire is based not so much on derision as on solicitude. In this respect Mr. Eberhart is to be associated with Eugene O'Neill and many other modern American dramatists who have, in their plays, composed manifestos repudiating the unrestrained cult of Progress. In a wider context *The Visionary Farms* and *The Emperor Jones* are protests against the excesses, the perversions, of those assumptions which have dominated post-Renaissance civilisation. These assumptions, as they have been described (with some bias) by Professor Krutch, are as follows. First, that Man is a creature capable of dignity. Second, that life as lived in this world, not merely life as it might be lived either in the Christian's City of God or the Marxist's Socialist State, is worth living. Third, that the realm of human reason is the realm in which man may most fruitfully live. An astonishing proportion of serious modern literature, he laments, implies the rejection of one or more of these premises: "When determinism, psychological or economic, has deprived man of even a limited power of self-determination and at the same time denied the validity of any of the ethical beliefs to which he may be attached, then man has ceased to have dignity." Similarly, Professor Krutch declares, when the radical pessimist or the Utopian reformer has represented life "under the present social system" as being inevitably frustrated, then the Renaissance thesis that life in this world is worth living is denied. The modern drama, he asserts, is open to the same charge that may be levelled against modern literature as a whole. Its tendency has been to undermine the foundations of post-Renaissance civilisation.[4]

Professor Krutch has reported the situation with tolerable accuracy, though one may find his exaltation of post-Renaissance civilisation unacceptable. One may argue, with a greater show of reason, that modern literature is largely a protest against the inadequacy of secular fideism. On this issue the author of *The Visionary Farms*, like D. H. Lawrence on a higher level, is

[4] Joseph Wood. Krutch, *"Modernism" in Modern Drama*, Cornell University Press, 1953, pp. 130-31.

close to the radical pessimist whom Professor Krutch posits. *The Visionary Farms* implies that if ordinary, day-to-day life continues to be based exclusively and fanatically on current "progressive" values it will at some unspecified date look very like the pathetic, monstrous life of the Parkers and the "Hurricane" Ransomes in 1919. Thus the satire and the solicitude.

The rhetorical intent of *The Visionary Farms*, as we have outlined it, seems naïve and oversimplified. It is true that neither *The Visionary Farms* nor *This Music Crept By Me on the Water* attains a "perfect" judgment of its material. *The Visionary Farms* is committed to a strong but simple rhetoric by its use of "planned derangement." Similarly in *Look Back in Anger* John Osborne withholds eloquent expression from any attitude other than that of the hero, Jimmy Porter. The latter, like Stephen Dedalus in *A Portrait of the Artist as a Young Man*, is shielded from ironical scrutiny. In achieving an immediate expressive aim, these works miss the higher success of complete presentation: they express, but do not penetrate, their material. One regrets this all the more in the case of *The Visionary Farms* because there is evidence that in recent years protests against machine-made "progressive" values, such as we find in that play, have become the stock-in-trade of inferior writers. The integrity of motive represented by *The Waste Land* is now being preempted by lesser writers as evidence of good faith. Even if one shares the artist's disgust with "progressive" values, one must recognise that the movement from *The Waste Land* to E. L. Mayo's *Orpheus on B Deck* is a lapse from genuine exploration to mere fashionable pose. There is often a narcissist ingredient in one's role as Sensitive Plant.

*The Visionary Farms* is a play in fifteen continuous scenes. The story which concerns the Parkers, Ransome, and Fahnstock is presented in twelve scenes as a play-within-a-play shown to a group of people in the home of Robin Everyman. In the first scene this story is introduced to Robin and the guests by the Consulting Author:

I carry a delicate, mystic, silken wand
To clear the air on these cloudy occasions.
I wave this now before your eyes and minds
To purge the qualities of every day,
And take your disbelieving personalities.
Each thus becomes a part of Everyman.
What is, is what might happen to him.
And each can share in the scenes of fabulous life
As if imagination were reality,
For reality is strange as imagination.

At the end of the thirteenth scene the Consulting Author addresses the group in the Everyman home:

Thank you, ladies and gentlemen, that is all.
We are going to leave the action at this point.
All of these gentlemen have become madmen,
Due to the enormity and gross enchantments
Of the times, astonishing products of America;
Each might soon be at the other's throat
And lay some bloody forms about our stage
Not unlike the old, gross days of Elizabeth.
Now let us enjoy what's done, and let's construe.
Let us keep vile actions off, and bring on thoughts
To estimate these matters to a standstill.
We are not going to have the usual climax;
Originality is to leave it to your imaginations.
Homer is more realistic than Shakespeare.
You continue beyond the high peaks to the lowlands,
Violent actions are flattened out by the years.

Robin asks the obvious question:

You pay a tribute to the time's confusions
We confess our lethargy and inability
To conclude the action dramatically.
Do we not owe fidelity to action?

The consulting Author answers:

No, we owe fidelity to talk.
It is the temper of our times to rage
And talk tragedy into comedy;
Now Adam Fahnstock could kill Mr. Parker,
But all these men were too intelligent,
The matters too complex, too thoroughly understood
In one way, yet not understood in others . . .

Robin then explains the formal procedure of the play as a design to talk these matters to a standstill. The audience must construe and contemplate what they have seen:

> We have shown the brutal spectacle of the world,
> Evading the true awe of reality,
> To plumb down into blood-deep savagery,
> But we would throw out scenes of the passional
> And weave around them pleasing ideation,
> Evoke, and leave the rest to contemplation.
> Thus, in our modernistic, small society
> Handle chaos, and keep a balance of sanity.

Selden Rodman, citing this passage, observes that *The Visionary Farms* deliberately, but not merely in its conclusion, is undramatic. Yet it is difficult, he says, to rebuke the author for what he cheerfully admits.[5]

Mr. Eberhart's procedure is deliberate, but it must still be assessed. Here the dramatist has gone astray. The comments of the Everyman group (which may be regarded as, collectively, choric) are designed to "bring on thoughts / To estimate these matters to a standstill." But the last scene, which might possibly stand being "undramatic," falls by being uncreative. The choric comments are forced on a dramatic fable which does not substantiate them. Such comments as

> But all these men were too intelligent,
> The matters too complex . . .

[5] Rodman, *supra*, p. 40.

are inadequately supported by a play whose very essence was the clarity which arises from distortion and simplification. As we have seen, realism has been set aside, in the Fahnstock story, in favour of one-dimensional expressionism, and with a high degree of short-term success. This success has been achieved primarily by Mr. Eberhart's "simplifying vision."[6] Not content with this modest achievement, the author has tried to insinuate, through the Chorus, ambiguities and complexities which are not *there* in the story of Adam Fahnstock.

For evidence we would point to the form of *The Visionary Farms*. Mr. Eberhart has deliberately withheld from his play the significance of form *as form*; indeed this is the *formal* counterpart of the play's thesis. Professor Krutch has argued, with reference to post-Strindbergian drama, that if one is going to argue that life is meaningless, one cannot make the point in a play where the play itself constitutes meaning. The violence and confusion of the play, he asserts, must express the violence and confusion which it proclaims. If life is a nightmare, then dramas must be nightmarish. It is impossible to deny that life is significant if the form which you impose upon a representation of it tends to give it meaning.[7] This argument is by no means overwhelming: the question of "expressive form" and the difficulties with which it bristles are outside the scope of the present study. It is enough to recognise that such arguments are the source of Mr. Eberhart's refusal to "tie a neat dramatic package." The story of Adam Fahnstock is presented with minimum emphasis on form *as form* because the mode of living which it represents is so weird and insane as to point away from meaning altogether. At all costs, therefore, Mr. Eberhart has avoided giving it the significance and "shape" implied by classic form.

Mr. Eberhart is a genuine, if remarkably uneven, poet. It is possible to see some of his qualities in his most popular poem *The Fury of Aerial Bombardment*:

[6] *Ibid.*
[7] Krutch, *supra*, pp. 115-16. Such views are strenuously rejected by Yvor Winters in *In Defence of Reason*, University of Denver Press, n.d.

You would think the fury of aerial bombardment
Would rouse God to relent; the infinite spaces
Are still silent. He looks on shock-pried faces.
History, even, does not know what is meant.

You would feel that after so many centuries
God would give man to repent; yet he can kill
As Cain could, but with multitudinous will,
No farther advanced than in his ancient furies.

Was man made stupid to see his own stupidity?
Is God by definition indifferent, beyond us all?
Is the eternal truth man's fighting soul
Wherein the Beast ravens in its own avidity?

Of Van Wettering I speak, and Averill,
Names on a list, whose faces I do not recall
But they are gone to early death, who late in school
Distinguished the belt feed lever from the belt
        holding pawl.

The "concretion" in the last stanza completes the statement
made tentatively—in "universal" terms—in the first. The entire
poem, however, exhibits a unity of tone which is reflective and
severe, though not quite "grand." The language of *The Visionary Farms* is a little lower than "mean." Particularly in the play-
within-a-play the representation of speaking voices is consistently realistic. A speech by Fahnstock:

Your conduct towards me is intolerable, despicable.
I feel that Ted has put you up to this.
I am the man who has made this company gigantic
    and famous.
We have worked together as a powerful team
Through the full years of our maturity.
You know that the bankers believe in me, not you.
You are saving your own face at the cost of mine.
You are making your right-hand man the scapegoat.
Roger, are you capable of such vile trickery?
Neither you nor I was to blame for Hurricane.

You hired him, promoted, believed in him,
I with you. We both trusted him implicitly . . .

Comparing the two passages and trying out Eliot's distinction between the three voices of poetry: *The Fury of Aerial Bombardment* exhibits the first voice, "the voice of the poet talking to himself—or to nobody." The "you" in the poem, the person who is confronted with the large philosophic questions, is the speaker himself, since in meditation one dissociates oneself into two roles, speaker and listener. The degree of formality in the tone which Mr. Eberhart adopts arises from his decorous sense of the issues involved. It is a fairly "high" occasion.

The speech by Adam Fahnstock exhibits—so Eliot would argue—the third voice, "the voice of the poet when he is saying, not what he would say in his own person, but only what he can say within the limits of one imaginary character addressing another imaginary character."[8] But this is difficult to prove—perhaps impossible. In the passage quoted the only voice one hears is that of Adam Fahnstock; one would be bold to hear in it an echo of the voice which one recognises from *The Fury of Aerial Bombardment* and other poems as Mr. Eberhart's own. If this voice speaks in *The Visionary Farms* it is audible only in the role of the Consulting Author. One can hardly profess to hear in this play that "more impersonal voice still than that of either the character or the author" which Eliot posits: the voice which issues only from an entire dramatic universe, such as the universes of Shakespeare or Racine. Mr. Eberhart has not created his universe.

The differences between the first and the third voices are differences of tone, not requiring differences of versification. In *The Visionary Farms* the regular end-rhymes of *The Fury of Aerial Bombardment* have gone, but the line of four stresses remains, as in

Roger, are you capable of such vile trickery?
Neither you nor I was to blame for Hurricane . . .

[8] T. S. Eliot, *The Three Voices of Poetry*, Cambridge University Press, 1953, p. 4.

By using an identifying vocabulary, syntax, and rhythm, Mr. Eberhart has caused Adam Fahnstock's role to emerge, valid and capacious, from the situations in which he is placed.

Mr Eberhart has given much thought to these questions. In fact, his second *Preamble*[9] contains one of the best discussions I have found of the appropriate speech for a play like *The Visionary Farms*. Here is a fragment torn from the poem:

> About the style. Should we make it
> Fluid and florid, in full verbal spate
> To touch on tongue ten thousand times,
> As it were, the richness of our English,
> Organ of shifting, grassy syllables,
> Or taste of rich and savage splendors
> Which, like the blood itself, that feeds
> The tongue, come out to tell the world
> All's a lush hectic in our English.

But the Consulting Author favours restraint, especially when the Author longs to render all the dynamic energies of the age that would burst forth in natural compulsions:

> Another style would be more daring now,
> The spare, the lean, the chaste, a Greek
> Of Doric, pure and strong restraint,
> Where reason and imagination
> Stay in sculptured elegance.

Neither is convinced. The play of ideas goes on. But the Author asserts that he will keep his style "quite American." In *The Visionary Farms*, at its best, this comes out as talk-with-character.

[9] "Preamble II," *Sewanee Review*, LXII, I, January-March, 1954, pp. 84-100.

# CHAPTER FIFTEEN. ON SPEAKING THE VERSE

DRAMATISTS and actors, with a few distinguished exceptions, have devoted very little thought to the problems involved in speaking verse. Many verse dramatists compose with little regard for the virtues and limitations of the human voice. Many actors, suspicious of verse, ignore the factors which make it such.

On the vexed question of the reading of verse we would agree with Professor Winters that a poem calls for a formal reading, partly because the poem is of its own nature a formal statement, and partly because "only such a reading will render the rhythm with precision." It follows that conversation is not the proper mimetic basis of verse reading, since conversation is the least rhythmical form of expression. Also, that an adequate reading is one "in which the rhythm of the poem is rendered intact, without the sacrifice of any other element."[1]

The speaking of theatre-verse presents special problems with which Professor Winters has not dealt, but we would show that here a similar set of emphases apply, though with important modifications. It is apparent, for example, that in a play the pressure of the fable and the activity of the various agents will reduce to some extent the degree of formality in the speech. Since each passage spoken by an actor in a play is of its nature "incomplete," it can hardly be spoken with that air of finality which one ought to require in the rendering of a sonnet. There is also the convention that we, the theatre-audience, are not so much hearing as overhearing the words of the agents. This factor again tends to reduce the formality which is proper in the direct address of verse-speaking. But there are limits. On no account should an actor speak so informally, so "conversationally" as to undermine the rhythmic integrity of the verse. If the text is verse the features which make it such ought not to be obliterated.

[1] Yvor Winters, "The Audible Reading of Poetry," *Hudson Review*, Vol. IV, No. 3, Autumn 1951, pp. 434, 436.

Of these, the rhythmic variations on metrical patterns are normally among the most important.

The responsibilities of the verse-dramatist to the actor (the first half of the problem) begin with the following: that in any passage a pattern of sound exist and be readily ascertainable; that this pattern be inherent in, and therefore sanctioned by, the mechanical properties of the words, or, otherwise stated, that it be unnecessary for the actor to impose an artificial pattern on the speeches. These responsibilities are virtually ignored in *The Lady's Not for Burning*, to cite a single example. There are several passages in that play from which no metrical pattern emerges even after prolonged study:

> Let Humphrey go and officially
> Bury himself. She's not for him.
> What does love understand about hereinafter—
> Called-the-mortgagee?
> An April anarchy, she is, with a dragon's breath,
> An angel on a tiger,
> The jaws and maw of a kind of heaven, though hell
> Sleeps there with one open eye; an onslaught
> Unpredictable made by a benefactor
> Armed to the teeth—.

We must be pedantic about this. The number of syllables in each line varies from five to thirteen; the number of stresses, according to my guess, from two to five. There are no verse-differentia of any kind. Except for an occasional detail such as the rhetorical pause between "officially" and "Bury" (with valid emphasis on "Bury"), it makes no difference if one simply reads the passage according to the syntax, ignoring line-endings and yielding up entirely the pursuit of metrical pattern. This may be exactly what Mr. Fry wants; if so, he bears the onus of naming the features in the passage which make it verse. We assume he would not claim that such writing is verse, or poetry, solely on the strength of the flamboyant diction exhibited in the last four lines. He should also indicate in what respect passages "written down in this way because I find it convenient"[2] will be found "helpful" by those who speak them. For instance, we have suggested that the pause between "officially" and "Bury" is rhetorically valid, but one can hardly find similar point in the pause between "little" and "while" in this passage from the same play:

> But what are you afraid of, since in a little
> While neither of us may exist? Either or both
> May be altogether transmuted into memory,
> And then the heart's obscure indeed . . . Richard, . . .

Here there is neither metrical pattern nor rhetorical point. Since grammar and syntax are in full accord with normal prose usage, one is strongly tempted to delete the text and write: "But what are you afraid of, since in a little while neither of us may exist? Either or both may be altogether transmuted into memory; and then the heart's obscure indeed." I hear no difference. The revised version is not particularly good prose, but at least it is free from unnecessary confusion.

A further responsibility of the verse dramatist to the actor is that the sound pattern shall not conflict with the rhetorical pattern. Sound factors should operate in the service of the rhetoric. This requirement is not commonly understood by verse dramatists, but it was constantly in Eliot's mind in *The Cocktail Party* and *The Confidential Clerk*. Here is a passage from *The Cocktail Party*:

REILLY: . . . But when I said just now
That she would go far, you agreed with me.
JULIA: Oh yes, she will go far. And we know where she is going.
But what do we know of the terrors of the journey?
You and I don't know the process by which the human is
Transhumanised: what do we know
Of the kind of suffering they must undergo
On the way of illumination?

[2] Foreword to *The Lady's Not for Burning*, Oxford University Press, 1949, p. v.

REILLY:                          Will she be frightened
  By the first appearance of projected spirits?
JULIA: Henry, you simply do not understand innocence.
  She will be afraid of nothing; she will not even know
  That there is anything there to be afraid of.
  She is too humble. She will pass between the scolding hills,
  Through the valley of derision, like a child sent on an errand
  In eagerness and patience. Yet she must suffer.
REILLY: When I express confidence in anything
  You always raise doubts; when I am apprehensive
  Then you see no reason for anything but confidence.
JULIA: That's one way in which I am so useful to you.
  You ought to be grateful.
REILLY:                          And when I say to one like her
  "Work out your salvation with diligence," I do not under-
    stand
  What I myself am saying.
JULIA:                          You must accept your limitations.

There is splendid craft in this writing. To speak the passage
well requires that actor and actress appreciate the flawless mesh-
ing of rhythm, syntax, and rhetoric; to do justice to one is to
find all three acting together. But the actor and the actress,
speaking these lines, should constantly be guided by the rhythm;
rhythm alone, not syntax or even rhetoric, will prompt the
actress to recognise the eloquent, preparatory pause before the
expanding wonder of "transhumanised." Nothing in the syntax
needs this pause, but it is crucial in the tone of the entire speech.

We would propose this passage as one of the most distinguished pieces of theatre-verse written for many years. How
varied the writing is; how wide the range of feeling explored
within a mode, as a whole, urbane; how delicately and yet how
firmly the increasing density of Reilly's questions

Will she be frightened
By the first appearance of projected spirits?

is reduced by Julia's

239

Henry, you simply do not understand innocence.

The movement of feeling is beautifully repeated when the slight whine in Reilly's later protestations is cleared away by the affectionate formality of Julia's "You must accept your limitations."

The responsibilities of the actor to the verse dramatist are equally onerous. If an actor ignores the sound patterns in the text, he cheats the dramatist and the audience just as gravely as if we were to speak the lines inaccurately in any other respect. When Orestes says to Hermione in the second Act of *Andromache*:

> Je vous entends. Tel est mon partage funeste:
> Le coeur est pour Pyrrhus, et les voeux pour Oreste—[3]

the most authentic "quality" of feeling is that which emerges from the sonal and rhetorical collocation of "Oreste" and "funeste," from the precise placing of "Le coeur" and "les voeux" on a similar level of stress, and from the actor's fidelity to every detail of the rhythm.

The actor, then, must convey all the effects of emphasis and rhetorical nuance indicated by the metrical structure. An example from Austin Clarke's *The Flame* will illustrate the point:

> Then, halfway in the wood, I saw
> A fair-knee'd youth that had been trumpet-blown
> Among those leaves and would escape them
> On golden elbows, but he was betrayed
> And buckled by the anger of his hair—
> Great hair that glittered like the tightened strings
> When the long nails of the harp-player live
> In the dark clef and the pale.[4]

---

[3] *Théâtre Complet de Jean Racine*, Paris, Garnier Freres, n.d., p. 143. In a personal letter of 16 August 1956 Professor Winters expressed the view that rhymed drama (Racine, Tirso) should be read in a manner approaching the formal reading which he recommends for lyric verse.
[4] *Collected Poems*, Allen and Unwin, 1936, pp. 121-22.

An adequate reader of this passage should have little difficulty in rendering the blank verse, intact, without obscuring the syntax. He should be careful to take account of the rhetorical emphasis, suggested by the metre and by their position, on such words as "saw" and "betrayed." If he reads the passage as— "Then halfway in the wood / I saw a fair-kneed youth / that had been trumpet-blown among those leaves / and would escape them on golden elbows / but he was betrayed and buckled / by the anger of his hair . . ." the reading, though it makes quite good sense, will be rhythmically null and rhetorically deficient. (To be fair, one should concede that the original version is not metrically flawless, but at least it uses metre authentically to relate the words more sensitively to the nature and feeling of the speaker.)

Perhaps we may try a simple test. A careless reader of theatre-verse will have Brutus say: "Between the acting of a dreadful thing / and the first motion / all the interim / is like a phantasma, or a hideous dream /." A good reader will speak the words precisely in accordance with their lineation in the text:

> Between the acting of a dreadful thing
> And the first motion, all the interim is
> Like a phantasma, or a hideous dream[5]

where, among other details, the slight pause after "is" has the same kind of rhetorical point as the similar nuance in the passage quoted from *The Cocktail Party*. The moment of silence, by fiction, is the moment in which Brutus conceived the expansive, awed speculation of the simile. Longinus should be behind the reading, somewhere.

Lineation does not, of course, reveal everything. In the lines from *Julius Caesar* the reader must not only know the customary arrangement of stresses in blank verse but must also take account of the traditional variations. Robert Bridges has dealt

---

[5] *Julius Caesar*, II. 1. lines 63-65, edited by J. Dover Wilson, Cambridge University Press, 1949, p. 25. The commas, which I have inserted, are defensible, I think, in view of the point at issue.

with three of these in *Milton's Prosody*. First, two unstressed syllables could replace the one which the iambic foot allows, if elision were possible whether actually in speech or only theoretically. Second, an extra unstressed syllable could appear after the fifth foot, making a feminine ending. Third, in any foot except the last the iamb could be replaced by a trochee. Professor Ransom has shown[6] that we must add a fourth: any two successive iambic feet might be replaced by a double or ionic foot:

> Let me not to thĕ márrı̆age ŏf trúe mínds
> Admit . . .

The metrical arrangement of the lines from *Julius Caesar* would therefore be as follows:

> Bĕtwéen thĕ áctĭng óf ă dréadfŭl thíng
>
> Ănd thĕ fírst mótiŏn, áll thĕ ínterı̆m ís
>
> Líke ă phăntásmă, ór ă hídeŏus dréam.

This indicates the *metre*, but not the precise degree of stress on each syllable. Clearly, the degree of stress on "or," on the second syllable of "between," and on the first syllable of "acting," technically identical, will not be identical in a reading which takes account of the weight of meaning borne by each word. It would be quite impossible to indicate the precise degree of stress appropriate to each syllable, however elaborate one's system of notation. And unnecessary, since the rhetorical factor provides enough hints to guide the intelligent reader.

6 "The Strange Music of English Verse," *Kenyon Review*, Summer 1956, p. 471ff.

# CHAPTER SIXTEEN. THEATRE POETRY
## AND DRAMATIC VERSE

BEGINNING with a commonplace: Yeats will provide a text; Allen Tate will indicate its scope; no serious writer in our time has been unaware of its implications.

In June 1903 Yeats, committed for the time being to an "aristocratic" drama, a theatre for the elite, declared: "Almost the greatest difficulty before good work in the ordinary theatres is that the audience has no binding interest, no great passion or bias that the dramatist can awake."[1] To Allen Tate thirty years later (in *Reactionary Essays on Poetry and Ideas*) it seemed— and surely it is even more apparent today—that the age provided for the poet no epos or myth, no pattern of well-understood behaviour, which the poet could examine in the light of his own experience. The ages which have produced the greatest drama, he observed, are those which offer to the poet a seasoned code: drama would seem to depend on such a code for clarity and form. It matters little whether it is a code for the realisation of good or of evil. The important thing is that it shall tell the dramatist how people try to behave, and that it shall be too "perfect," whether in good or evil, for human nature. By adhering strictly to the code the dramatist exhibits a "representative" action. The tension between the code and the hero makes the action also specific, unique. The code is at once broken and affirmed, the hero's resistance at once clarified and defined by the limits thus set to his conduct. Macbeth asserts his ego in terms of the code before him, not in terms of courtly love or the idealism of the age of Werther: he has no choice of code. The modern character has the liberty of indefinite choice, but not—like Macbeth and Antigone—the good fortune to be

[1] *The Letters of W. B. Yeats*, edited by Allan Wade, London, Rupert Hart-Davis, 1954, p. 406. Letter of June 28, 1903.

chosen. Mr. Tate also argued that with the disappearance of general patterns of conduct the power to depict action that is both single and complete also disappears. The dramatic genius of the poet is held to short flights, and the dramatic lyric is a fragment of a total action which the poet lacks the means to delineate.[2]

The problem is pretty well understood by now as a breakdown in the range of communication. It has been defined for the present generation in Ionesco's plays and Empson's poems. (Indeed the line from Chekhov's *The Three Sisters* to Ionesco's *Chairs* is the very enactment of the breakdown). Here is Empson:

> though you
> Look through the very corners of your eyes
> Still you will find no star behind the blue;
> This gives no scope for trickwork. He who tries
> Talk must always plot and then sustain,
> Talk to himself until the star replies,
> Or in despair that it could speak again
> Assume what answers any wits have found
> In evening dress on rafts upon the main,
> Not therefore uneventful or soon drowned.[3]

If we are reduced to "assuming" and "feigning," the great traditional prop of drama has collapsed: Faith (in *something*), or a body of provisional beliefs (in *something*). Empson has learned a noble, if precarious, style from a despair, but in drama such a venture is doomed. The meditative poet may speak for a long time without adverting to the fact that no one else is listening. Not so the dramatist.

Yeats, tackling the problem with his own insights, brought off a drama of formal purity which has practically nothing to say to modern theatre audiences. Trusting in its own fine validity it hovers in mid-air over a society with which it has barely estab-

[2] *Reactionary Essays on Poetry and Ideas*, New York, Scribner, 1936, pp. 199-201.
[3] *Collected Poems*, London, Chatto and Windus, 1955 edition, p. 47.

lished diplomatic relations. Yeats showed what can be achieved even after one has despaired of the Common Man; and the limits of this achievement. (Mrs. Brown always has her revenge.) Eliot's approach—so different—has been equally suggestive. He has rarely been happy with coterie-drama, and he has acknowledged the necessity of meeting the Common Man. But snags persist. In Eliot's strategy the dramatist uses the Common Man's words, but makes them accommodate elitist meanings. He tries to assume at least the remnants of a code, the Christian one, and to conceal all trace of the assumption from his audience. But it is an inhibiting device, complicated still further by Eliot's innate distaste for the Common Man. Eliot's dialectic, in fact, differs very little in this respect from Yeats's.

### LANGUAGE: ELIOT AND ARISTOTLE

In this situation Eliot placed his trust in language, specifically in dramatic verse, not only to effect communication but to impose artistic order on experience. In 1950 he argued (*Poetry and Drama*) that it is a function of art to give us some perception of an order in life by imposing an order upon it. It seemed to him that beyond the classifiable emotions and motives of our conscious life when directed toward action there is a fringe of feeling which we can only detect, so to speak, out of the corner of the eye, and can never completely focus, feeling of which we are aware only in a kind of temporary detachment from action. This peculiar range of sensibility, he thought, could be rendered by dramatic poetry, at its moments of greatest intensity.[4]

This confidence in language is dangerously excessive, but one can easily see where it fits in. Eliot's own success in the direct manipulation of words is an obvious factor. Again there is his conception of language as not only the guardian of one's tradition but the means by which one names feelings and atti-

[4] *Poetry and Drama, Selected Prose,* London, Penguin Books, 1953, p. 85.

tudes.[5] Furthermore, as a literary historian Eliot has pointed to certain dramatists (Dryden, for one) whose plays have been kept alive mainly by their language, their "pure magnificence of diction." In the same context he conceded that "drama is a mixed form; pure magnificence will not carry it through," and that the poet who tries to achieve a play "by the single force of the word" provokes comparison with poets of other gifts. Corneille and Racine, he noted, do not attain their triumphs by magnificence of diction: ". . . ; they have concentration also, and, in the midst of their phrases, an undisturbed attention to the human soul as they know it."[6] This dates from 1924; its insight has been largely shelved in Eliot's recent theory of drama. The etiolated clarity of that theory is disturbing, particularly the wishful suggestion that despite indications to the contrary pure magnificence of diction *will* carry the play through.

The issue is tricky, though. In those parts of Shaw's theatre which retain their strength, the vitality issues mainly from the sharpness of the argument, the athletic vigour of the prose. Think of *On the Rocks, Getting Married*, and *Heartbreak House*. Beddoes, too: whatever impact he continues to make as a dramatist arises solely from his flair for language. No one dreams of studying Beddoes for any other reason, and there are some who are so impressed that they jump to untenable conclusions. Louis O. Coxe, for instance: "[Beddoes] had grasped what too few dramatists today believe, that the vehicle of a play is not character but language, a particular language that is theatrical in that it conveys the immediate action while it points ahead to impending tragedy. He knew that language can be dramatic of itself and was able to make it so."[7] But language cannot be dramatic "of itself." The most acclaimed speeches in the history of the theatre are "dramatic of themselves" only because while reading them we recall or imagine the situations in which they

---

[5] "The Social Function of Poetry," *Adelphi*, July-September 1945.
[6] *Homage to John Dryden*, London, Hogarth Press, 1924, pp. 20-22.
[7] "Beddoes: The Mask of Parody," *Hudson Review*, Vol. VI, 2, Summer 1953, pp. 253-56.

are uttered. This applies also to *Death's Jest Book* and *Sweeney Agonistes*.

Eliot's preoccupation with dramatic verse (to the neglect of more basic problems involved in the composition of a play) arises, I should imagine, from two considerations. First, the failure of nineteenth-century verse dramatists presented itself to him (wrongly, in my view) as a linguistic failure, a failure to provide "the special language necessary for drama." Again, as a practising verse dramatist he found that there were no established traditions—or none that he regarded as still viable—no charted ways of exploiting the full resources of language in the theatre. Hopkins's editor W. H. Gardner has claimed that it was the verse-form of Caradoc's soliloquy in *St. Winefred's Well* "that provided the most significant hint to future dramatic poets,"[8] citing *Murder in the Cathedral*. But where is the evidence? The Alexandrine blank verse of the soliloquy has several qualities which theatre-speech requires: muscle, throbbing energy, and, above all, the power at one thrust to close the gap between thought and speech:

> Yes,
> To hunger and not have, yet hope on for, to storm and
> strive and
> Be at every assault fresh foiled worse flung, deeper dis-
> appointed,
> The turmoil and the torment, it has, I swear, a sweetness,
> Keeps a kind of joy in it, a zest, an edge, an ecstasy,
> Next after sweet success. I am not left even this;
> I all my being have hacked in half with her neck: one part,
> Reason, selfdisposal, choice of better or worse way,
> Is corpse now, cannot change; my other self, this soul,
> Life's quick, this kind, this keen self-feeling,
> With dreadful distillation of thoughts sour as blood,
> Must all day long taste murder.

[8] W. H. Gardner, *Gerard Manley Hopkins: A Study of Poetic Idiosyncrasy in relation to Poetic Tradition*, Vol. II, London, Secker and Warburg, 1949, p. 191.

Caradoc's energy and the energy of the language are one. It is a happy occasion. But there are moments in which one hears, while Caradoc speaks, only the voice of the poet who wrote *The Wreck of the Deutschland* and *Felix Randal*. And surely it is inconceivable that Eliot or any other dramatist would take his bearings from a soliloquy which runs to such barbarous quirks of syntax as this:

> What stroke has Caradoc's right arm dealt?/What done?
>                         Head of a rebel
> Struck off it has; . . .

or this:

> Wiped I am sure this was;/it seems not well; . . .[9]

In confronting the problem of language in modern verse drama, Eliot has shown that the verse which "works" in the modern theatre is as different from *La Figlia Che Piange* as from *The Blessed Damozel* or *The Lake Isle of Innisfree*. Indeed, *insofar as the problems of verse drama are linguistic problems,* Eliot has done more than any other dramatist to lay down genuine lines of development. He has indicated the necessity and the possibility of refurbishing theatre-speech, whether verse or not. It is a commonplace that the modern theatre condones remarkably inept handling of language; the sheer bad writing to be found in the plays of O'Neill, to cite one instance, points up the debt the modern theatre owes to Eliot as a devotee of scrupulous speech.

And yet—to be basic or banal—there is more in a play than words. Drama is like poetry and fiction inasmuch as it uses words; unlike poetry and fiction inasmuch as words alone are not enough. Eugene O'Neill, however elephantine in manipulating words, was a better dramatist than Henry James; I don't relish the fact, but there it is. Perhaps we may generalise to this extent, that great plays are never lyric notations. Yeats was a better *poète de théâtre* than Eliot or James or Joyce—for several

[9] *Poems of Gerard Manley Hopkins*, edited by W. H. Gardner, Oxford University Press, 1948, pp. 153-59.

reasons: (1) he knew the differences between a poem, a play, and a nouvelle, (2) he had a finer sense of the theatrical organism, (3) he had the intelligence to exploit a valid relation between the Noh plays and certain shapes vaguely discernible in the legendary anecdotes which he chose as substance of his theatre. The measure of his superiority is the structural finesse of the *Plays for Dancers*.

The dramatist who has started as a poet or a novelist is often loath to concede that words alone are not enough. His natural impulse is to trust the words to carry all his burdens: action, plot, agency, gesture, and more than these. Alternatively he refuses to acknowledge that the composition of a play requires new skills which he, however expert in words, may not command. His hope, in fact—it is Eliot's—is to deduce a play from a poem. He may even have been encouraged in this fancy by those critics who have been in the habit of presenting Shakespeare's plays "as poems," as sheer verbal artifacts. The appropriate corrective, of course, is Aristotle, recalling the implication in the tangled *Poetics* that a play is not in the first instance —to use Francis Fergusson's gloss—"a composition in the verbal medium." At its deepest level it is a sequence of acts, whose nature is indicated partly by words, partly by gestures, partly by the "context of situation," by the "scene" itself.

Eliot and the keenest modern critics have of course studied Aristotle, but their ideas of drama have been largely determined by Coleridge, a closet-dramatist! This is partly why Eliot has not felt the relevance, the sheer resonance, of the *Poetics*, or indeed of Pound's endorsing marginalia in the *ABC of Reading*: "Ultimately, I suppose, any man with decent literary curiosity will read the *Agamemnon* of Aeschylus, but if he has seriously considered drama as a means of expression he will see that whereas the medium of poetry is WORDS, the medium of drama is people moving about on a stage and using words. That is, the words are only a part of the meaning and the gaps between them, or deficiencies in their meaning, can be made up by 'action.' "[10] This blurs the special meaning of "action" which Kenneth Burke and Francis Fergusson have been at pains to preserve for use, but its general slant is impregnable. Eliot with Coleridge against the devotees of Aristotle: a crude reduction but not too inaccurate. It would be pleasant if we could throw in our lot with either party, without serious qualifications or misgivings, but it is hardly feasible. What we must regret in Professor Fergusson and in M. Cocteau if not in Aristotle is the hovering implication that the words do not greatly matter; if the plot is sound the "verses" will look after themselves. In the Preface to *Les Mariés de la Tour Eiffel* we find Cocteau saying: "Car je supprime toute image et toute finesse de langue. Il ne reste que la poésie. Donc, pour les oreilles modernes, il ne reste rien."[11] This is perverse. Yes of course the plot is primary; no "words" can take its place. But this does not mean that *poésie de théâtre* in Cocteau's sense—what every serious dramatist is striving to achieve—has no use for the full resources of language, for language as a penetrative instrument, *toute finesse de langue*. A play is more than its scenario, just as it is more than its text. Eugene O'Neill would have been a finer dramatist if in addition to his theatrical sense —which itself was strong though not profound—he had been gifted with the arts of language and the powers of mind on which they depend. Recall too that one of the special concerns of modern critics has been to show that metaphor and image, far from being mere decorations on an already given, wrapped-up meaning, are often the essential ways of bringing meaning to birth. How then can *poésie de théâtre* be *fully* articulate unless it utilises all the exploratory potentialities of words? Susanne Langer has observed (in *Feeling and Form*) that a dramatist who writes only the words uttered in a play marks a long series of culminating moments in the flow of the action;[12] and surely

---

[10] *The ABC of Reading*, London, Faber and Faber, 1951, p. 46.

[11] *D'un Ordre Considéré comme une Anarchie*, 1923, *Le Rappel à l'Ordre*, Paris, Stock, 1926, p. 255.

[12] *Feeling and Form*, London, Routledge and Kegan Paul, 1953, p. 315.

the culminating moments require for presentation nothing less than the ultimate skills of language. Mark Twain, providing in *Huckleberry Finn* a profound sequence of acts, still needed something very close to the ultimate skills of language in order to *render* those acts. It would seem that in *poésie de théâtre* (and in the effort to comprehend it) we need the kind of insight that might emerge from the juxtaposition of Aristotle and Coleridge. R. P. Blackmur has already proposed this juxtaposition for his own purposes. For us Aristotle would endorse the primacy of plot, and he would force Coleridge to scrutinise his whole idea of drama, to see whether it was not fundamentally flawed. He would warn us, graciously, that the determining fact about a play is that one thing is represented as happening after another; that the features which give us an impression of the play's *simultaneity* are local enrichments contributing their versions of unity to support the quite different kind of unity which issues from the sequential coherence of the play; that this sequential thrust is the source of the *dynamic*. In turn, Coleridge would define, with solicitude, the role of language in drama. And perhaps a third force, which we will call Kenneth Burke, might persuade both critics to assign a more creative role to the *scene* in which an *act* is performed. All in the service of an ideal theatre and the entelechial myth by which we would define it.

## TOWARD EVALUATION

Twentieth-century verse drama in English (or in American, in deference to Dr. Williams) has been very slow in becoming a "modern" movement: it has trailed far behind crucial events in poetry and fiction. One anachronism, of several: up to 1932 verse-drama in England meant Masefield, Flecker, Phillips, and Bottomley. Such writers, having made nothing at all of Yeats's theatre (those who knew it), clung to the "high" example of Shakespeare's tragic soliloquies and affected the "sublime" in those terms. Since Shakespeare never took quotidian reality tragically, and since the tragic and the sublime were prerogatives of the great, the Georgian verse dramatists sought the sublime through heroic characters and mythic situations. Yeats's chosen level as dramatist was also "high"—though not in a neo-Shake-spearean tradition—in keeping with his own heroes and myths, which have their own validity because of the virile if limited ethos that sustains them. Eliot, trusting otherwise, has enlarged the range of modern verse drama, and strengthened it, by en-forcing some of the sharp movement of the "low" style which he mastered in his early poems, cutting away the Georgian *fat* by means of language exact, ascetic, transparent.

We would speculate on Eliot's activity—without invoking "influences" or qualitative comparisons—alongside three writers, Dante, Flaubert, and Ibsen. Eliot's procedure in his plays, like Dante's in the *Commedia*, involved the mingling of styles, keep-ing common idiom as the basis of diction and rhythm. In the letter to Can Grande, Dante said of the style of the *Commedia*: " . . . remissus est modus et humilis, quia locutio vulgaris, in qua et mulierculae communicant."[13] The programme is Eliot's rather than Yeats's; one does not account for it by listing differ-ences between comedy and tragedy.

Eliot's situation in regard to early twentieth-century verse drama was similar to that of Flaubert confronting the loose, expansive ardours of French Romanticism. In one of the finest of the letters to Louise Colet Flaubert—for the time being self-critic and author of the *Dictionnaire des Idées Recues*—gave an account of his aesthetic which she was unlikely to relish: "Il faut ecrire plus *froidement*. Mefions-nous de cette espece d'echauffement, qu'on appelle l'inspiration, et ou il entre souvent plus d'emotion nerveuse que de force musculaire."[14] In modern verse drama there is room for a lot of work in this direction. Eliot has secured a certain amount of *force musculaire* for

[13] *Dantis Alagherii Epistolae*, edited by Paget Toynbee, Oxford, Claren-don Press, 1920, p. 177. Erich Auerbach argues that "locutio" here means "style," not "the Italian language." See *Mimesis*, Princeton Uni-versity Press, 1953, p. 186.

[14] *Correspondance: 1852-1854*, Paris, Conard, 1927, p. 104. Letter of 27-28 February, 1853.

verse drama—indeed, it is one of the most enlightening things to say on the subject—but there is still an air-lock that is blocking verse drama from some of the deepest areas of experience. Some years ago Dr. Williams (the most acute critic in diagnosing such weaknesses) complained that Eliot's approach to actuality was still only partial.[15] There is no getting around this; the defect is *there*: Eliot's is very much a Paleface theatre.

Unlike Ibsen's, which has a certain warm *thickness*. Eliot is like Ibsen in conceding extremes of experience to persons in social rank far below "the great." But a temperamental blockage has prevented him from making the most of Ibsen's theatre-poetry. Is it not emerging more clearly than ever that modern theatre poetry, finding the Shakespearean example inspiring but, in the long run, unemployable, may take its formal bearings more rewardingly from Ibsen? If so, it is peculiarly unfortunate that Ibsen's achievement has been so radically misunderstood by such dramatists as Yeats, Synge, and Eliot himself, and so attenuated even by Joyce in the lyric purgation of *Exiles*. In the long run it will matter less that Ibsen's *haute bourgeoisie* has become unrecognisable than that he has provided for our time the most viable emblems of theatre-poetry. What Eliot requires, what verse drama requires, to substantiate a Flaubertian finesse of language, is a sense of the theatrical organism comparable to Ibsen's.

In present circumstances there is little hope of developing a drama characterised by the range, concentration, and precision of awareness which astonishes in *Antony and Cleopatra, King Lear*, or *A Winter's Tale*. Modern drama seems fated to be a mirror in fragments. Francis Fergusson has reminded us (in *The Idea of a Theater*) that beyond the problem of tapping the roots of our culture for the revival of the actual theatre there is the general cultural problem in its thousand forms, the preoccupation of Joyce, Mann, Yeats, and Eliot: what is the relation between the divided modern awareness and that "or-

---

[15] *Selected Letters of William Carlos Williams*, New York, McDowell, Obolensky, 1957, p. 249. Letter of 30 October, 1946 to Ezra Pound.

ganisation of the sensibility" which we feel in Shakespeare, Dante, and Sophocles? We do not know.[16] All we can see is the condition of the contemporary theatre: a profusion of talent and goodwill issuing in plays composed on the margin of a blank page; almost total confusion as to the nature of tragedy; almost total inability to find order or meaning in an individual life; the misunderstanding of *entelechy*; a failure of nerve issuing in the mood play; the sheer gimmickry of "theatre," cut off from genuine theatrical invention.

We have glanced at Yeats's version of modern heterogeneity. Eliot's is equally suggestive. In studying the Elizabethan dramatists, he observed, we feel that they believed in their own age, in a way in which no twentieth-century writer of the greatest seriousness has been able to believe in his. And, accepting their age, the Elizabethan dramatists were in a position to concentrate their attention, to their respective abilities, upon the common characteristics of humanity in all ages, rather than upon the differences. We recognise an "assumption of permanence" in Shakespeare, in his minor fellows, in Dante, and the great Greek dramatists.[17] Eliot's account is homely but just as valid as several more pretentious theses. It is clear that even in the work of such theatre-satirists as Hall and Marston there is a commitment to the solidity, the reality of the world. What Marston "says" about the world in *Antonia and Mellida* is sufficiently mordant for anyone's taste, but it does not undermine the image of that world as *real*, however corrupt. Shakespeare could take certain positive values for granted, while enacting their perversion; the only things Eliot can assume are negations or, at best, "neutralities."

The phrase "assumption of permanence" strikes a painful note in our time and illustrates the position of contemporary drama. One well-documented result is that there are no longer any heroes, any "capable men" (Wallace Stevens's phrase) as

[16] *The Idea of a Theater*, Princeton University Press, 1949, pp. 195-96.
[17] "John Ford," *Selected Essays*, London, Faber and Faber, 1934, p. 202.

distinct from arbitrarily chosen characters to which things happen. Harry Levin has noted in his study of Marlowe that Faust in the twentieth century is the decadent aesthete of Mann or the intellectual snob of Valery. The hero of the modern artist is Flaubert's Saint Anthony, the resigned protagonist who secludes himself, yet is haunted by the desires he has resisted. His watchword is Renunciation; his favourite figure of speech is *meiosis*. Only through mystical correspondences can the modern artist link the symbolic world of poetry with the actual world of experience. Marlowe succeeded in bringing the two worlds close together because his background was still sustained by the mythical and the universal, even while he was engaged in bringing the factual and the personal into the foreground.[18] Recalling Marlowe we can hardly avoid noticing that the symbols of modern drama, as compared with those of the heroic *auto* (Northrop Frye's term) are attenuated to the point of invisibility. Eliot has given us more than one version of the heroic; and yet these, if anything, support our point. In Eliot's early plays there is a disconcerting parity between the degree of moral action possible to Man and the extent of his estrangement from the quotidian world. To act, this Man must transcend Mankind, becoming Meta-Man. In the later plays Man acts not to the extent that he is *human*—with Reason and Will—but only insofar as he is *religious*. Or, in an extreme version, it amounts to this: only Christians can act. Eliot's plays, with the fine exception of *The Elder Statesman*, do not share our conviction that this day-to-day world—in itself, and without apology—is still the glowing locus of value. The habit of implying that the human being can no longer *act* has already had a debilitating effect on the novel and the drama: we applaud such writers as Joyce Cary, Cozzens, and Herbert Gold for resisting, for asserting the value of human choice and action. In the theatre the regressive habit has tended to substitute the static for the dynamic, to exalt the "interesting" or the decoratively anaemic. *Pathos* rather than *Praxis*.

[18] *The Overreacher*, London, Faber and Faber, 1954, pp. 188-89.

In the face of this situation the modern dramatist can work only with the materials available. It is even more difficult for him than for the novelist to endorse the minority assumption that human life is valuable. Society must recover or formulate some kind of code before the dramatist can use the code as a member of the dramatic tension. In a recent study of *Don Perlimplin* as *poésie de théâtre* Francis Fergusson observed: "When a national culture revives, its art forms seem significant, filled with immediately relevant moral and spiritual content; and that seems to have occurred in Lorca's Spain. When that happens, the theatre in its play with images from art may be allusive without being merely arty."[19] *Don Perlimplin* did not create the society; when the culture revived, the play helped to define it, became its focus, its emblem, thus contributing to the revival its own form and meaning. In this case, as in *Hamlet,* we feel a reciprocal relation obtaining between the society and its drama. No confident feeling of this kind arises from the plays of Yeats or of Eliot. Can we not say this—that our theatre is full of individual insights, "characteristically" partial images of man, insights all the more extreme because they feel themselves caught in a trap? What we lack is an image of man, in the medium of theatre, which we can acknowledge as somehow representative, somehow central: we lack "harmonies." Modern drama is all Behaviour (Mr. Blackmur's term, from another context), but Behaviour cut adrift from any "theoretic form," of Manners or Morals, which would test its vitality. There are still, of course, "certainties," which retain their validity because they are *prior* to the embarrassments of idea and belief: the senses, for example, and the biologic imperative—these undercut the level of existence which painfully in our time has involved radical fragmentation, isolation. And these certainties are indeed available as substance of an image of man. But this image is at least as partial as any other, since by programme it excludes the essen-

[19] "Don Perlimplin: Lorca's Theater-Poetry," *Kenyon Review,* Vol. XVII, 3, Summer 1955, p. 346.

tially human level of existence, existence in terms of Reason, Intelligence, Idea.

What are we to do, then, with these partial, extreme images? With Beckett's image, for instance, or Brecht's, or Kafka's; or Eliot's parade of D.P.'s? Reject them? Endorse them? Argue about them as if they were instances of dialectic (which, obliquely, they are)?—or, as a protective or ironic gesture, place them against some equally extreme but more engaging images, hoping thereby to redeem their partiality? Our idea of the representative image is constantly forcing us, as it were, to compose (by ourselves) the "perfect" image of man—and the "perfect" modern play—by setting up many partial images to redeem the supple confusions of each.

Eliot's drama, seen with these preoccupations, is not so much a number of good or bad plays as a body of interim drama, *essays* in drama rather than drama itself. And as essays they are probably, in their own way, as fine as can be managed until the conditions of society change. Indeed it may well be that their value is to keep the lines of severe intelligence open in the commercial theatre, waiting for such a change. If society changes, it will also provide "central" motives for the dramatist; relevance will gather into new patterns involving the whole of man. At present each dramatist does the best he can with his own little corner. We recall, with Francis Fergusson, that drama can flourish only in a human-sized scene, generally acknowledged as the focus of the life or awareness of its time.[20]

This being so, since there is no "centre" there can be no "tone of the centre," no single authoritative style, no mode of vision emblematic of our time. I take it that this is the context which has propelled Dr. Williams's lifelong search for "a redeeming language," a new measure consonant with our time, just as it has compelled every serious modern writer to be an experimental writer, trying anything at least once. It is possible to argue from literary history that the most fruitful eras were

[20] *The Idea of a Theater*, p. 225.

those in which a supply of viable conventions was available to an
artist in any medium, and that literature today suffers from the
lack of such conventions. In the meantime we are exposed to the
bizarre, the oblique, the grotesque, the extreme, the raw insight.

If new actions somehow acquire relevance, if, somehow,
society acquires a determining motive or code—and this is a
tune we whistle desperately to ward off the ghosts—it will be
desirable to have a verse style capable of playing its part in
"poésie de théâtre." We cannot afford to let the words take care
of themselves: hence the justification, even at this stage, of
trying to understand the question of dramatic verse.

The rules which Eliot has proposed in regard to dramatic
verse are few and modest. They amount to this: the proper verse
is one in which everything that has to be said may be said with
"ease" and grace. The speeches must satisfy the requirement of
strict dramatic relevance. We would argue, further, that the
dramatist who writes a "contemporary" play is compelled to
take his bearings from the habits of speech in the section of
society with which he is dealing; Eliot has shown that one can
do this and still write with distinction. The difficulty is to decide
how rigorously this commitment is to be interpreted: my own
feeling is that it must be taken fairly severely. Paul Valery spoke
of the poet as a maker of *deviations*, artifacts constructed from
a special poetic language which stands over against the language of practical day-to-day speech. Eliot has held out against
the invitation, and rightly, sensing that the risk of artificiality
and spuriousness is too great. This applies to an even greater
extent in the theatre. I imagine most people would concede
that experiments in the imposition of an artificial verse-manner
in modern drama have been unrewarding. The trouble is that
the conventions of the theatre do not leave the dramatist completely free to choose, nor are they sufficiently "of our time"
to provide adequate signposts for a dramatist investigating
contemporary experience. The conditions are most favourable
for the writer of fiction. We may cite, close at hand, a passage

from the conversation between Isaac McCaslin and his cousin in *The Bear*:

" 'All right. Escape.—Until one day he said what you told Fonsiba's husband that afternoon here in this room: *This will do. This is enough*: not in exasperation or rage or even just sick to death as you were sick that day: just *This is enough* and looked about for one last time, for one time more since he had created them, upon this land this South for which he had done so much with woods for game and streams for fish and deep rich soil for seed and lush springs to sprout it and long summers to mature it and serene falls to harvest it and short mild winters for men and animals, and saw no hope anywhere and looked beyond it where hope should have been, where to East North and West lay illimitable that whole hopeful continent dedicated as a refuge and sanctuary of liberty and freedom from what you called the old world's hopeless evening, and. . . ' "[21]

This, one part elegy, one part jeremiad, dissolves realistic terms in a strong solution of ceremony. It is acceptable, however "artificial," because a sustaining decorum, the decorum of ceremony which is so deeply involved in the meaning of the story, has been established by the tone of Faulkner's prose in earlier pages. We accept it all the more readily, realising that something essential is being revealed about Isaac, in words attributed to him though he, if we could imagine him apart from the story, would not have conceived those words. It is an equivalent of the convention of the omniscient author stepping forward to comment, but the novelist can get away with it provided he reveals the rules at the beginning of the story, when we are getting our bearings. No satisfactory way has yet been found to give the dramatist similar latitude. In *The Family Reunion* Harry's "poetical" speeches are out on a limb because nothing in the decorum of the play sustains them. Even in *Requiem for a Nun* (the Courthouse Scene) when Gowan

[21] *The Portable Faulkner*, edited by Malcolm Cowley, New York, Viking Press, 1946, pp. 316-17.

*259*

suddenly starts talking in a High Style very like that monopolised
by Gavin Stevens the bucolic Cincinnatus:

> From the past. From my folly. My drunkenness.
> My cowardice, if you like—

the conventions of drama start yelling: the nearer the thing
comes to being a play, with actors who look like real people,
the more difficult to sustain radical departures from credible
speech. It may have something to do with the simple fact that
one doesn't need to visualise Ike McCaslin or Boon Hogganbeck;
if one responds to the force of will behind their words and acts,
that is good enough. In *The Bear* Faulkner can affect the sublime or the apocalyptic—and get away with it—because he
seizes the opportunity—richly available in fiction, not as richly
in drama—of framing one's own rules. He knows, as Henry
James knew, that the novelist to a much greater degree than
the dramatist enjoys the privilege of composing a self-subsistent
universe; his only obligation—which is also a prime means of
persuasion—is internal consistency.

The freedom of expression which Faulkner's stories exhibit
is not as readily available to the dramatist. Probably the main
snag is that no satisfactory convention—that is, a set of procedures to which theatre audiences respond with ease—has yet
been developed by which the dramatist may indicate more of
the truth about an agent than that agent may be expected to
know. Eliot's experiments in this direction have not been fruitful and in recent years he has abandoned them. The problem
persists, however, and some interesting experiments are being
made. I would mention one: Reuel Denney in *September Lemonade* has tried a procedure which allows him frequently, though
not arbitrarily, to transcend the probable. In that play Irene
talks to her younger sister Janet on a warm autumn evening; at
a certain point she moves toward Janet and takes her hand:

> You know, if a hand should hold this season's mouth,
> Someone would hear it anyway? Would call the birds back
> With drummed tattoos on hollow beams and elms

Into the cypress balconies of the South?
Where no one on a terrace weeps in armchairs.
Or turns a fluid lake to ice of snakes.
Or tries the blue between-tones of this time.
Or tunes like that Blue Diesel of the horn.

Janet moves off to the right, saying:

Terraces you talk about, while we put up with porches.
You know, the way not to give what you don't want to keep
Is to tell them you'll kiss but you'll never sleep?
Miss Diesel, you blue consultant, what color polish
Shall I put on my toes? My wave has been to wash
And my toes are scrunchable. Have some candy!

Janet sits on the settee, pulling her legs up snugly. Irene lolls
in the chair beside the table, saying: "When are you going to
try to stop being a menace to work at gas stations and naviga-
tions in any narrow channels where the bridge-keepers are under
forty-five? You don't have to act thrown together that way with
a one-piece sit-down and eyes rolling on weights like a doll's
head; that is, unless you want to. Maybe you want to."

Then Janet, from the Frankie Addams stable: "I like to toss
myself around like a rag doll, that's all. I feel better that way.
I can't talk like you; so how can I say to myself how I feel? I
have to just move the way I feel. I just like to feel, for example,
like taffy on one of those machines on the beach. Remember
how that taffy goes around the arms of the machine, two ways
at once? Oh, to be as daffy as that taffy! Here comes your
friend!"[22]

Four speeches, the first two quite improbable. But each of
those is the verbal sign of a "movement of the psyche" which
the girl herself, if limited to the probable, would be unable to
render. Here the words move far beyond the probable because
they insist on finding out how accurately they can represent,
stand for, the girl's otherwise inexpressible feelings. The change

[22] *New World Writing, 7th Mentor Selection*, 1955, p. 20.

from verse to prose endorses the movement from full expression to partial expression—from "the whole truth" to "as much of the truth as the girl knows and can speak." Much of the meaning of the play is enacted in transit between the two fictive worlds.

These verse speeches do not, of course, suddenly or wildly break through the probable. If they were to do so, they would be disastrous, like some of Oliver's speeches in *This Music Crept By Me on the Water*, or the irruption of a smart remark by Cliff Lewis in *Look Back in Anger*. Rather, they have been sanctioned by the ritual formality insinuated since the beginning of the play:

IRENE: So am I. It's a good dress for sitting around in waiting
    for someone else to smile first. . . . If it only fit me like
    these ambitious vines fit these candy porches!
JANET (*offstage*): Did you say like delicious lines fit dandy
    wenches?
IRENE: Yes. . . . In the long absence of the city gardener in
    winter,
    When snow alone blooms on the corner boulder,
    And the barked wood whitens, and the cleansers
    Of the rained light and the luminous sleet
    Divide the sight of the street from the sight of the stairs . . .
    I wonder why I make, where winds arrive,
    Each weightless husk hold endings like a hive?

If the audience responds to these procedures easily and without distraction, the dramatist can force open the doors of the mind which tend to close on the familiar fragment of experience and insight. And in *September Lemonade* when these speech-procedures have been insinuated, the dramatist can have Jack apologise to Irene in words which stand very suggestively for the "quality" of his feeling; he has built up a decorum which sustains this version of the improbable:

    I feel as wrong as a King of Egypt
    With his money of time gone on:

My hand was rough; I'll tend, mend
The frail forsythia of your mood,
Make amends to your mere might
Fallen into my hands like spring.

There is something here of that density of reference which a dramatist may reasonably seek. Self-denial in a dramatist is a good thing, but not every form of self-denial. We would welcome, in its proper place, such language as Jack's in *September Lemonade* because it encompasses a range of expression that realistic drama has tended to suppress, and because in suppressing it this drama has helped to render modern audiences insensitive to words. Mr. Denney had this in mind when he complained that "the Word" does not stand on its own feet within "the Naturalistic convention of today's theatre." Hence he felt driven to concern himself with those themes "which depend, in the last analysis, on making the word a higher variable than any other aspect of the spectacle."[23] The emphasis has its own dangers, which he understands as well as anyone.

In the linguistic procedures of *September Lemonade*—no masterpiece, a slight play, but suggestive—there are intriguing possibilities. The play demands, of course, that the audience rise to the verbal occasion, fairly strenuously from moment to moment, and this response is quite different from the surrender to bardic lushness requested by *Under Milk Wood*. But Mr. Denney's strategy is not as factitious as our account of it may suggest; since the play contains only two "kinds" of speech, and these sharply differentiated, audiences might respond without too much fuss. It is hard to say. We remind ourselves, warily but with hope, that in the past audiences have responded to extensions of procedures at least as radical as this.

[23] "A Note on Poetic Language in the Theater," an unpublished essay which Mr. Denney kindly made available to me.

## DRAMATIC VERSE: A TRIAL DEFINITION

Eliot made his most direct attempt to specify the qualities peculiar to dramatic verse in *The Three Voices of Poetry*,[24] where he envisaged the first as the voice of the poet talking to himself, or to no one; the second, that of the poet addressing an audience, whether large or small; the third, the voice of the poet when he creates a dramatic agent speaking in verse, saying only what he can say within the limits of one imaginary agent addressing another. This distinction is less rewarding than one had hoped: it provides no solution to what Eliot calls "the problem of the difference between dramatic, quasi-dramatic, and non-dramatic verse," especially as Eliot remarks rather gnomically in the same context that in "poetic drama" all three voices are audible. It is obvious that a lyric or meditative poet who sets out to write a verse play needs a new set of procedures, but the precise nature of these procedures remains elusive.

We should avoid being precious about this. Dramatic verse is different from other kinds of verse, but the differences are not, we would argue, in matters of image, syntax, metaphor, diction, or metre. Only its context makes "Ripeness is all" a dramatic statement, and one could envisage a non-dramatic context such as *The Vanity of Human Wishes* in which the same statement would fit neatly enough. Again, there is nothing in such lines as "Farewell! thou art too dear for my possessing" or

> My lady's presence makes the roses red,
> Because to see her lips they blush with shame

which would debar them from supporting the burden of *some* dramatic situation. Indeed Romeo might have tossed Constable's lines to Benvolio in the opening scene without our feeling that they were inappropriate or undramatic, *in context*.

If this is so; if we cannot distinguish between dramatic and non-dramatic verse in such terms—what then? I should argue that a vital difference remains. Susanne Langer has pointed out that literature projects the image of life in the mode of virtual

[24] *The Three Voices of Poetry*, Cambridge University Press, 1953, p. 4.

memory; language is its essential material. The sound and meaning of words, their familiar or unusual use and order, create the
illusion of life as a realm of events—completed, lived—events
that compose a past. Drama, on the other hand, presents the
poetic illusion in a different light: not finished realities, not
"events," but immediate, visible responses of human beings,
make its semblance of life. The basic abstraction in drama is
the act, which springs from the past but is directed toward the
future and is always great with things to come. The distinction
is that as literature creates a virtual past, drama creates a virtual future. This tension between past and future, the theatrical
"present moment," is what gives to acts, gestures, and attitudes
the peculiar intensity known as "dramatic quality." In drama,
speech is an act, motivated by visible and invisible other acts,
and like them shaping the oncoming future.[25] What distinguishes
dramatic verse from lyric or meditative verse, therefore, is nothing as tangible as diction or syntax or versification, but rather a
bias, on the part of dramatic verse, toward the fulfillment of a
form whose completion lies ahead. The completed form may
be seen to have developed in a straight or crooked line, but
throughout the play there is a force which presses *forward*, and
the verse must answer to that pressure. Kenneth Burke had
something like this in mind, I imagine, when he spoke of the
dramatist building up "potentials," giving the audience a more
or less explicit or vague "in our next" feeling at the end of each
scene, and subsequently transforming such promises into ful-
fillments. The potentialities of one scene would in this way become the actualisations of the next, while these in turn would
be potentialities from the standpoint of unfoldings still to come.[26]
This is the kind of sequence that Hopkins professed to find in
Bridges's *The Growth of Love*; he felt that the work excelled
"in phrasing, in sequence of phrase and sequence of feeling on
feeling." By "sequence of feeling" he meant "a dramatic quality

[25] *Feeling and Form*, pp. 306-08, 315.
[26] "Othello," *Hudson Review*, Vol. IV, 2, Summer 1951, pp. 189-90.

by which what goes before seems to necessitate and beget what comes after."[27] The idea is pretty much the same.

It may be possible to indicate the characteristically dramatic sequence more precisely by taking account of Aristotle's distinction in the *Rhetoric* between three kinds of oratory. First, forensic oratory, which is oriented toward the past, as in a speech designed to establish someone's guilt. Next, demonstrative or epideictic oratory, the motivation of which is dominated by the desire to display one's skill as an orator; it is oriented toward the present-in-itself, "purely," like acrobatics. Finally, deliberative oratory, oriented toward a future in which the audience will act as persuaded.[28] The literary equivalent of forensic oratory would be narrative, the epic, the novel. Epideictic, in its concern for the present moment in itself, would correspond to lyric. The deliberative would link itself with drama, engendering in the audience "sequences of feeling." This correlation may also indicate the typical defect of such a dramatist as Christopher Fry, whose work exhibits a kind of inertia arising from the habit of substituting epideictic for deliberative writing.

Arguing thus; an essential requirement of dramatic verse is that throughout the play it shall be agile in miming the "movements of the psyche," and at the same time in generating contexts of future acts within a "theoretic form"; the thrust of the potential to realise itself in the actual. We would praise a passage of dramatic verse by indicating how its rendering of the present moment is simultaneously creating an emotional demand for fulfillment. Throughout the play the verse must be occupied in "shaping the oncoming future" and in persuading the audience to desire its "perfect" enactment.

We would illustrate this in speeches which are not obviously "dramatic"; to cite Cleopatra's "They do not go together"

[27] *The Correspondence of Gerard Manley Hopkins with R. W. Dixon*, edited by Claude Colleer Abbott, Oxford University Press, 1935, p. 8. Letter of 13 June 1878.

[28] Cp. Kenneth Burke, *A Rhetoric of Motives*, New York, Prentice-Hall, 1950, reprint by George Braziller, Inc., 1955, pp. 70-71.

would be inappropriate. Here is a fair example, all the more relevant because its dramatic quality has been questioned:

> Alas that Love, whose view is muffled still,
> Should without eyes see pathways to his will!
> Where shall we dine?—O me! What fray was here?
> Yet tell me not, for I have heard it all:
> Here's much to do with hate, but more with love:
> Why, then, O brawling love, O loving hate,
> O anything of nothing first create!
> O heavy lightness, serious vanity,
> Misshapen chaos of well-seeming forms,
> Feather of lead, bright smoke, cold fire, sick health,
> Still-waking sleep, that is not what it is!
> This love feel I, that feel no love in this.

The words—we make an obvious point—render a certain "movement of the psyche." It is possible to laugh at the speaker, and Romeo is uneasily aware that he is talking like a Petrarchan sonnet or like a poem from Watson's *Hekatompathia*:

ROMEO: Dost thou not laugh?
BENVOLIO: No, coz, I rather weep.

The oppositions persist: the syntax is not "merely verbal." Simultaneously, the lines evoke in the audience (who are deemed to be free from Romeo's confusions) a desire to have Romeo's mode of feeling confronted by the sharper realities of experience. The speech is designed *like* an Elizabethan love-poem so as to call out from the audience an appropriately critical response; if Romeo is to be tossed out of his enclosed garden of love-sickness it must be because the audience somehow wants this to happen. Hence the rich, if interim, fulfillment when Mercutio from outside the garden applies his salacious critique. Hence, here, these words which evoke in the audience a critical desire to put Romeo's seemingly fragile heart to the test. The lines press forward, not—like a Johnsonian sentence—closing and nailing down the matter, but expanding, as their energy

*267*

strains to enact such a test. The audience's desire is appeased in v, i when Romeo says, "Is it e'en so? Then I defy you, stars." It is a resonant assertion, Romeo has passed the test—a sequence of feeling has been "perfected." What we respond to, therefore, is the organic and extrinsic quality of Romeo's early speeches: their "poetical" nature is at once a rendering of feeling and a critique of that feeling; as critique it generates a characteristically dramatic sequence.

This, I am happy to say, is in line with Kenneth Burke's wavering distinction, in his *Grammar*, between the attitude as preparation for action and the attitude as substitution for action. He points out that if Aristotle's world is essentially a dramatic one, his God—as a pure act identical with perfect rest—is essentially lyrical. From the dramatic point of view, the moment of arrest that characterises the attitude is a kind of "pre-act." But the lyrical attitude is rather the kind of rest that is the summation or culmination of action, transcending overt action by *symbolically* encompassing its end. In drama, he notes, there is the intense internal debate prior to the moment of decision, but from the lyric point of view the state of arrest is itself an end-product, a resolution of previous action rather than a preparation for subsequent action.[29] Romeo's speech is a "pre-act" which, far from being the transcendence of his role in the enactment, is the "motive" for his subjection to a new series of trials. The series is inaugurated now because the audience wants it; and their wanting it is determined by the "quality" of the speech itself, since it exhibits a mode of feeling too fragile to be condoned.

Continuing: in Coleridge's *Remorse* the inferiority of the drama is accompanied by an almost continuously intrinsic and retrospective use of language. In iv, iii, for instance, Teresa says:

> The moon is high in heaven, and all is hushed.
> Yet, anxious listener! I have seemed to hear

[29] *A Grammar of Motives*, New York, Prentice-Hall, Inc., 1945, p. 245.

A low dead thunder mutter thro' the night,
As 'twere a giant angry in his sleep.
O Alvar! Alvar! that they could return
Those blessed days that imitated heaven,
When we two wont to walk at eventide;
When we saw nought but beauty; when we heard
The voice of that Almighty One who loved us
In every gale that breathed, and wave that murmured!
O we have listened, even till high-wrought pleasure
Hath half assumed the countenance of grief,
And the deep sigh seemed to heave up a weight
Of bliss, that pressed too heavy on the heart.
And this majestic Moor, seems he not one
Who oft and long communing with my Alvar,
Hath drunk in kindred lustre from his presence,
And guides me to him with reflected light.[30]

This limp aria, typical of *Remorse*, dissolves drama into a lyric moment, just as the typical speech in *Zapolya* tends to enforce an epic perspective; in both cases the essential defect is the same. There is no point in arguing that the verse is too close to the kind of lyric verse, such as *To the River Otter,* which Coleridge wrote in imitation of Bowles's sonnets—that begs the question; the real fault is that it looks *back* without simultaneously pressing *forward* to fulfill a "theoretic form." It provides "explanations" rather than raising emotional "problems" which demand solution. Even if the speech adequately mimes Teresa's feeling, its activity is merely local: it generates nothing from its blocked-off "present moment."

In contrast here is a passage from *The Confidential Clerk,* part of the conversation between Lucasta and Colby at the beginning of the second act:

LUCASTA: But it's only the outer world that you've lost:
    You've still got your inner world—a world that's more real.

---

[30] *The Dramatic Works of Coleridge,* edited by Derwent Coleridge, London, Moxon, 1852, pp. 57-58.

That's why you're different from the rest of us:
You have your secret garden; to which you can retire
And lock the gate behind you.

COLBY: And lock the gate behind me?
Are you sure that you haven't your own secret garden
Somewhere, if you could find it?

LUCASTA: If I could find it!
No, my only garden is . . . a dirty public square
In a shabby part of London—like the one where I lived
For a time, with my mother. I've no garden.
I hardly feel that I'm even a person:
Nothing but a bit of living matter
Floating on the surface of the Regent's Canal.
Floating, that's it.

The plot of this, moving from the "outer world" to the "inner world" and equating the latter with "a world that's more real," prepares us for the otherwise excessive weight of significance in "garden." When this word has taken the strain, its greatly increased momentum carries it through the rest of the play, extending its scope and supporting the spiritual burden of such lines as:

But for Eggerson
His garden is a part of one single world.

In Lucasta's speech the juxtaposition of "garden" and "dirty public square" endorses that of "person" and "matter"; the nexus of insight thus formed radiates through the entire play: outer, inner; public, secret; matter, person. The lines mime Lucasta's feeling with precision, "placing" her particular kind of self-consciousness. What they exhibit is a beautifully controlled rhetoric, similar in kind to that which Eliot admired (*"Rhetoric" and Poetic Drama*) in those situations in Shakespeare's plays in which a speaker *sees himself* in a dramatic light. There are the examples which Eliot cites:[31] Othello's "And say, besides,—that in Aleppo once . . .": Coriolanus's

[31] *Selected Essays*, p. 39.

If you have writ your annals true, 'tis there,
That like an eagle in a dovecot, I
Fluttered your Volscians in Corioli:
Alone I did it. . . .

to which we would add Timon's

Come not to me again: but say to Athens,
Timon hath made his everlasting mansion
Upon the beached verge of the salt flood.

The superbly directed stress on Coriolanus's first "I," thrust
forward by the sense of drama and history in "annals," vibrates
with his self-awareness. Lucasta's words do not affect this level
of magniloquence but their fine rhetoric operates similarly in its
own context. It issues in

Floating on the surface of the Regent's Canal.
Floating, that's it . . .

where the repetition indicates the dramatic light in which
Lucasta, for the time being, sees herself.

"Dramatic" is a eulogistic term, like "poetic," and, like
"poetic," often used to praise an effect which we like but do
not understand. We often speak of a dramatic element in a
poem, without indicating very precisely what this means. We
need an example. Compare Donne's:

Show me deare Christ, thy Spouse, so bright and clear.
What! is it She, which on the other shore
Goes richly painted? or which rob'd and tore
Laments and mournes in Germany and here?
Sleepes she a thousand, then peepes up one yeare?
Is she selfe truth and errs? now new, now outwore?
Doth she, and did she, and shall she evermore
On one, on seaven, or on no hill appeare?
Dwells she with us, or like adventuring knights
First travaile we to seeke and then make Love?

271

Betray kind husband thy spouse to our sights,
And let myne amorous soule court thy mild Dove,
Who is most trew, and pleasing to thee, then
When she'is embrac'd and open to most men.[32]

with Arnold's *Written in Butler's Sermons*:

Affections, Instincts, Principles, and Powers,
Impulse, and Reason, Freedom and Control—
So men, unravelling God's harmonious whole,
Rend in a thousand shreds this life of ours.

Vain labour! Deep and broad, where none may see,
Spring the foundations of the shadowy throne
Where man's one Nature, queen-like, sits alone,
Centered in a majestic unity.

And rays her powers, like sister islands, seen
Linking their coral arms under the sea:
Or cluster'd peaks, with plunging gulfs between

Spann'd by aerial arches, all of gold;
Whereo'er the chariot wheels of Life are roll'd
In cloudy circles, to eternity.[33]

To what are we responding when we feel that Donne's poem is more dramatic than Arnold? Not, surely, to any differences between the substance of the poems, the moral issues involved; or even, perhaps, to the fact that Donne's language is closer to spoken idiom, more sinewy, more Chaucerian. We recognise that the realism of speech in Donne's poem arises from the vigour of the speaker's piety, interpreting piety in Santayana's sense—larger than the usual one—of "loyalty to the sources of one's being." The speaker in Donne's poem is striving to acknowledge the prime source of his being and to unite himself with it. At once, then, a relationship is effected, by *fiat*, and this relationship is potentially a dramatic situation. In Arnold's lines,

[32] *The Poems of John Donne*, edited by Herbert J. C. Grierson, Oxford, Clarendon Press, 1912, Vol. I, p. 330.
[33] *Works*, London, Macmillan, 1910, p. 4.

on the other hand, we merely overhear someone meditating at large. Arnold's poem, a meditative lyric, presents the speaker gathering up his life's experience into a single moment of critique. It is the end of something rather than the beginning; it looks back upon experience, distilling its meaning. The poem does not attempt to persuade by involving us in a close or urgent relationship; its tone is that of a man making a trial account of his experience purely for his own benefit—we have not been invited to attend. We enter into the experience of Donne's poem directly, meeting no obstacles. Our entry into the experience of Arnold's poem is likely to be inhibited by our recalling other literary habits, such as those of the moralistic essays which Johnson weaves into *Rasselas*. Donne's plot and characterisation are much keener than Arnold's, the plot being of course the movement of words which testifies to subtle developments in the relationship of the speaker to Christ, the brusque tone of "What!" for example, being a new "situation," a development from the humble address of "deare Christ." May we not say, then, with these instances before us, that a speech is dramatic to the extent that it directs attention immediately and vigorously to a fictive personal relationship in the process of enactment? Hopkins seems to have had something of this in mind in one of his letters to Bridges when he used the word "bidding," describing it as "a nameless quality which is of the first importance in oratory and drama." It is "the art or virtue of saying everything right *to* or *at* the hearer, interesting him, holding him in the attitude of correspondent or addressed or at least concerned, making it everywhere an act of intercourse—and of discarding everything that does not *bid*, does not tell . . . witness Greek plays—and Shakespeare's."[34] There is very little bidding in Arnold's poem.

Perhaps now we may add a further characteristic of dramatic verse: that it attracts primary attention to the mind speaking

[34] *The Letters of Gerard Manley Hopkins to Robert Bridges*, edited by Claude Colleer Abbott, Oxford University Press, 1935, p. 160. Letter of 4 November 1882.

rather than to the language being spoken. But we must be careful with this. Horatio's

> But look the morn in russet mantle clad
> Walks o'er the dew of yon high eastward hill . . .

may seem to draw our attention away from Horatio as speaker to the language as such; we may be inclined to "explain" the lines as being designed primarily to answer to a deep desire in the audience at that moment, other claims being in abeyance. But this is unnecessary here, though it applies to several other speeches in Shakespeare. Even Eliot's comments on Horatio's speech fall away from the real point. He declares (in *Poetry and Drama*) that the scene in which these words are spoken "is great poetry, and is dramatic," and is something more. There emerges, he suggests, a kind of musical design also which reinforces and is one with the dramatic movement; it has checked and accelerated the pulse of our emotion without our knowing it. When we hear Horatio's words, Eliot says, we are lifted for a moment beyond character, but with no sense of unfitness of the words coming, and at this moment, from Horatio: "The transitions in the scene obey the laws of the music of dramatic poetry."[35] Poetry, drama, and then as if things were not sufficiently complicated already, music, each curiously evanescent. If Mr. Eliot intended to say why and how these lines are dramatic, it seems to me he failed. But the hint we need is in the earlier tribute, which we have already met, to "the really fine rhetoric in Shakespeare." "Where a character in the play *sees himself* in a dramatic light": or, translating to fit Horatio's case, where a character in the play *sees the occasion* in a dramatic light. In the word "walks" Horatio's sense of Being, activated to a Wordsworthian degree by contact with the Ghost, imparts a corresponding heightening to the felt nature and appearance of the morning: "state" is pointed up as "act." I imagine the procedure comes within the terms of *prosopopoeia* as interpreted by Elizabethan poets generally. Coriolanus sees himself in a dramatic light, likewise Othello and Timon; Horatio sees in a

[35] *Selected Prose, supra,* p. 73.

274

dramatic light the situation in which he, Marcellus, and Bernardo find themselves. Read in this way, of course, the lines exhibit our second characteristic of dramatic verse: they mime a movement of Horatio's psyche.

A convenient illustration of another attribute of dramatic verse is provided by *Samson Agonistes*. Robert Martin Adams has discussed the Latinate element in *Samson* with particular reference to the words "popular" and "capital," arguing that when Samson speaks of himself as "retiring from the popular noise," the adjective carries—and is meant to carry—contemptuous feelings from the Latin "populus." In the same way when Samson refers to his "capital secret," he is pointing out the importance of his secret, that it resided in or on his head, that like the Capitol in Rome it was the centre of his power and the residence of a deity. The effect, he argues, is that of an overlay, dear to Jonson as well as to Milton: one is aware of a Latin word behind the English with its own impact.[36]

But the two cases are not quite the same. Take the first:

> This day a solemn Feast the people hold
> To Dagon thir Sea-Idol, and forbid
> Laborious works, unwillingly this rest
> Thir Superstition yields me; hence with leave
> Retiring from the popular noise, I seek
> This unfrequented place to find some ease.

The contempt which issues in "popular" is deep and strong in Samson's feeling, the culmination of that bitterness which reveals itself in "Sea-Idol," "the people," and "Superstition." Similarly Samson's association of himself with "This unfrequented place." In context, therefore, the full meaning of "popular" mimes Samson's feeling with precision. (This applies also to the irruptions of Latinity which Mr. Ransom has examined[37] in Gertrude's description of Ophelia's death; the Latin renders the regal element which is still active in Gertrude's role and in

---

[36] *Ikon: John Milton and the Modern Critics*, Cornell University Press, 1955, p. 191.
[37] *Poems and Essays*, New York, Vintage Books, n.d., p. 128.

the feelings which testify to that role.) But the second piece from *Samson* is quite different:

> Thrice she assay'd with flattering prayers and sighs,
> And amorous reproaches to win from me
> My capital secret . . .

Here any Latinate meaning of "capital" over and above the primary meaning "chief" issues not from Samson's role or from his feelings at this moment, but from Milton as commentator. Milton, from without, offers an increment of comment which we may apprehend: the Latinate overlay is not in Samson's consciousness or in the habits of speech which testify to his role; it is an expansive gloss by Milton on the meaning of Samson's destiny. The procedure is very dangerous in a drama which has not set up a decorum to sanction it; it comes very close to the ventriloquism that bothered Coleridge.[38] The point may appear petty, and one can traffic ungracefully in details of this kind, but we have been concerned to examine it at a stage in which it has been carried down so thoroughly into the texture of the verse that it is barely noticeable. Instances which we might cite from *Venus Observed* would show the thing much more blatantly. In Fry's early comedies the language—much of it—is undramatic because it sets up verbal barriers between the audience and the relationships which are in process of exploration and enactment. Attention is diverted from the relationships to the opaque language itself.

Tying up the threads: the essential characteristics of dramatic verse would seem to be that the language is generative, answering to a pressure *forward* (which is in the movement of the acts imitated) toward the fulfillment of the play's "theoretic form"; that it is continuously agile in miming the speaker's "movements of the psyche"; that it compels primary attention to the mind speaking rather than to the language being spoken; and that its sharpest focus is directed on the minutiae of changing relationships within the play.

[38] *Biographia Literaria*, edited by J. Shawcross, Oxford University Press, 1907, Vol. II, p. 109.

# ACKNOWLEDGMENTS

I AM GRATEFUL to the editors of *Sewanee Review, Essays in Criticism,* and *Studies* for permission to reprint material from Chapters 3, 11, and 16, respectively, which first appeared in their pages. Also to the following publishers who have generously given permission to quote from copyright material:

From *Collected Poems of William Empson,* copyright, 1935, 1940, 1949, by William Empson, reprinted by permission of Chatto and Windus Ltd.

From *Reactionary Essays on Poetry and Ideas,* by permission of Allen Tate.

From *Collected Poems* and *Collected Plays* by W. B. Yeats, published by Macmillan and Co. Ltd., and reprinted here by permission of Messrs. A. P. Watt and Son.

From *The Shakespeare Apocrypha,* edited by C. F. Tucker Brooke, by permission of the Clarendon Press.

From *The Poetical Works of John Keats,* edited by H. W. Garrod, by permission of the Clarendon Press.

From *The Poems of John Donne,* edited by Sir Herbert Grierson, by permission of the Clarendon Press.

From *Selected Poems,* by Richard Eberhart, reprinted by permission of Chatto and Windus Ltd.

From the New Shakespeare editions of *Antony and Cleopatra, Julius Caesar,* and *Romeo and Juliet,* reprinted by permission of Cambridge University Press.

From *Collected Poems,* by Austin Clarke, reprinted by permission of George Allen and Unwin Ltd.

From *Collected Poems,* by Dylan Thomas, reprinted by permission of J. M. Dent and Sons Ltd.

From the New Arden edition of *Cymbeline,* by permission of Methuen and Co. Ltd.

From *The Songs and Sonnets of John Donne,* edited by Theodore Redpath, reprinted by permission of Methuen and Co. Ltd.

ACKNOWLEDGMENTS

From *Don Juan*, by J. E. Flecker, reprinted by permission of Martin Secker and Warburg Ltd.

From *The Ascent of F6*, by W. H. Auden and Christopher Isherwood, by permission of Curtis Brown Ltd.

From the *Cantos, Women of Trachis*, and the *Classic Anthology*, by Ezra Pound, reprinted by permission of Shakespear and Parkyn Ltd.

From *Him* and *Santa Claus*, by permission of E. E. Cummings.

From *The Visionary Farms*, by Richard Eberhart, reprinted with the author's consent from *New World Writing*, published by the New American Library of World Literature Inc.

From *September Lemonade*, by Reuel Denney, reprinted with the author's consent from *New World Writing*, published by the New American Library of World Literature Inc.

From *Poems of G. M. Hopkins*, edited by W. H. Gardner, by permission of Oxford University Press.

From *J.B.*, by Archibald MacLeish, reprinted by permission of Houghton Mifflin Co.

From *Good Friday*, by John Masefield, with the permission of the author and the Society of Authors.

From *The Lady's Not for Burning, Venus Observed*, and *The Dark is Light Enough*, by Christopher Fry, with the permission of Oxford University Press.

From *Collected Poems 1909-1935; Four Quartets; Murder in the Cathedral; The Family Reunion; The Cocktail Party; The Confidential Clerk*; by T. S. Eliot, reprinted by permission of Faber and Faber Ltd.

From *V-Letter and Other Poems*, by Karl Shapiro, with permission of Random House Inc.

From *The Portable Faulkner*, edited by Malcolm Cowley, reprinted by permission of Random House Inc.

From *Shenandoah*, by Delmore Schwartz, reprinted by permission of New Directions.

I have also to thank Jeremiah J. Hogan, Lawrance Thompson, C. L. Wrenn, and the late Una Ellis-Fermor for their critical reading of the text at various stages of its development. They are not, of course, responsible for the defects which persist. To Kenneth Burke I am grateful for the continuous excitement of his books. I am indebted to Francis Fergusson for *The Idea of a Theater, The Human Image,* and *Dante's Drama of the Mind,* as well as for genial encouragement and assistance over a period of several years.

# INDEX

*281*

# INDEX